I0799920

IMAGES
of America

MARQUETTE

IMAGES
of America

MARQUETTE

Gabriel N. Downs
and Michael C. Downs

ARCADIA
PUBLISHING

ISBN 978-0-7385-0056-0

Published by Arcadia Publishing
Charleston, South Carolina

Printed in the United States of America

Library of Congress Catalog Card Number: 98-83145

For all general information contact Arcadia Publishing at:
Telephone 843-853-2070
Fax 843-853-0044
E-mail sales@arcadiapublishing.com
For customer service and orders:
Toll-Free 1-888-313-2665

Visit us on the Internet at www.arcadiapublishing.com

CONTENTS

ACKNOWLEDGMENTS

This book is a joint production by Gabriel Downs and his father, Michael Downs. We shared the work—and the pleasure—of collecting the images, organizing the material, researching and writing the captions, and learning more about Marquette, Michigan, a place we have visited often during many summers in the Upper Peninsula.

The images, all pictures from the past, come from three important sources: the State Archives of Michigan, the Peter White Library in Marquette, and the Marquette County Historical Society. Additional historical material for the book was gathered from these institutions, the State Library of Michigan, and the J.M. Longyear Research Library. At each of these places, we were warmly welcomed and generously accommodated, and we acknowledge with thanks the particular assistance of Mark E. Harvey of the State Archives, Sandy Pelto, Jane Boyer John, and Carolyn Jordon of the Peter White Library, and Linda Panian of the Historical Society and the Longyear Library. We urge readers to join the Peter White Library and to become members of the Marquette County Historical Society.

We have also used contemporary images, photographs taken by Gabriel Downs during 1998, to illustrate some of the continuities and discontinuities in Marquette's history. One of the most attractive aspects of pictorial histories is their easy application to the task of seeing change through time. But there are some frustrations involved. In reviewing more than 5,000 images, culling 525 for more careful consideration, and selecting 203 for final use, we are aware that many interesting and important events, structures, and people may have been left out. In the end, we did what we could, and the omissions and mistakes are ours, not those of the individuals and institutions that were so helpful to us.

We must also acknowledge the special work done by others in collecting and organizing information about Marquette: Kathryn Bishop Eckert, for the section on the city's architecture in *Buildings of Michigan*; the unheralded writers of the parts of *Michigan, A Guide to the Wolverine State* about Marquette and the Upper Peninsula, L.A. Chase, whose brief but informative "History of Marquette" has circulated widely, and John Voelker for many good stories in many good books.

Our manuscript typist, Barbara L. Blauvelt, and film processors, Elmer Denman and Courtney Nardin, provided excellent service under great pressure. They have first call, and great claims, on our gratitude. We give thanks as well to Indiana University-Purdue University at Fort Wayne for help and support.

INTRODUCTION

One of the most evocative descriptions of Marquette, Michigan, and the most accurate—considering the time at which it was published—was written by an author writing fiction, not fact. With the right substitutions (Marquette County for Iron Cliffs County; Marquette for Iron Bay; Ishpeming for Chippewa; and Cleveland Cliffs for the Iron Cliffs Ore Company), the following passage from Robert Traver's *Anatomy of a Murder* holds up well: "Iron mining is the red lifeblood of Iron Cliffs County. The raw iron is mined and coasted downhill by rail from Chippewa to Iron Bay, on the Lake, and thence boated down the Great Lakes to the distant coal deposits and blast furnaces. This makes a handy money-saving arrangement, and for once even nature seems to have conspired on the side of free enterprise. If it weren't for mining I suppose the county'd still belong to the Indians. Instead it now belongs mostly to the Iron Cliffs Ore Company and the other smaller mining companies and, what's left over, to the descendants of the Finns and Scandinavians, the French, Italians and Cornish, and the Irish and a handful of Germans . . . who luckily landed here. . . ."

Robert Traver was the pen name of John Voelker, a descendant of that handful of Germans. He was writing about Marquette and its environs at a time (the 1950s) when the iron-ore industry was in steep decline, a decline that appears all but terminal today. In the early 1990s, however, Marquette was still flourishing—without its "red life blood." The city had become, as mining slowed, a center for providing government services. The K.I. Sawyer Air Force Base, established in the 1950s, and two older government institutions, the state prison and Northern Michigan University, became large employers, along with the expanding Marquette General Hospital. Even after the demise of the Soviet Union led to the closing of the air force base, the city's vitality and talent for adaptation persisted.

It is worth our while to recall, during the year of Marquette's sesquicentennial, that even a triumphant city has times that are bleak and unpromising. In 1868, the core of the city was destroyed by fire. The entire business district and most of the residential area disappeared in the tragedy. But to find the good within the bad, fire was the 19th century's method of urban renewal, and Marquette, like Chicago, used the opportunity to replace its flimsy and primitive wooden-built city with a solid and permanent city of brownstone. This effort gave life to a new industry—the quarrying of native stone. It provided employment for many and created a renewed and reinvigorated community. For more than 30 years thereafter, Marquette County's quarries provided red and purplish-brown variegated sandstone to builders throughout the Midwest.

A few years later, Marquette's economy was devastated during the financial panic of 1873, and the resulting depression lasted for five years. The price of pig iron plummeted from $12 to $5.50 per ton, and Marquette's population dropped by almost 11 percent during the period from 1874 to 1880. None of this was extraordinary in a region so dependent upon extractive industries, but the city produced what was an extraordinary expansion at the same time; some of its finest public buildings and private homes date from the same period. The government, local entrepreneurs, and Marquette's leading citizens all contributed to this counter-trend, and the harbor breakwater, a brewery, the Opera House block, and the Episcopal church were all built in defiance of the dismal present with confidence in the future.

Iron-ore production hit its peak in 1919, and in 1929, when there were only 16 mines still active, the industry was being written off. With the industrial run-up to World War II, however, mining made a comeback that lasted through the Korean War. Even during the Great Depression, the city demonstrated its resilience. It sustained itself during that economic crisis through diversification, manufacturing woodenware, dimension lumber, chemicals, machine parts, and mining equipment. Its tourist industry grew and became increasingly important.

To say that there is a recurring theme in the history of Marquette is to make romantic what is prosaic; we will say there is a pattern. People learn and then adjust, at least the successful people—the survivors—do. Buildings, if they are still standing and useful decades, or a century, after their construction, exhibit these traits, and so do institutions such as churches, corporations, and schools.

In the 150 years since Robert Graveraet arrived at Carp River, a little south of Marquette proper, and Amos R. Harlow founded the city itself, learning and adapting has been the process of its development. All of the original reasons for Marquette's existence (lumber, iron ore, and shipping) have disappeared or faded. The alternatives that grew up as responses to the volatility of the markets for extractive industries, including brownstone quarrying, railroading, specialized heavy manufacturing, and the Air Force base, have not always endured. Marquette, unlike other lumbering and mining towns and cities in the Upper Peninsula and the rest of the Midwest, has continued to move onward and upward.

The elements that create the basis of the city's sustainability are the industries that meet needs—education, health care, and correction—which exist everywhere; its setting, which is beautiful; its changing seasons, which are glorious and awesome and attract thousands of people to the area over and over again; and its people, who deserve a last, full paragraph of their own.

Today, Marquette belongs in some part, as John Voelker wrote, to the descendants of those "who luckily landed here," a remarkably diverse group that must be expanded to include the Native Americans who "landed" before anyone else. Together they have produced a city that is warm and hospitable without being particularly self-conscious about it. One of Voelker's characters is called an "Irishman," not, his narrator says, to demean or stigmatize him, but just to identify him toward "the simple end of getting along together." This quality, at last, may be at the very heart of Marquette's success.

One

MAIN STREETS

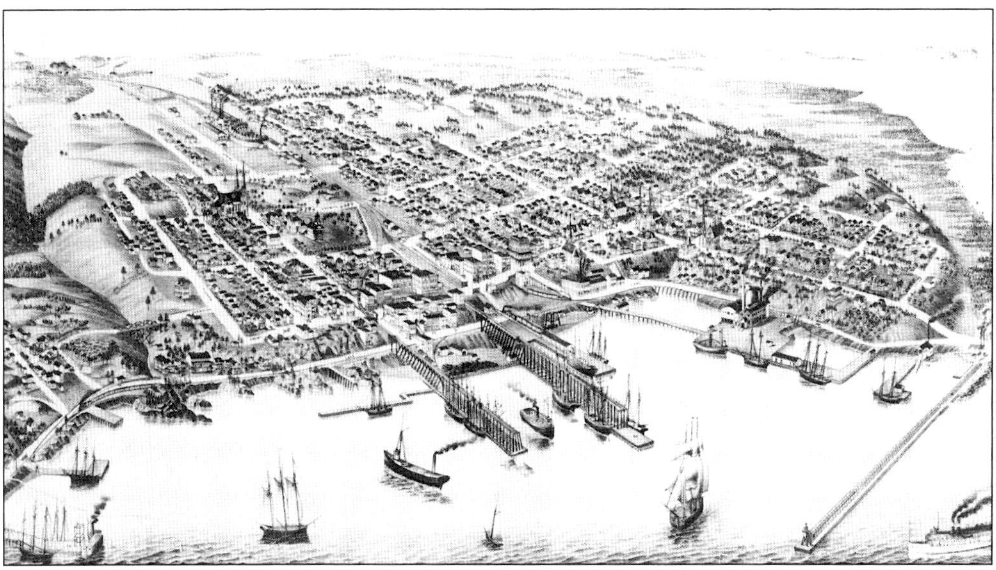

In 1881, Marquette was already filling the space between its northern and southern heights. The city's topography dictated that rail access to its port facilities would run along its shoreline or, from the west, through what might have been the center of the valley. Commercial development was pushed up the hills to allow the iron ore a right of way. (Courtesy State Archives of Michigan.)

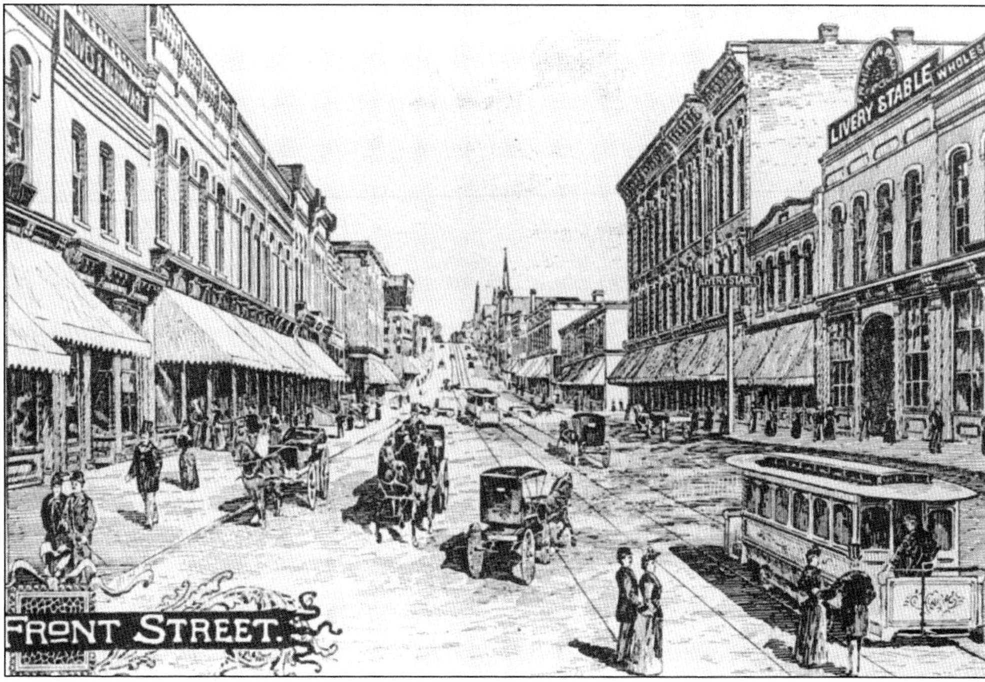

This lithograph is a companion to the photograph below. It was published in 1891 and shows the vitality of the mid-day scene. And what a change! Now there are double trolley-car tracks where there weren't any in the morning, and the people in the street are dressed as stylishly as if it were Sunday. Lithographers had more artistic freedom. (Courtesy Peter White Library.)

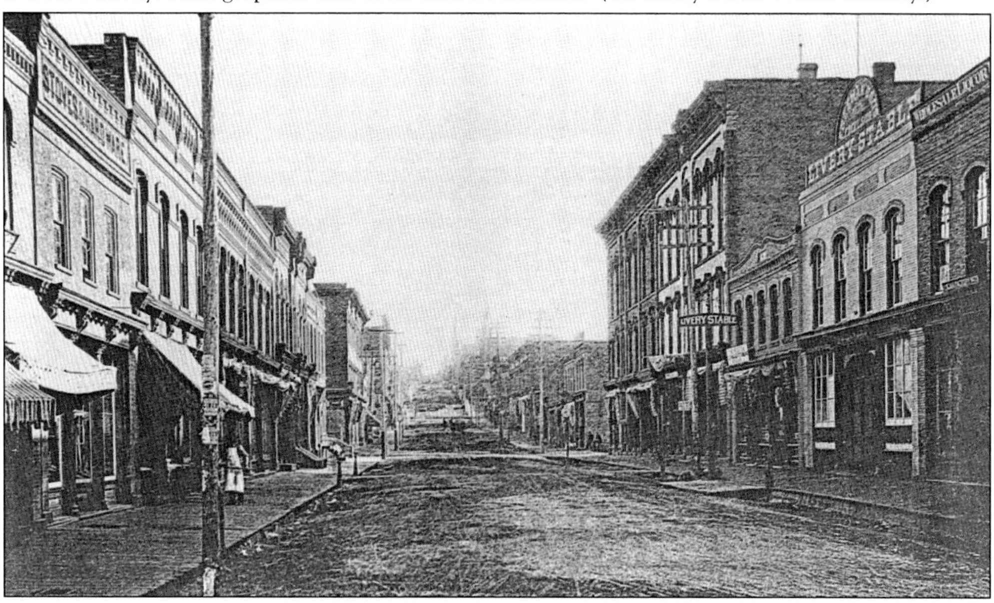

Front and Washington Streets, which intersect just several blocks north—or up the street—from where this photo was taken, were Marquette's main business thoroughfares in 1891. Despite competition, they still are today. This image of Front Street shows how it looked early on a summer's day. Awnings protect the stores on the west side of the street from the morning sun. (Courtesy Peter White Library.)

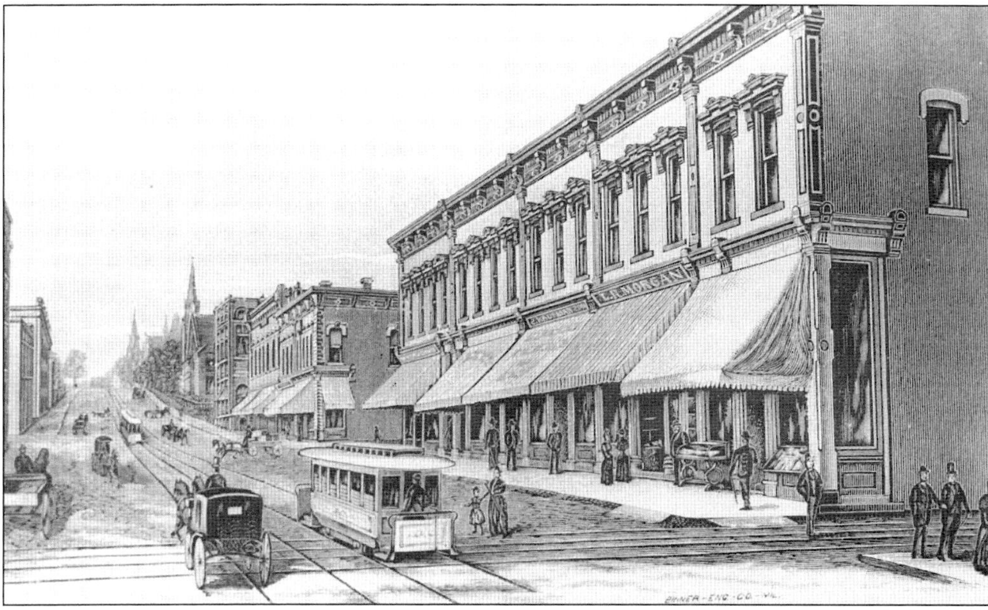

This is another example of the lithographer's art and imagination. This image is a copy of the Frasier Block photograph featuring the soon to be, although not yet running, trolley cars as well as a fashionable crowd (which differs from the casual loungers in the photograph below). The Citizens Association published the lithographs with a desire to put Marquette's best foot forward. (Courtesy Peter White Library.)

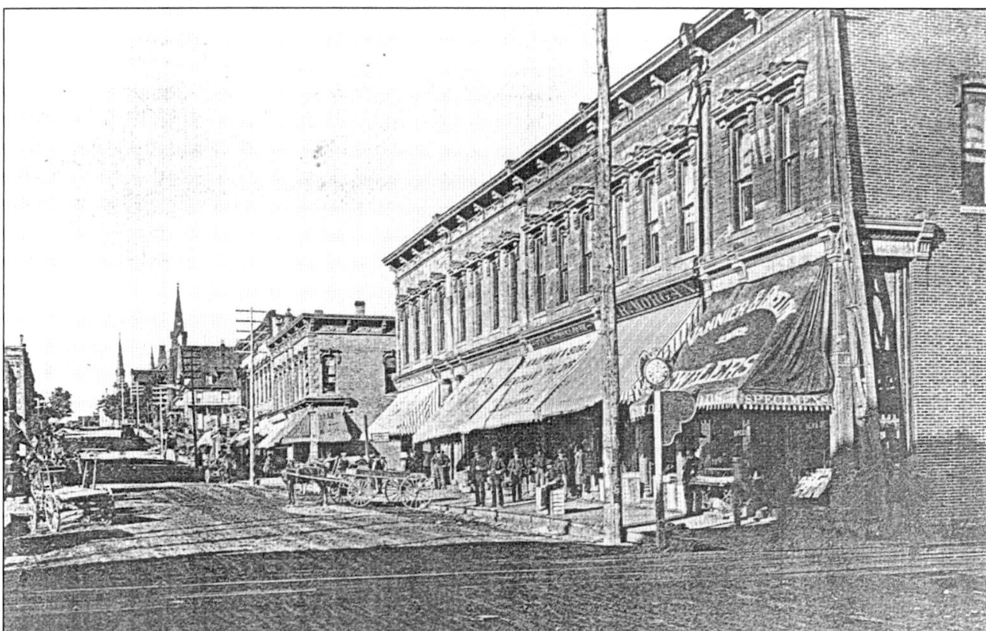

In this Front Street scene, the Frasier Block is shown south of the intersection with Washington. This picture was published in a photo folio of Marquette settings in 1891. The shadows and awnings indicate that it was late afternoon when the photographer took this shot. (Courtesy Peter White Library.)

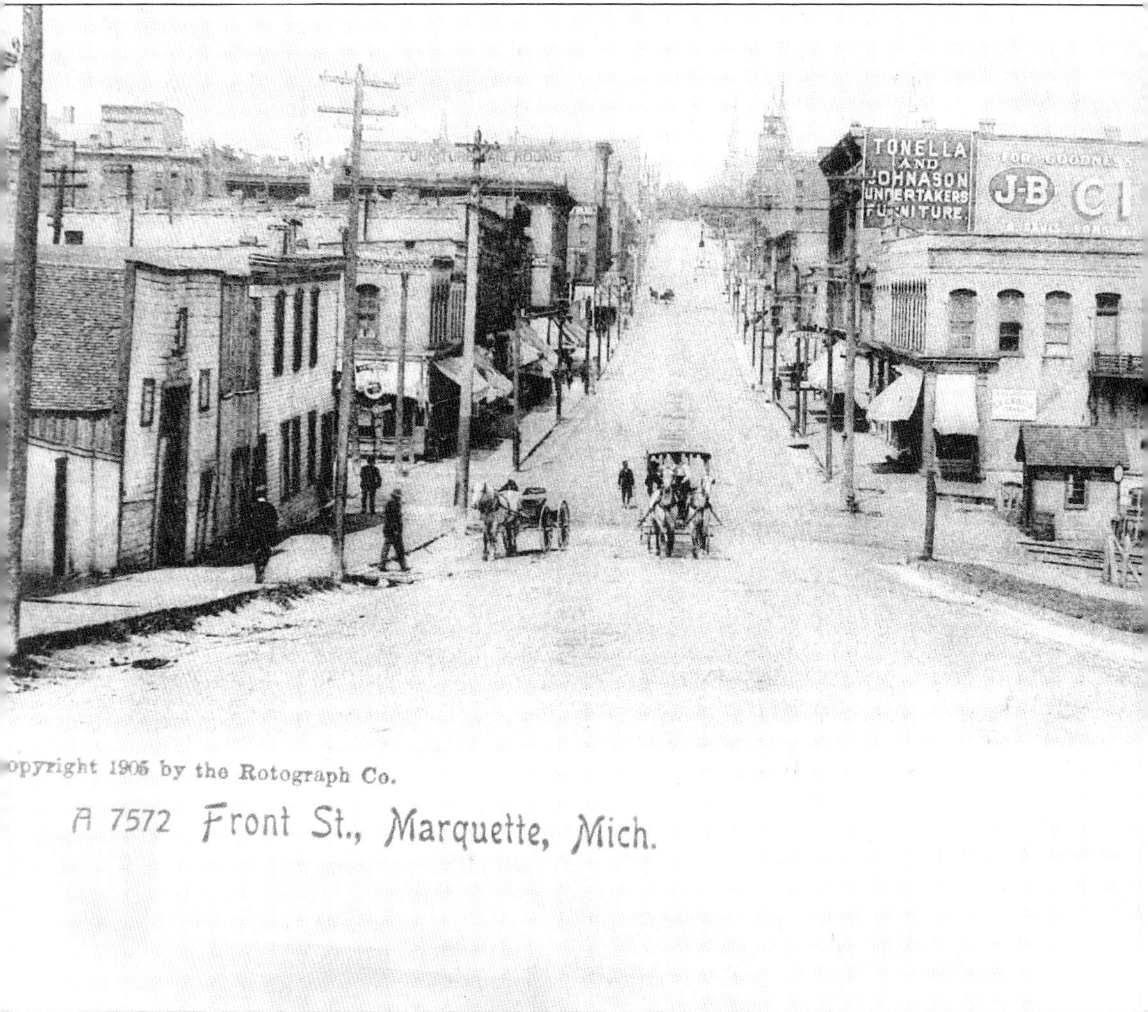

Most postcards try to make their subjects attractive and, at the turn of the century, lithographers took even greater liberties with the scenes they worked on, enhancing them and tidying them up in order to promote a business or a community. This 1906 postcard view published by the Rotograph Company presents South Front Street unvarnished. The buildings on the immediate left are sagging, and one has an obvious false front. Though the picture was snapped during the middle of the day, the street is nearly deserted; the figures and the vehicles do not convey movement with purpose. There are no trolleys, no well-dressed citizens, and no eager shoppers. This is the way it really looked at times. From the down-at-the-heels look of the foreground, however, the eye moves to the distant heights in the background and the familiar tower of the Marquette County Savings Bank, which lends every view of Front Street a touch of class. (Courtesy State Archives of Michigan.)

The tower of the old Marquette County Savings Bank Building is seen on the left in this 1998 view of Front Street looking south. The new and modern quarters of the First Bank of America, also on the left, occupy the site of its predecessors, the Wilkinson Bank and the Union Bank. The summer traffic was heavy on the day this photo was taken. (Photo by G. Downs.)

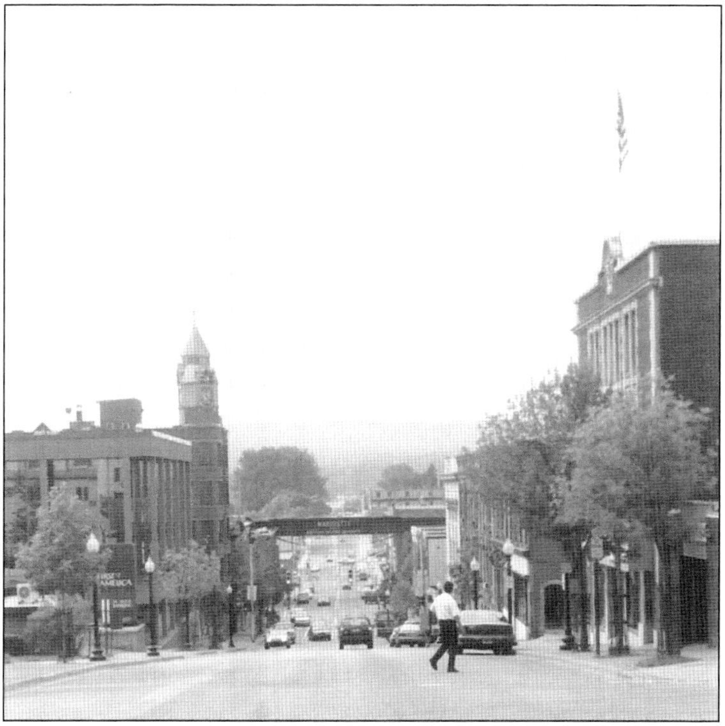

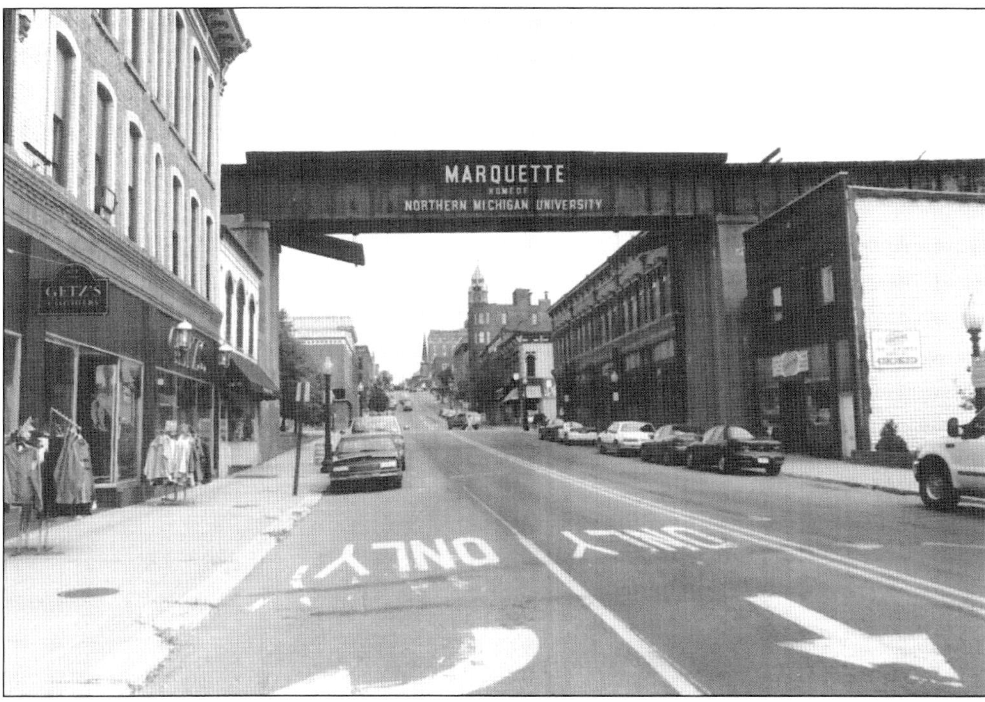

The Duluth, South Shore, & Atlantic Railroad trestle now advertises Marquette and Northern Michigan University. The Adams Block on the immediate left now houses Getz's Department Store, and what once was called the Frasier Block on the right is being remodeled into the Rosewood Hotel. Front Street is still a good business address. (Photo by G. Downs.)

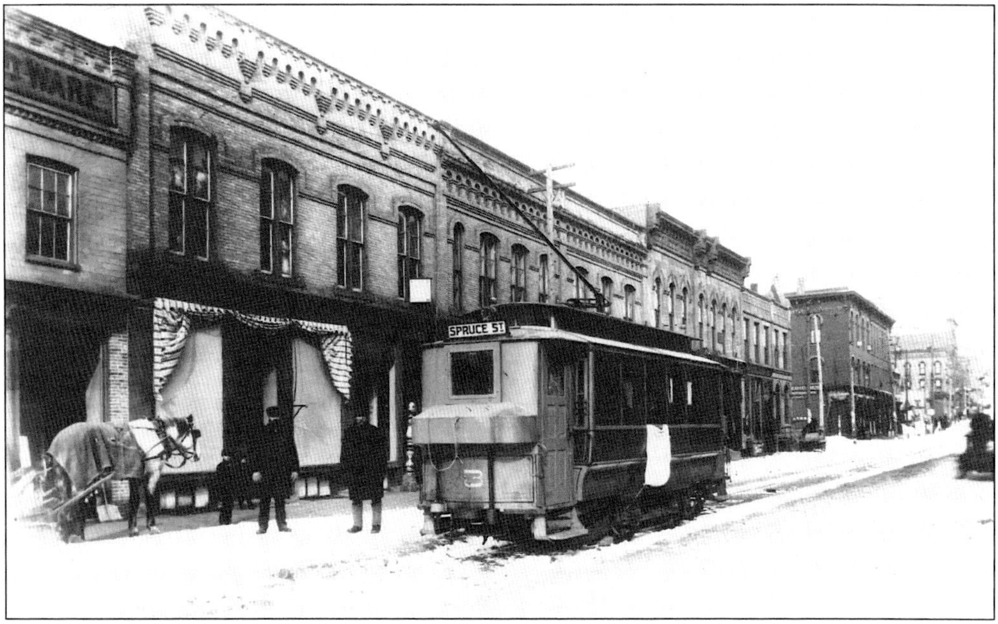

This Spruce Street Car is headed south on Front Street on a winter day in the 1890s. The cars of the Marquette City & Presque Isle Street Railway Company ran on Marquette streets from 1891 until 1935, when its equipment and tracks became too "dilapidated and dangerous to operate." The tracks were not torn up until 1942, when they became part of the war effort. (Courtesy Marquette County Historical Society.)

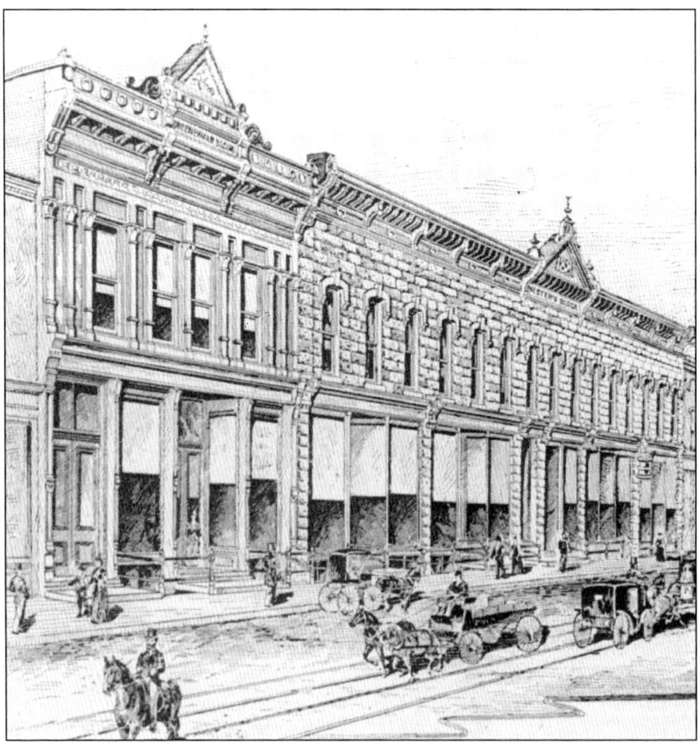

Pictured here is another somewhat misleading lithograph of Marquette street life in the 1890s. This time, the view depicts the Greenwald and Nestor Blocks on the south side of Washington Street. The lithographer had some difficulty with perspective and proportions. The wagons and carriages are smaller than they should be in relation to the buildings and other figures. (Courtesy Peter White Library.)

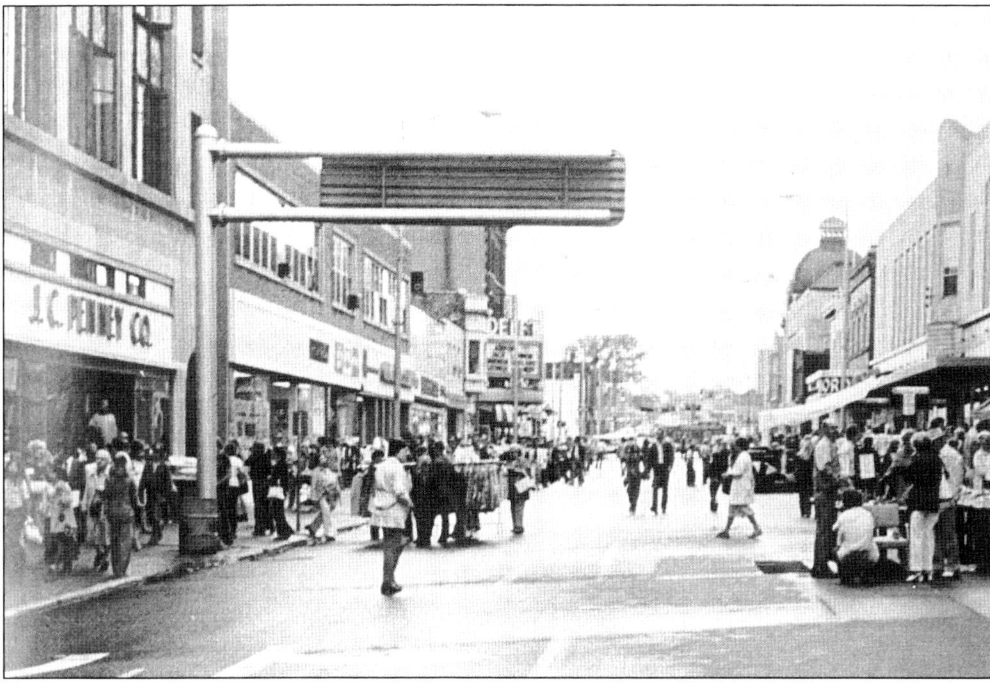

Downtown merchants reacted to the changing patterns of commerce by cooperative action. This example, a summer sidewalk sale in the 1970s, sought to attract shoppers by turning Washington Street into an outdoor outlet mall. There is a crowd, but in the end, even strenuous salesmanship couldn't create enough trade to keep Penney's and Montgomery Ward in business; by the 1990s, they were gone. (Courtesy Peter White Library.)

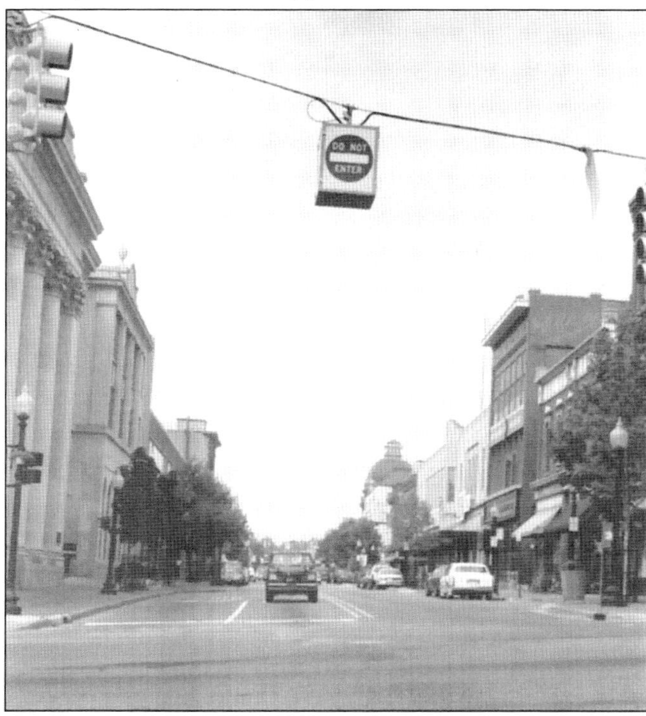

The photographer is facing west for this 1998 view of Washington Street. Traffic is light, and some shoppers are taking advantage of ample parking. The First National Bank and Trust Company still anchors this block (left), and specialty stores, providing goods and services not usually available in local malls, stretch along both sides of the street. The summer tourist business is usually heavy. (Photo by G. Downs.)

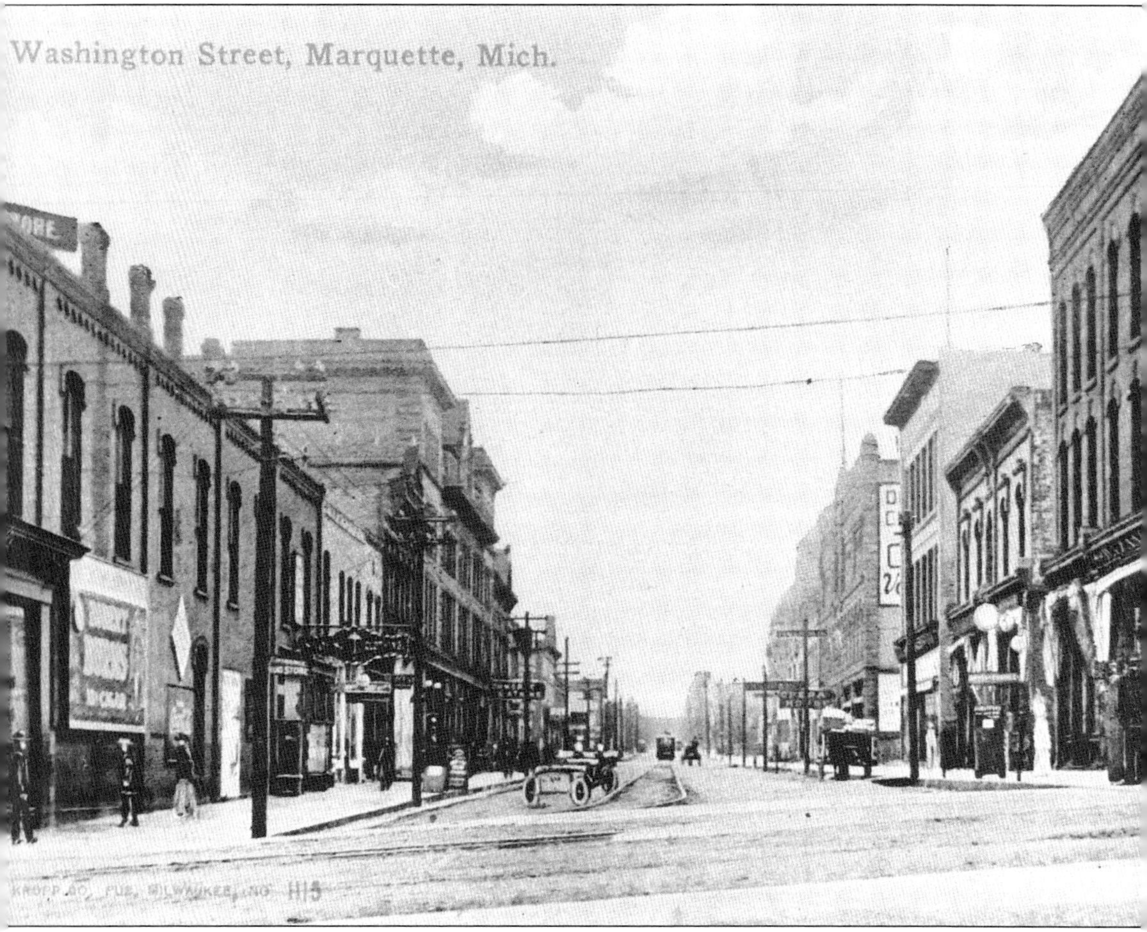

Pictured is a 1910 view of Washington Street, looking west. By this time, Marquette's two main streets had different, well-developed images. Front Street was crossed by the railroad tracks, the docks were close by, and the street, although commercial, was closely tied to the city's industrial base, especially mining, railroading, and shipping. Washington Street was located up the hill, was more commercial, less industrial, and featured the Opera House, a proud symbol of the city's cosmopolitanism. The Marquette City Hall and the post office also gave Washington Street a more respectable and substantial air. Transportation was in transition. In this picture, we can see a trolley in the distance, two horse-drawn vehicles, and, in the center of the frame, an automobile preparing to make a turn. Although the sidewalks are not crowded, the stores are ready for business with outdoor advertising on the curb side. (Courtesy State Archives of Michigan.)

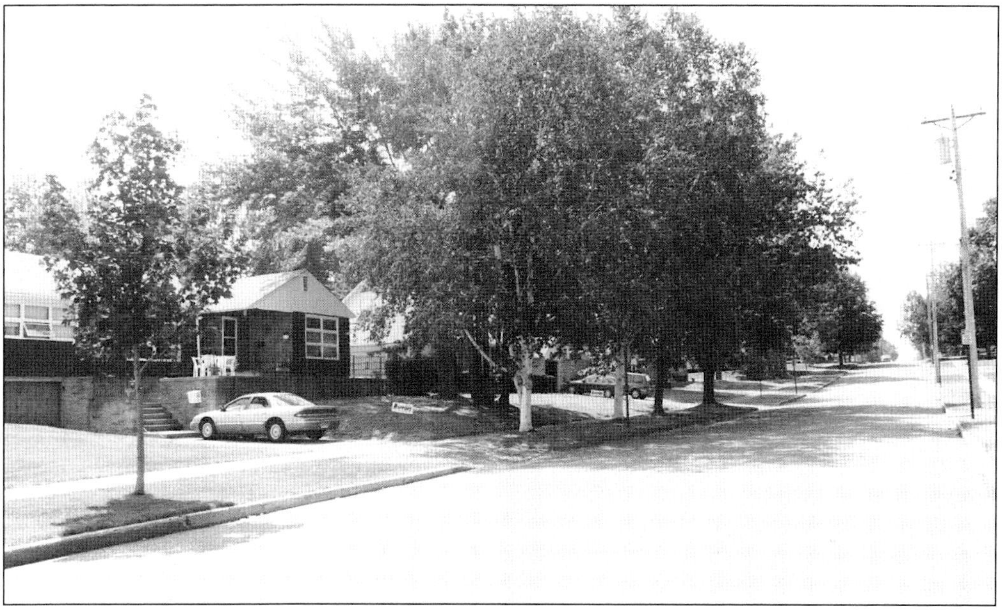

The homes in Marquette's newer neighborhoods conform to patterns formed years before. Trees and lawns, a leisurely atmosphere, neat and quiet, are all traits of the upper Midwest and its early settlers, including New Englanders, Scandinavians, Germans, and Finns. The pleasing landscape was easily taken up by the Irish, Italians, and others who moved in later. (Photo by G. Downs.)

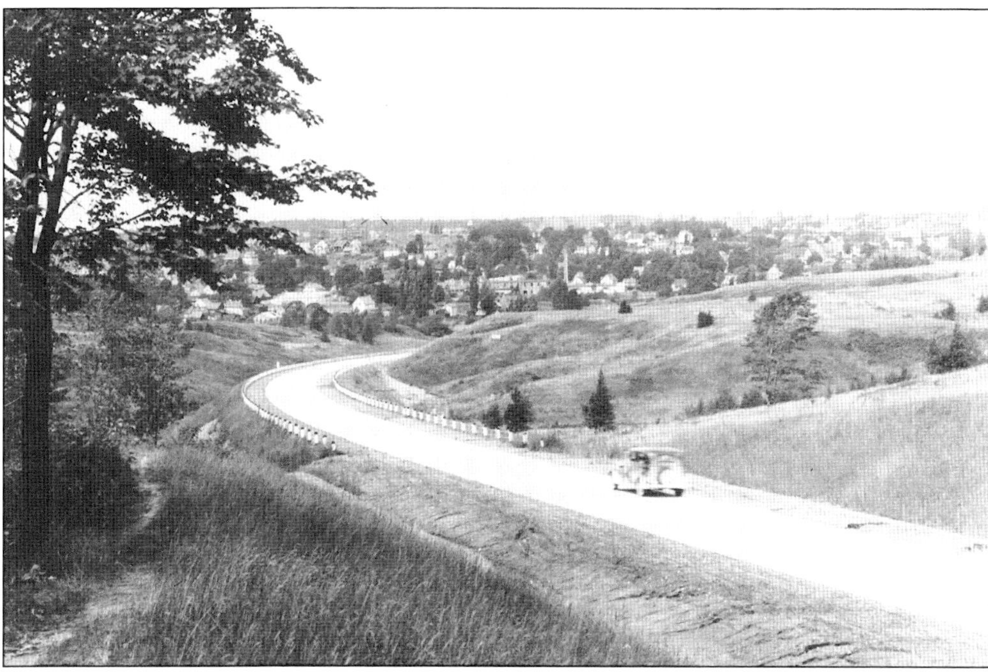

This car, approaching Marquette on U.S. 41 from the south on an improved modern highway, is a sign of many things to come. The lake and the railroads, though still vital in the late 1930s and throughout the 1940s, would soon be superseded by automobile and truck transportation as highway travel provided greater flexibility. (Courtesy State Archives of Michigan.)

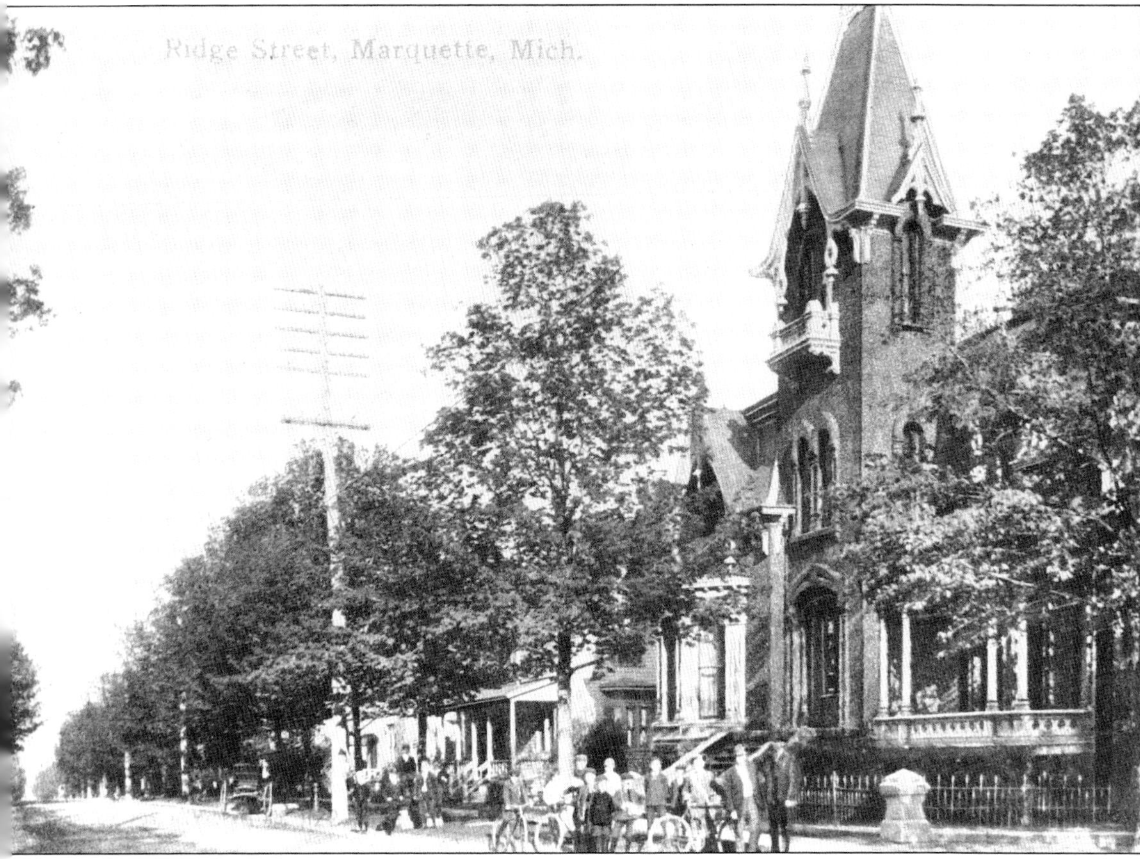

The sense that this neighborhood represented an important part of Marquette's identity is still strong today and grows out of the whole series of idyllic images from the period 1885–1915. In this *c.* 1910 view of Ridge Street, a group of bicyclists is gathered in the foreground, along with a few pedestrians. A little farther up the street, there is a horse and buggy pulled up to the curb. The house on the right is quite grand in a Victorian way, and the trees are in full leaf. It is morning in America; no one is in danger, and everyone has reason to be pleased. In 1910 the U.S. Census Bureau reported that 11,503 people lived in Marquette, but only a few of them lived in what is now called the Ridge, Arch, Michigan, and Ohio Streets Residential District. There are far fewer images of less favored neighborhoods. (Courtesy State Archives of Michigan.)

Two

PUBLIC PLACES

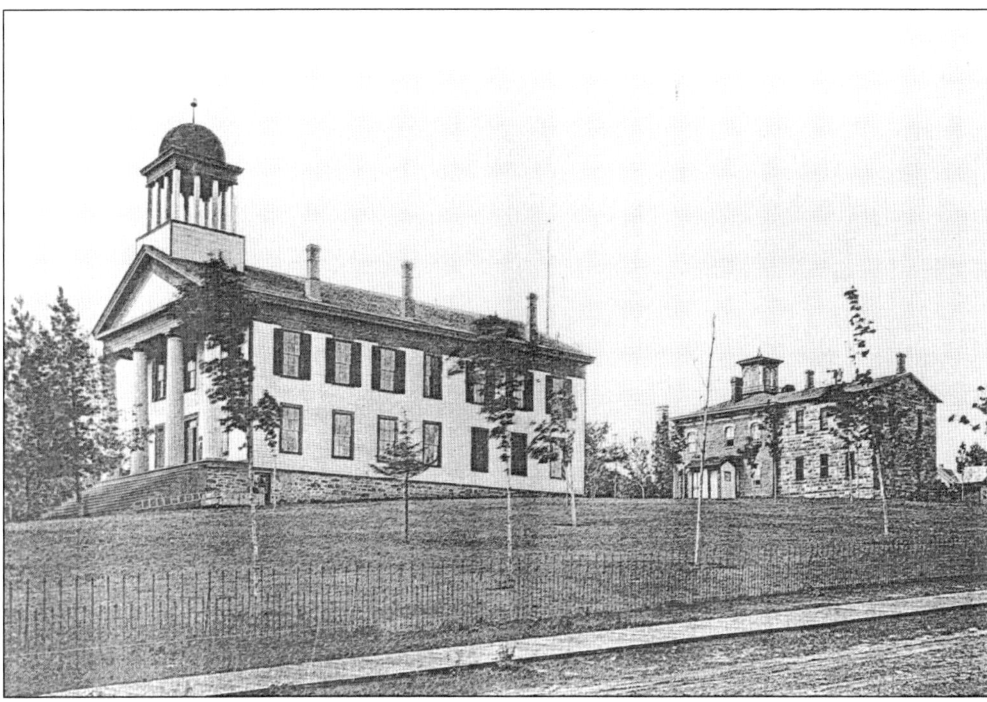

The old Marquette County Court House and Jail are shown here in an 1891 photograph. These buildings date back to a period before the widespread use of central heating; notice the multiple chimneys on the roofs of the buildings. Marquette's early city hall and the county courthouse, located on opposite sides of the city, faced each other from their hillside sites. (Courtesy Peter White Library.)

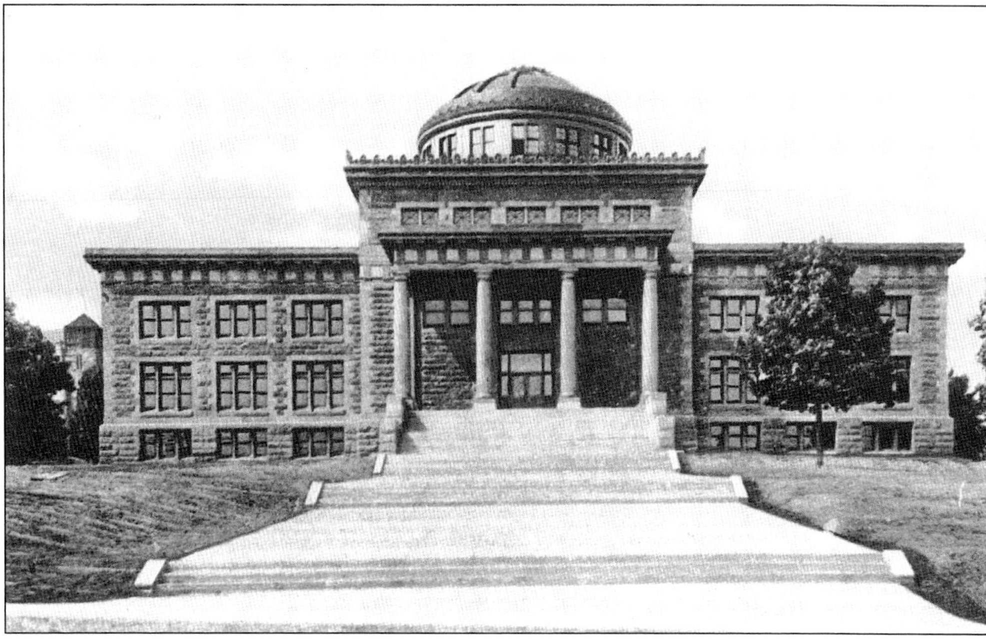

This is an early postcard photo of the "new" Marquette County Court House on its square. The front entrance faces Third Street. Built in 1902, its impressive symmetry persuades us that the law and justice are balanced and imperturbable. At that time, the courthouse created this effect without extensive landscaping and exterior ornamentation. (Courtesy State Archives of Michigan.)

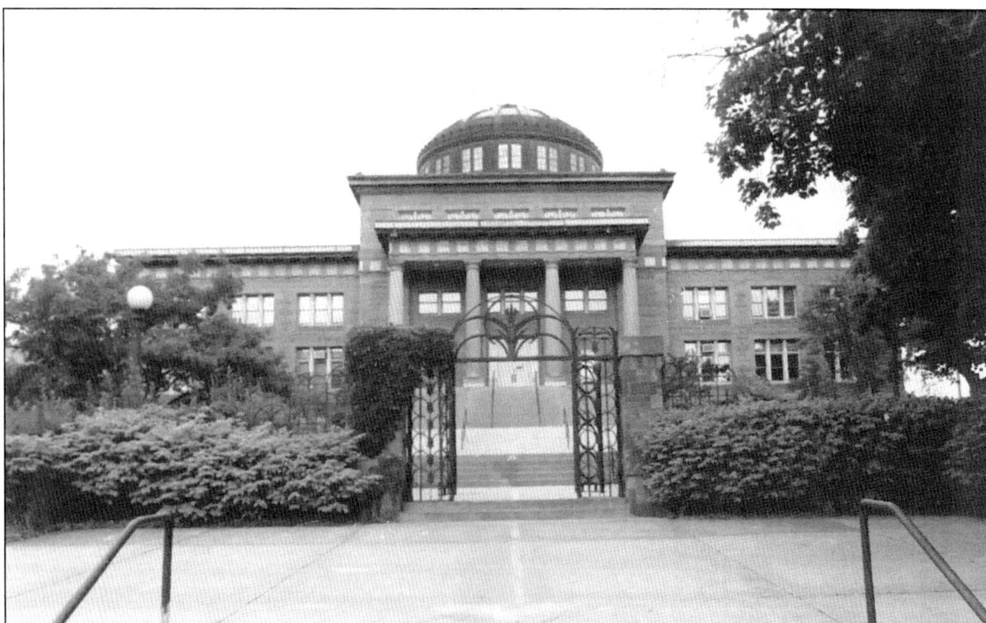

By 1998, the courthouse and its square had relaxed its awesome symmetry by using hedges and trees to create a park-like atmosphere. Beyond the camera's view are the various changes the building has undergone. An annex was built in 1977, and an attractive restoration was completed in 1984. (Photo by G. Downs.)

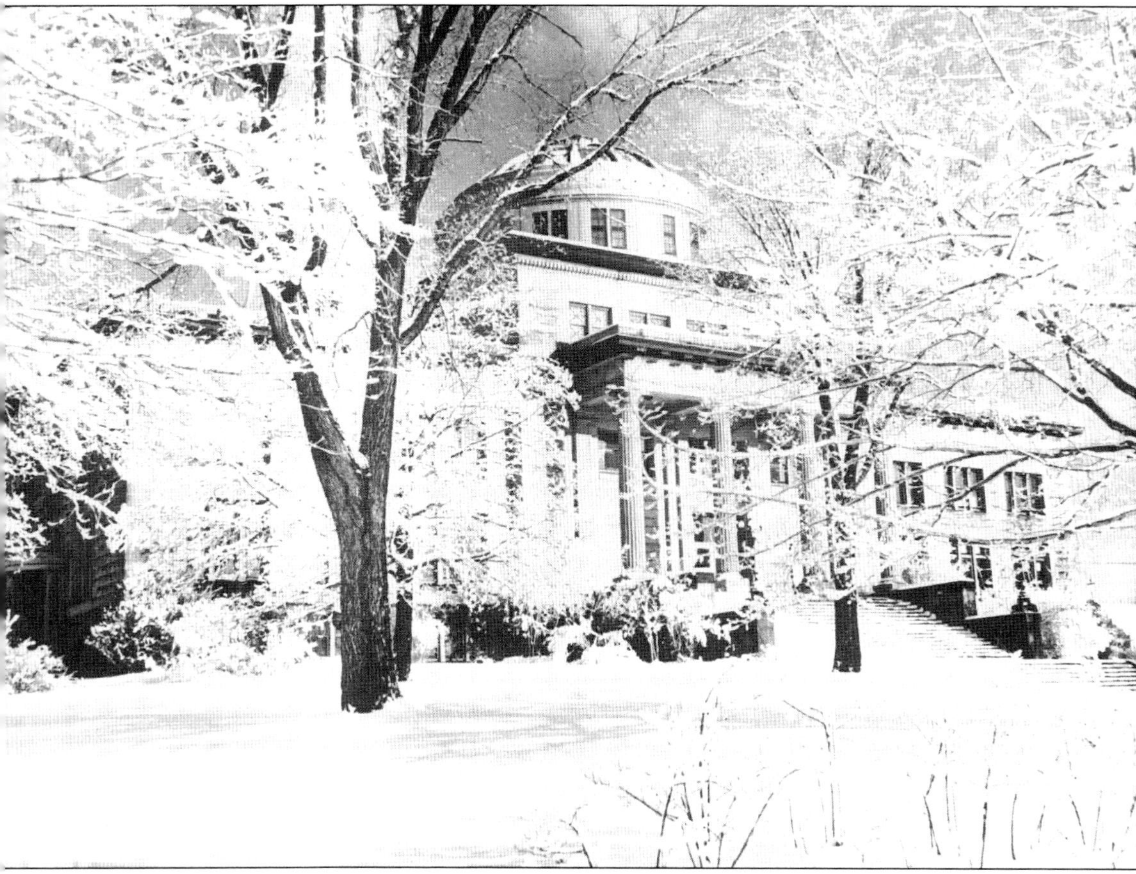

In this photograph, the courthouse, ordinarily a bulky, even brooding presence, gains some delicacy and is softened. The trees, their branches heavy with an unseasonable snowfall, make the old building look like the centerpiece in a Christmas card. The people of Marquette were probably not so enthusiastic about the beauty of the scene at the time. The snow that makes this image so attractive fell in May 1953, just when everyone thought that winter was finally over. There is a point in the long Upper Peninsula snow season when people say to each other, "It won't be long now," meaning that the snow will stop falling, melt away, and the trees will begin to bud. This beautiful but cruel storm delayed, briefly, that anticipated development. "The seasons change up here," one resident has said, "but they usually don't change fast enough." She was thinking of winter. (Courtesy State Archives of Michigan.)

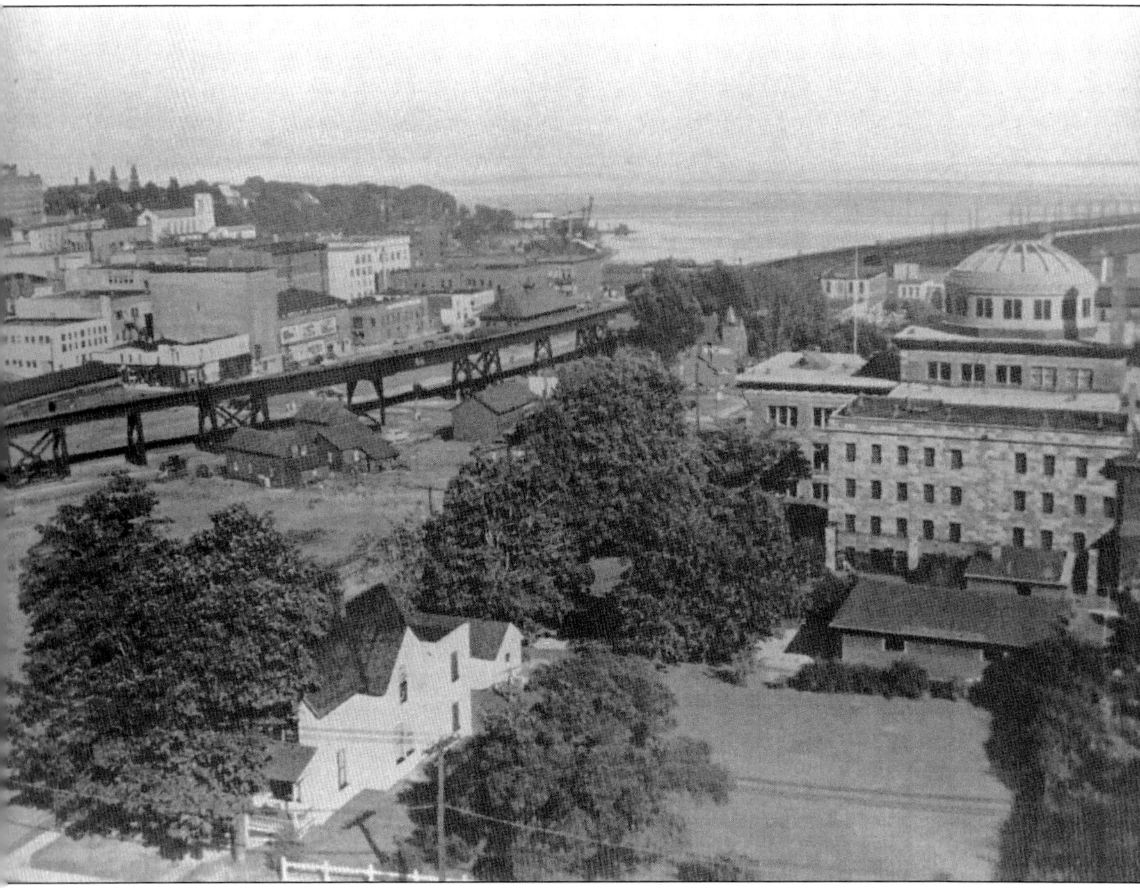

This photo of Marquette in the 1940s is an unconventional view because it shows the much less attractive rear of the otherwise handsome Marquette County Court House and the long expanse of the D.S.S. & A. trestle-and-ore dock from the land side instead of the lake side. Despite the time of day—the shadows are being cast by a late afternoon sun—and the pleasant weather, the city seems almost deserted. There are no trains, no visible traffic, and no people. It is interesting to note that the jail, the somewhat dilapidated buildings behind the courthouse, and the old houses nestled up against the trestle are now gone. (Courtesy Peter White Library.)

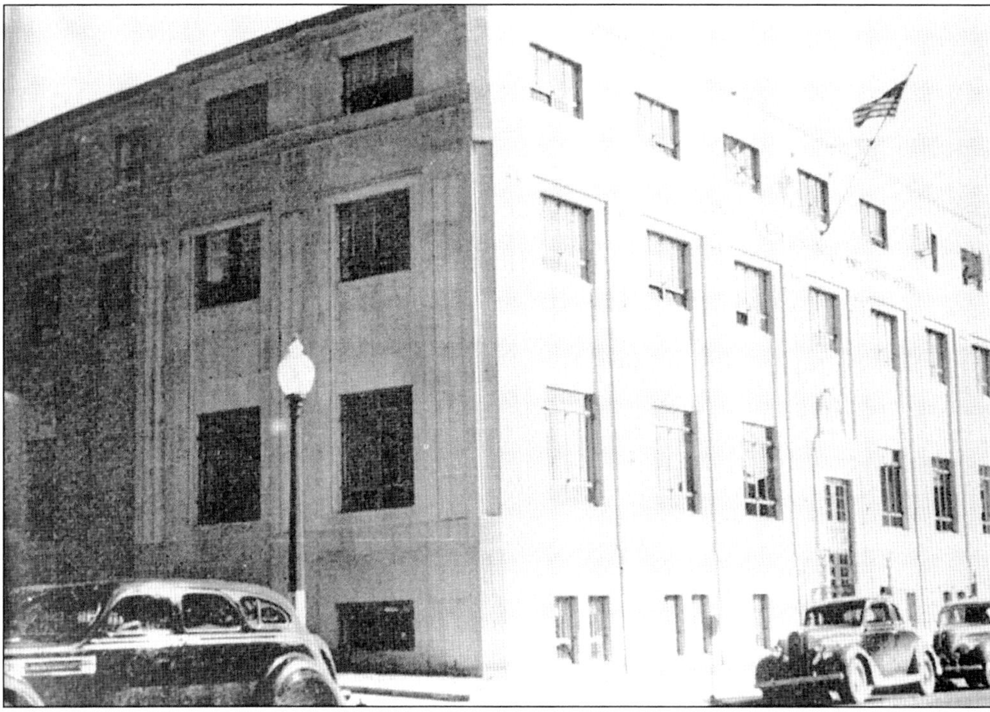

The automobiles, all models from the late 1930s, indicate that this picture of the U.S. Post Office and Court House was taken shortly after it was built. The exterior of the building has not changed much since then (see below). Interesting architectural touches soften the stark modernness of the structure; the fluted corners and the vertical pilasters, in particular, relieve the hard-edged appearance. (Courtesy Peter White Library.)

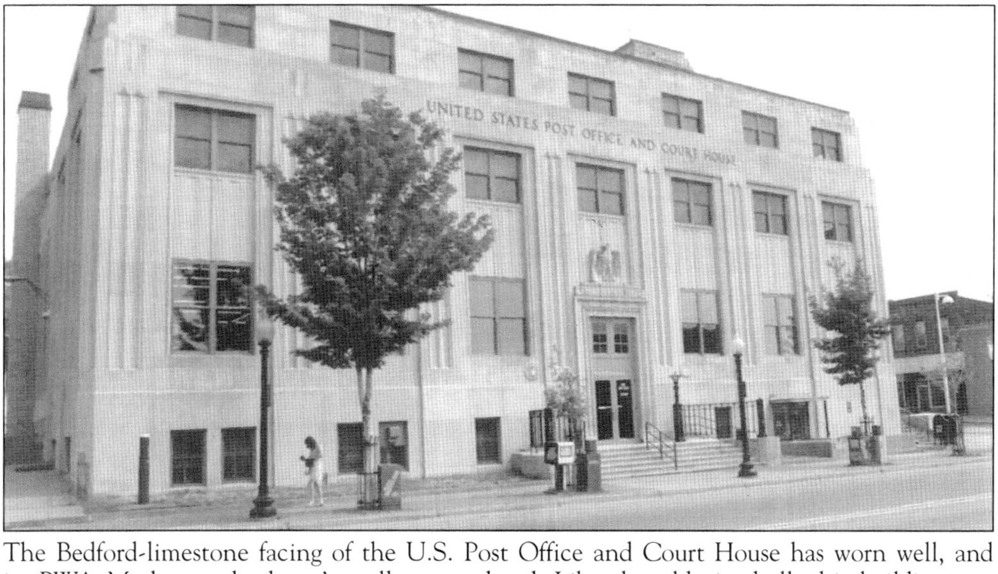

The Bedford-limestone facing of the U.S. Post Office and Court House has worn well, and its PWA Modern style doesn't really seem dated. Like the old city hall, this building was built during a serious economic downturn in the local economy and represented community confidence in the face of adversity. This is how the post office looked in the summer of 1998. (Photo by G. Downs.)

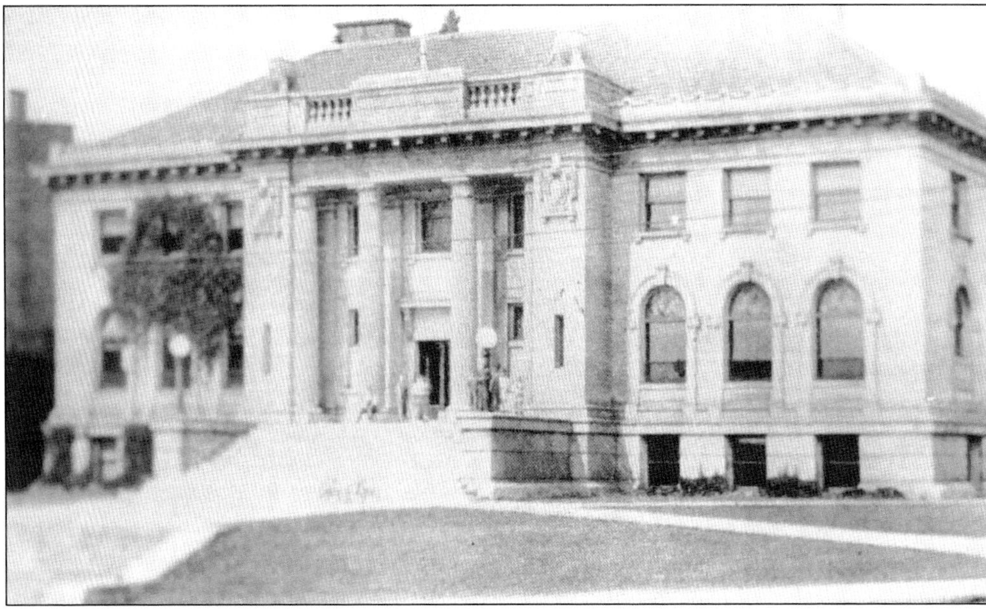

This early picture of the Peter White Library shows the restraint and dignity of its design. Its "whiteness" at the time of its construction in 1902 was a matter of note. In 1958, a western addition was built, and in 1982, the main entrance was moved to the north side of the building. This is a good example of how a well-thought-out plan can be modified to create new opportunities for use. (Courtesy Peter White Library.)

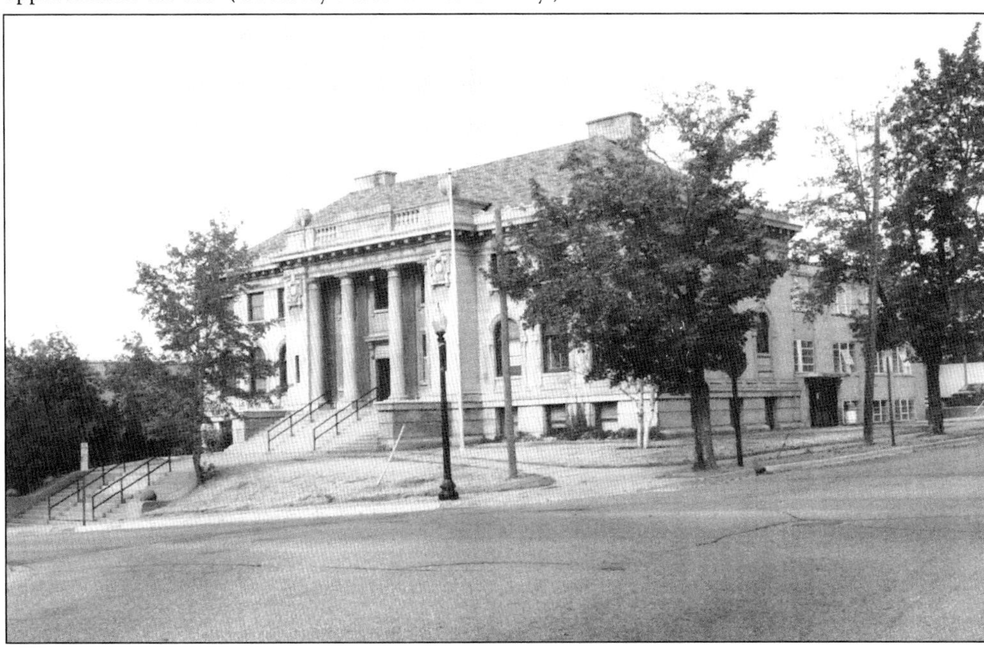

Built of limestone in 1904, the Renaissance-style Peter White Library building was unoccupied when this picture was taken in 1998. The library's resources and staff were temporarily housed on the Northern Michigan University Campus while this facility was redesigned and redecorated. The headquarters of the Marquette County Historical Society occupies the building on the left. (Photo by G. Downs.)

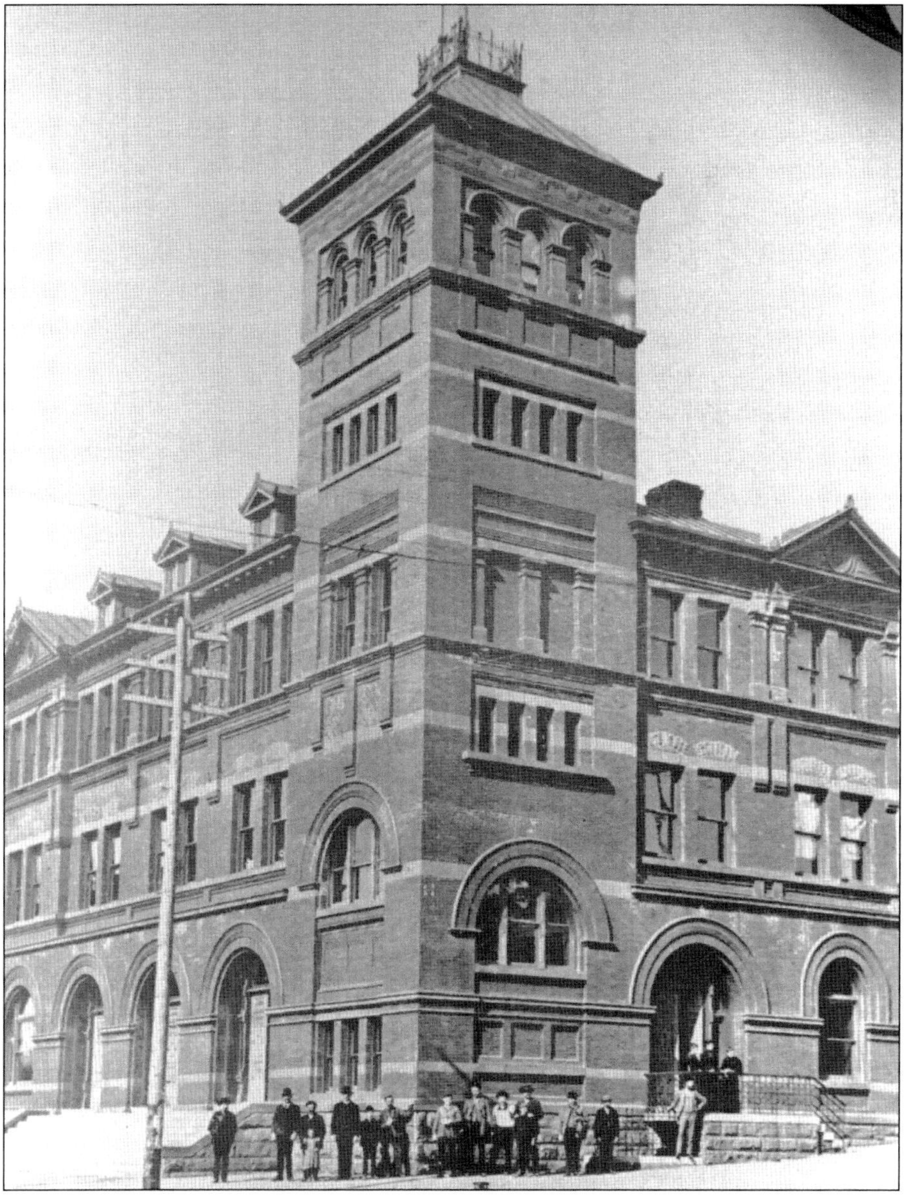

This large and imposing building, built by the federal government in 1889 and finished in 1891, stood on West Washington Street where the U.S. Post Office stands now. It was only one of a number of construction projects and services sponsored and paid for by the U.S. Government in Marquette during its early years. By the time this structure went up, the lighthouse, the breakwater in the harbor, and the lifesaving station had been built, and the list of federal functions included the weather bureau, post office, customs, land office, and courts. In 1886, the whole of Presque Isle had been given to the city for use as a park. The federal government was already an important contributor to Marquette's growth and development. This building signified the city's growing wealth and political influence and brought together in one place the post office, courts, customs, and land office. In 1900, there were still 60,000 acres of federal land available for claim in the country. The customs house alone employed 30 people. (Courtesy Peter White Library.)

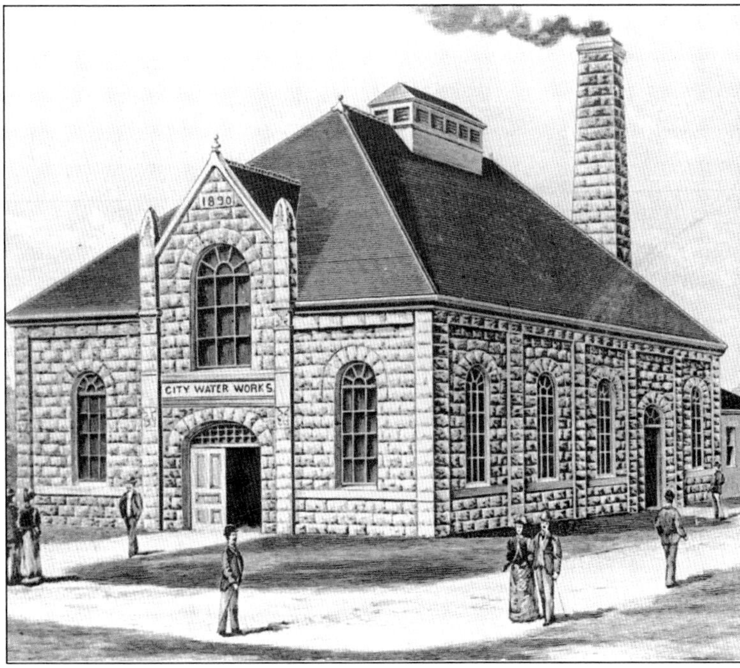

These images of the City Water Works provide a then and now perspective of the structure. The first, a lithograph from 1891, suggests that on Sunday afternoons the Water Works and its location near Lighthouse Point was a popular place for a promenade. With a pumping capacity of 6 million gallons daily, the facility was a technical marvel. (Courtesy Peter White Library.)

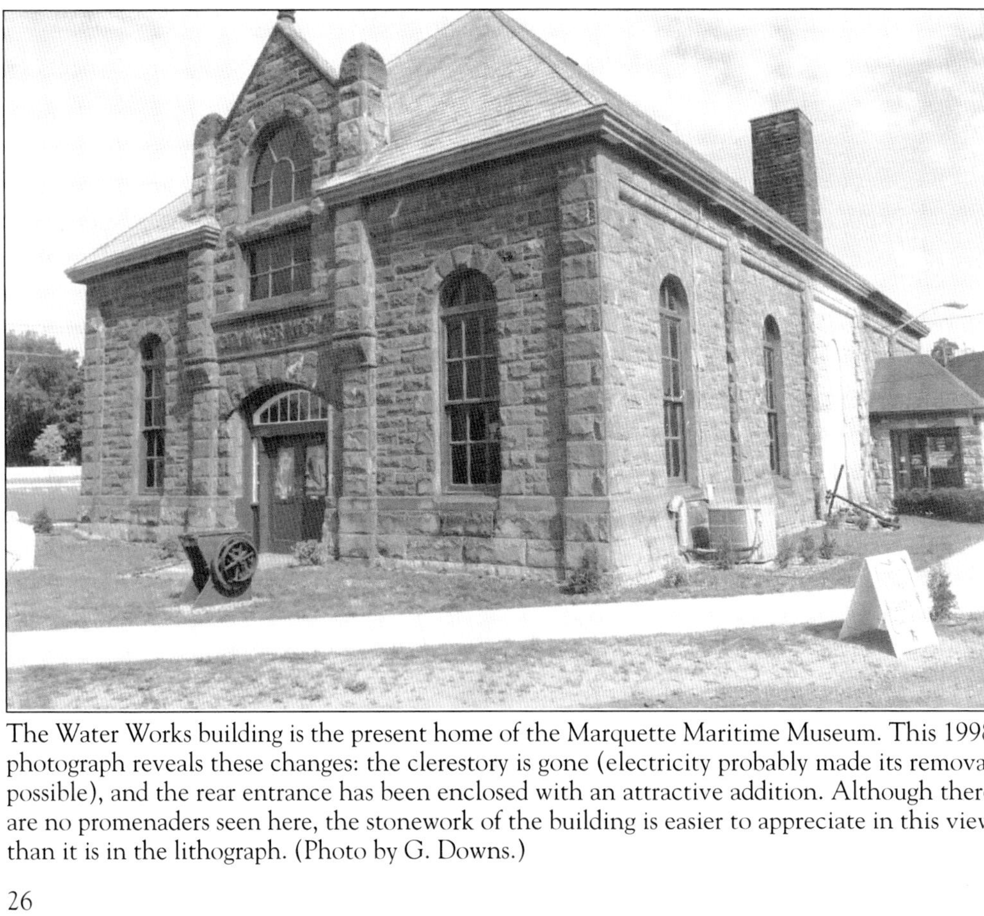

The Water Works building is the present home of the Marquette Maritime Museum. This 1998 photograph reveals these changes: the clerestory is gone (electricity probably made its removal possible), and the rear entrance has been enclosed with an attractive addition. Although there are no promenaders seen here, the stonework of the building is easier to appreciate in this view than it is in the lithograph. (Photo by G. Downs.)

The Old Marquette City Hall on Washington Street was built in 1893 of red brick and local sandstone. The heavy, purple-brown sandstone lent itself to use in Richardsonian arches, of which the building has several; a particularly handsome example is seen at its front entrance. This picture was taken shortly after the city hall was built, when it was still surrounded by residences and empty space. (Courtesy Peter White Library.)

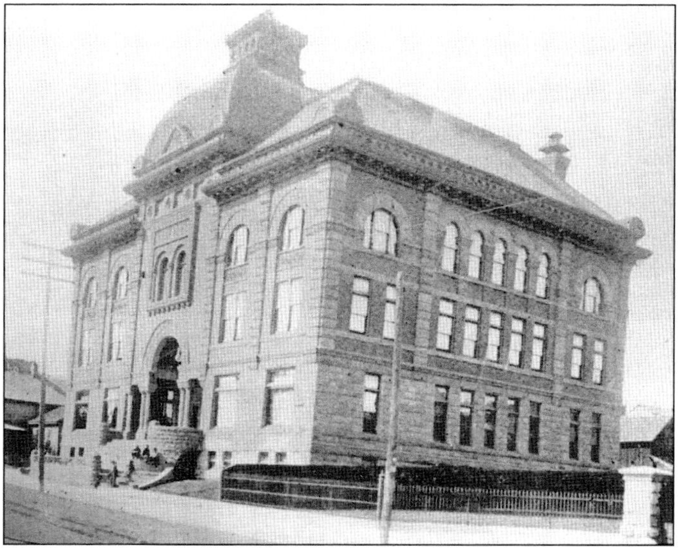

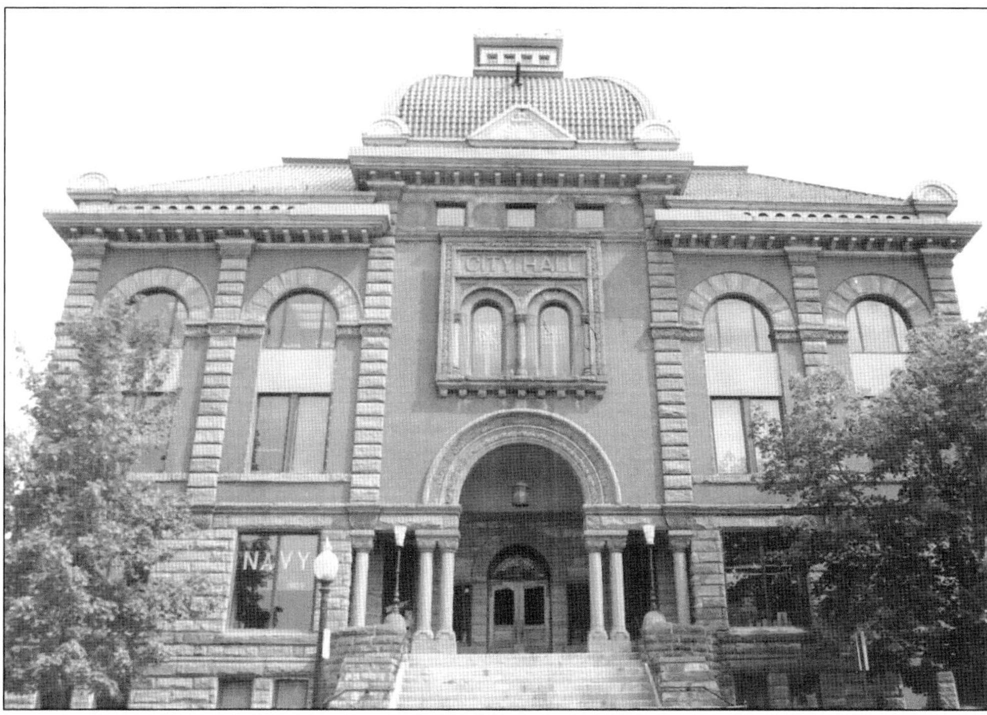

Imposing and still serving in 1998, the old city hall is no longer the center of Marquette city government but houses a variety of government offices, including the U.S. Navy recruiting station. Using local labor and materials kept the original cost of construction to $50,000, a sum recovered many times since 1893 in use and sheer visual pleasure. (Photo by G. Downs.)

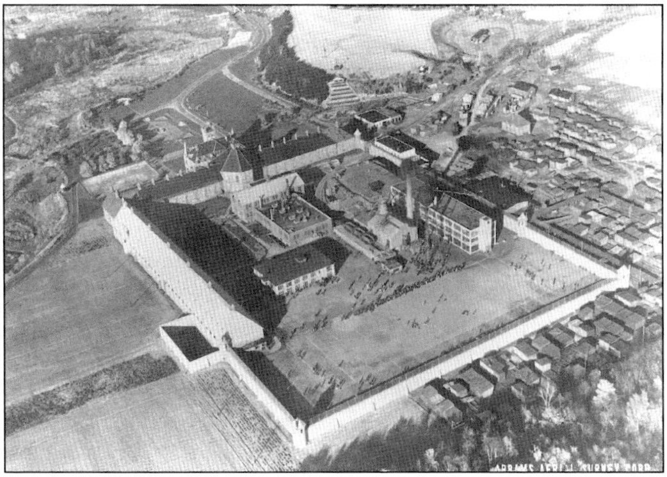

This 1975 aerial view of the Marquette Branch Prison gives a good idea of its size and the variety of structures that compose it. Toward the top of the picture is the Administration Building. Outside the walls, materials for the products made by the prisoners are stockpiled, and the prison farm fields are also visible. (Courtesy State Archives of Michigan.)

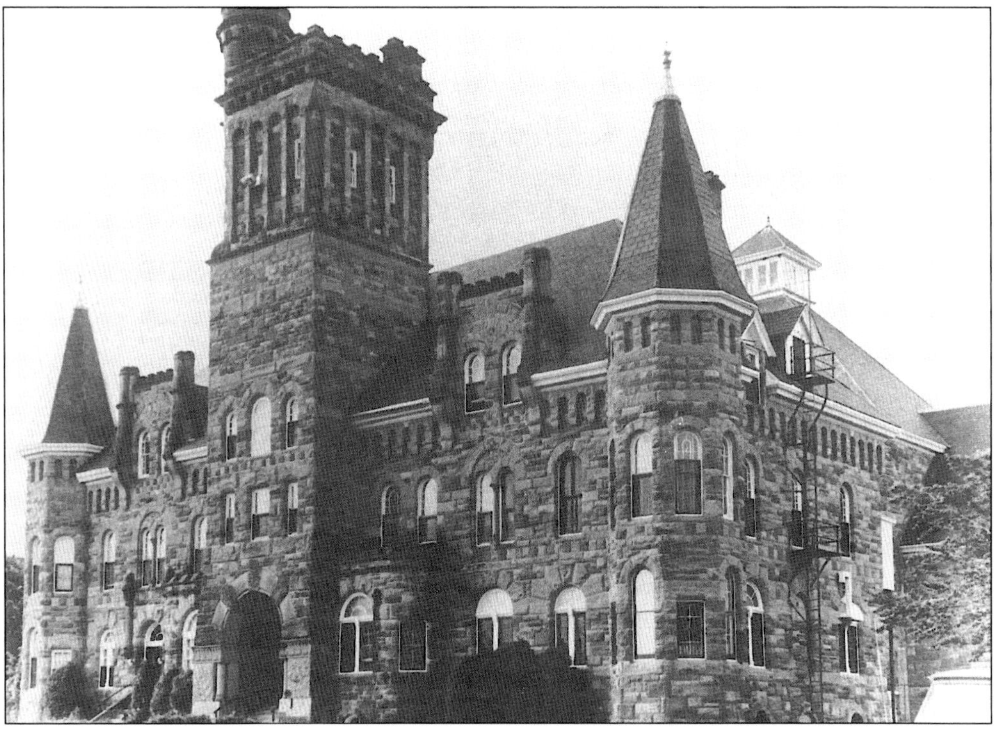

Pictured is the Administration Building at the Marquette Branch Prison in 1965, some 75 years after it was completed. The massive structure, built in what is called High Victorian Romanesque style, looks much like the administration building of an old university. Its reddish-brown walls are trimmed with red Portage Entry sandstone from the Keewanaw Peninsula, and the roof is covered with Lake Superior slate. (Courtesy State Archives of Michigan.)

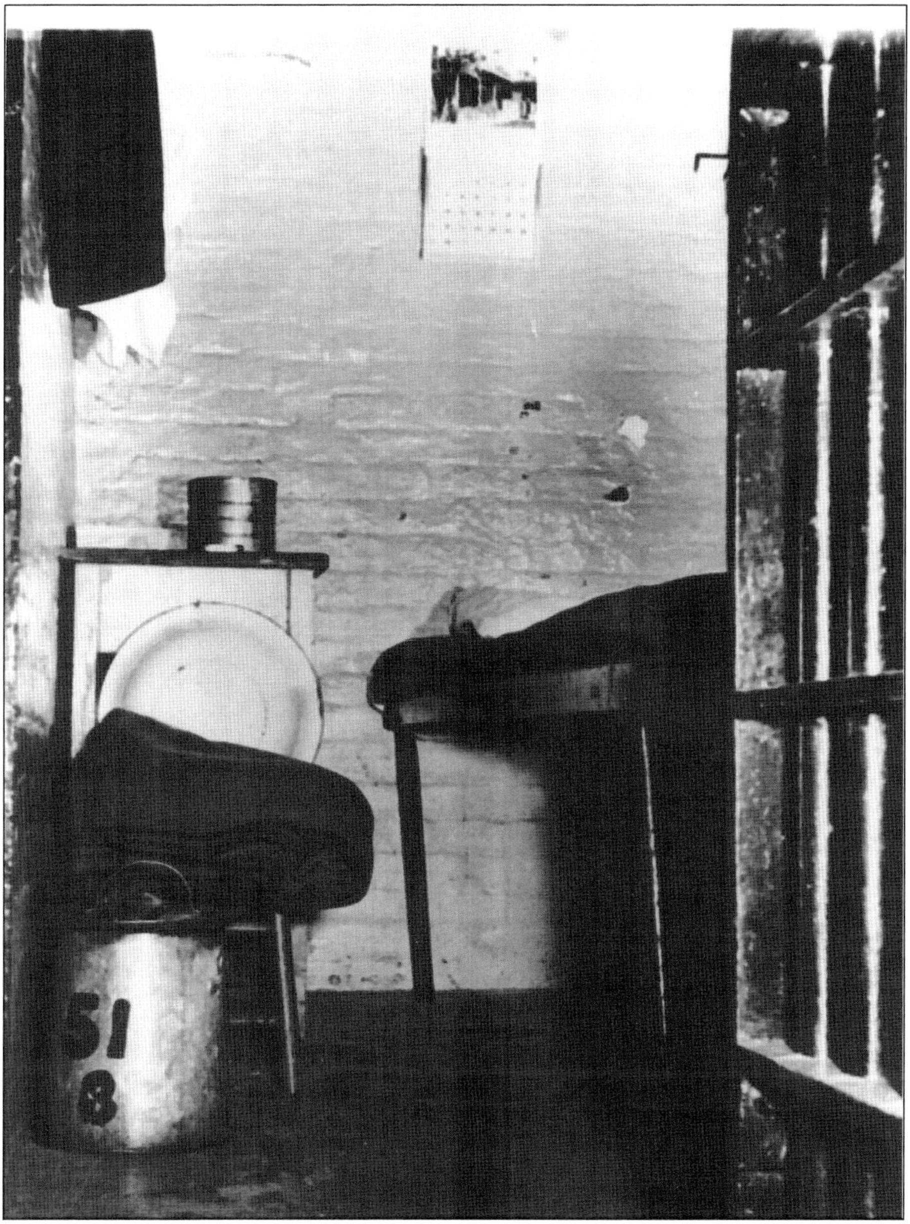

Shown here is the interior of a cell at the Marquette Branch prison shortly before the facilities were upgraded after World War II. It was no country club. The quarters were small, cramped, and smelly by all accounts, and the prison, because of its geographic isolation and the rigor of its drill, was reserved for hard cases and long-termers. Escape was difficult, or impossible, the winters were long, cold, and dark, and after a hard day in the shop, this was the cell you returned to. When the site near Marquette was selected, politicians complained that it was too beautiful for a prison, but they probably were not planning on doing time there. At times, the beauty of the setting must be all that sustains the prisoners. The grimness of the place was caught nicely by Robert Traver in the locally based novel *Anatomy of a Murder*. A petty thief says to a judge, "All I hope is that you send me any udder place but Marquette Prison. Any place a'tall but dat crummy joint." (Courtesy State Archives of Michigan.)

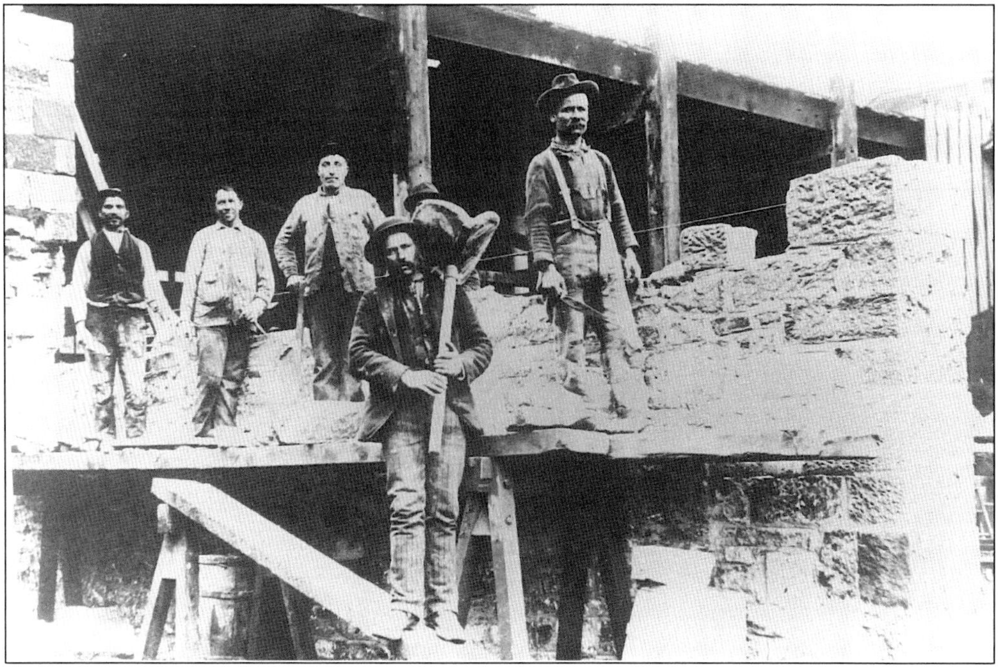

In 1885, the Michigan Legislature authorized the construction of a prison at Marquette to house residents of the Upper Peninsula convicted and sentenced to do time. This is the earliest picture in the state archives that concerns the Upper Peninsula Branch Prison and House of Correction. Workers are building the walls from the distinctive reddish-brown Marquette sandstone. It was not easy labor. (Courtesy State Archives of Michigan.)

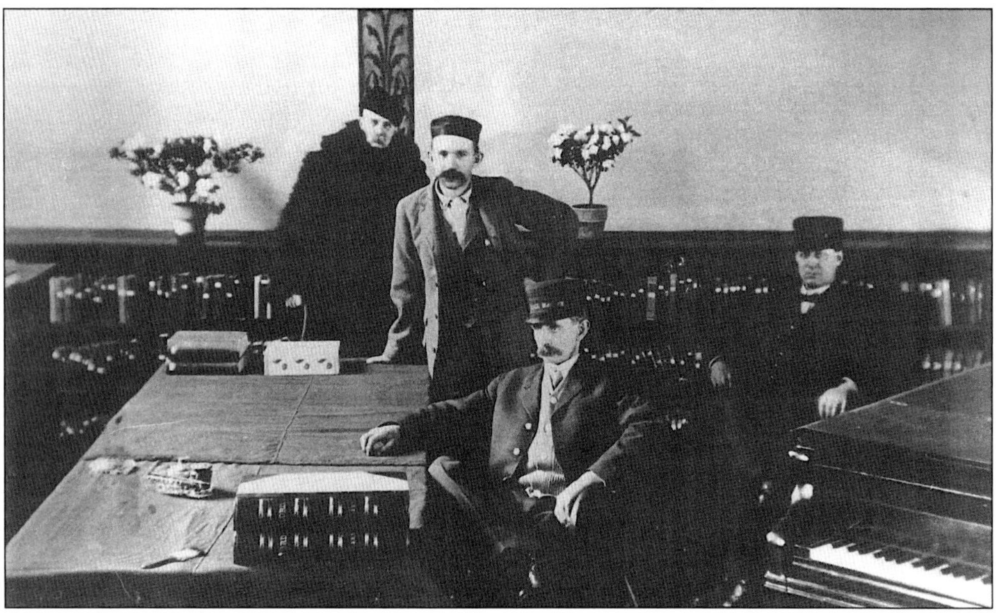

Did this picture seem as strange when it was taken in 1890 as it does today? These prison officials, somber and seated or standing near a grand piano, seem out of place in these surroundings. Note that three of the officials are dressed for indoor activity, but the fourth is wearing a large fur coat and hat. What could it mean? (Courtesy State Archives of Michigan.)

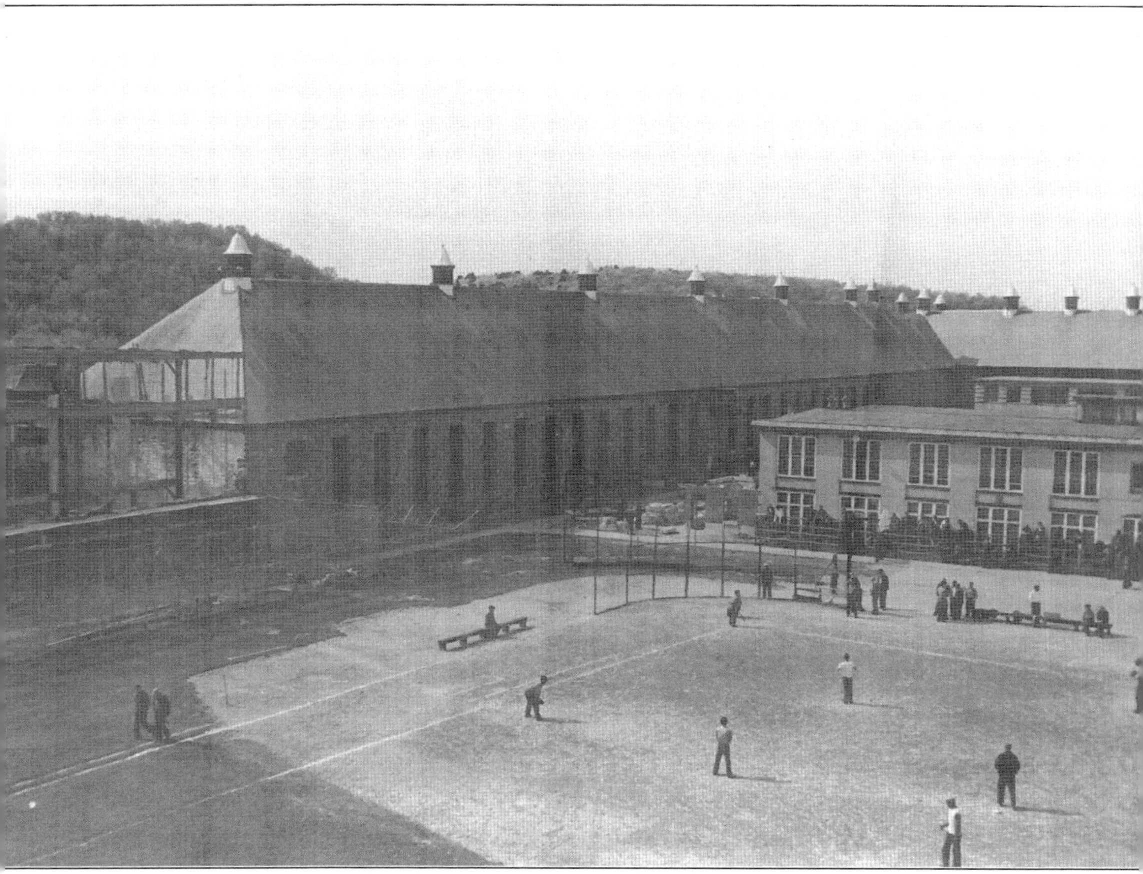

Shown here is a panoramic view of the playing fields at Marquette Branch Prison on a summer day in the 1950s. While the main administration building of the prison is often praised for its architectural distinction, the most recent construction in this picture, the building in the right middle ground, is utilitarian and prosaic. The routine at the branch prison is based on the Auburn penal system, which seeks to rehabilitate inmates through daytime work and exercise in common areas and less time spent in cells. (Courtesy State Archives of Michigan.)

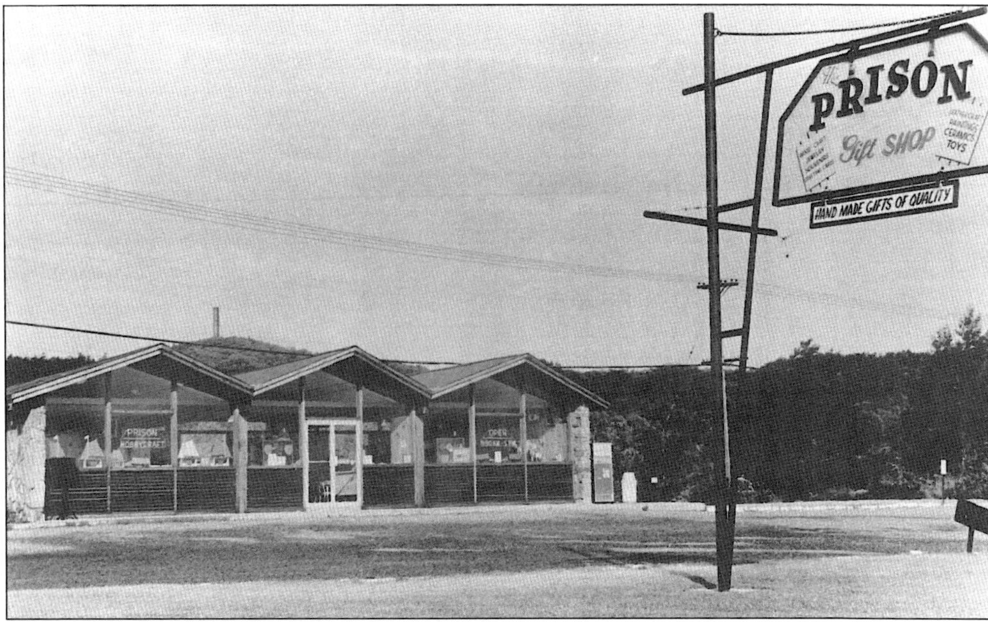

The Prison Gift Shop, located on U.S. 41 just outside prison grounds, is a popular tourist attraction. This photograph was taken *c.* 1959. Prisoners earn extra money from the sale of a variety of skillfully made handicrafts in leather and metal and other art objects such as paintings and woodcarvings. (Courtesy State Archives of Michigan.)

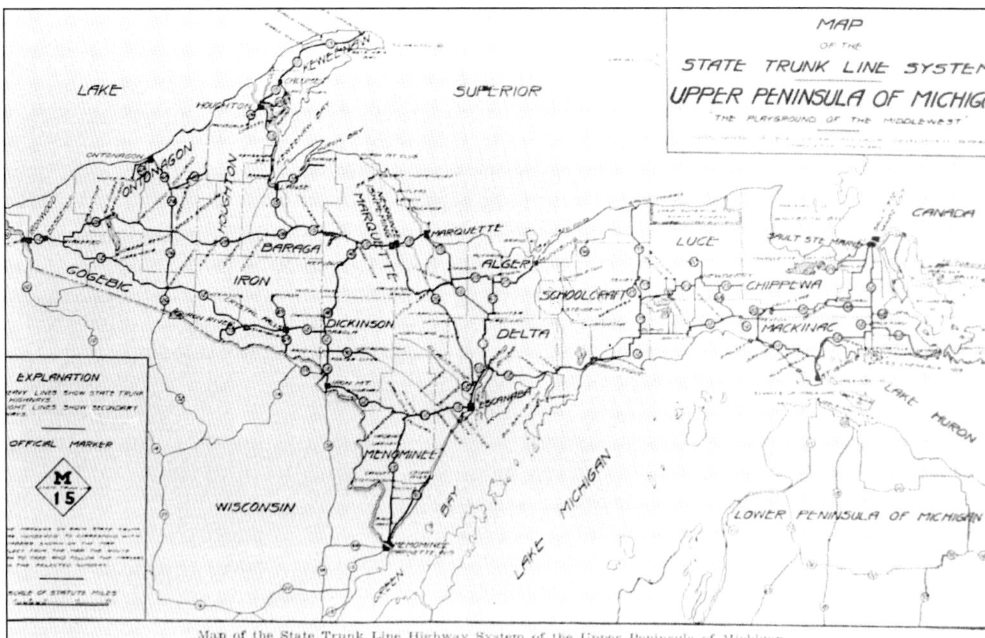

"The Playground of the Middlewest" reads the legend on this early state highway map. As early in the automobile age as 1923, the Upper Michigan Development Corporation was working to make the connection between roads and tourists. As extractive industries drove railroad development, the tourist business pushed the state to build roads. (Courtesy Peter White Library.)

Three

Commerce and Banking

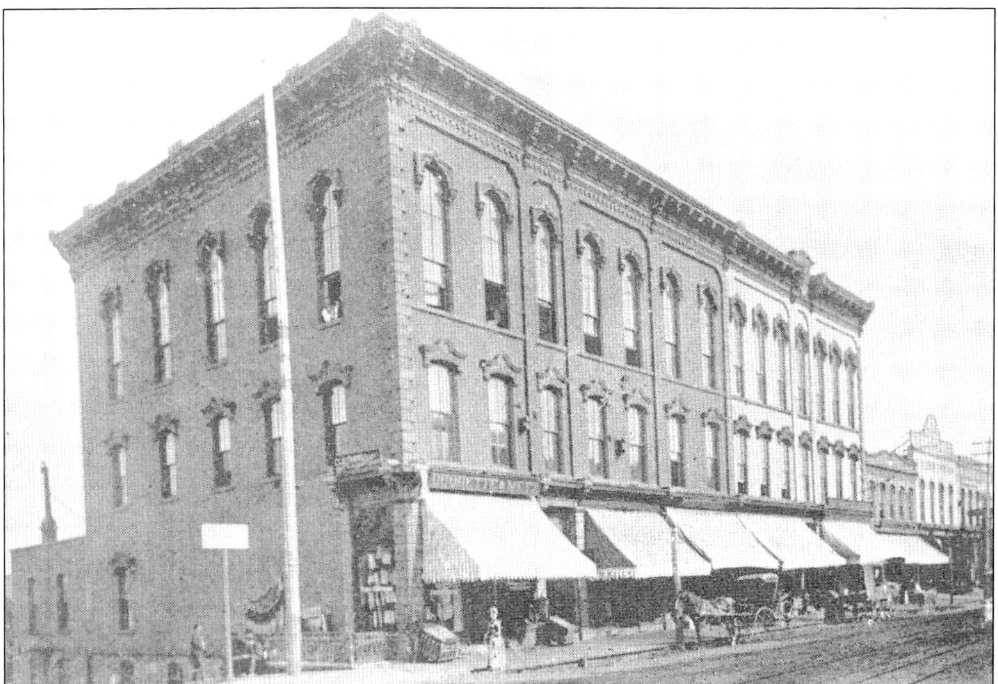

Pictured is South Front Street as it looked in the 1890s. This three-story building was located just south of the two-story block that later housed the Adams Hotel. South of the building, there are more buildings where the railroad tracks to the ore docks now cross the street. The tracks of the Marquette City & Presque Isle Railway Company (as it was called then) run in the foreground. (Courtesy Peter White Library.)

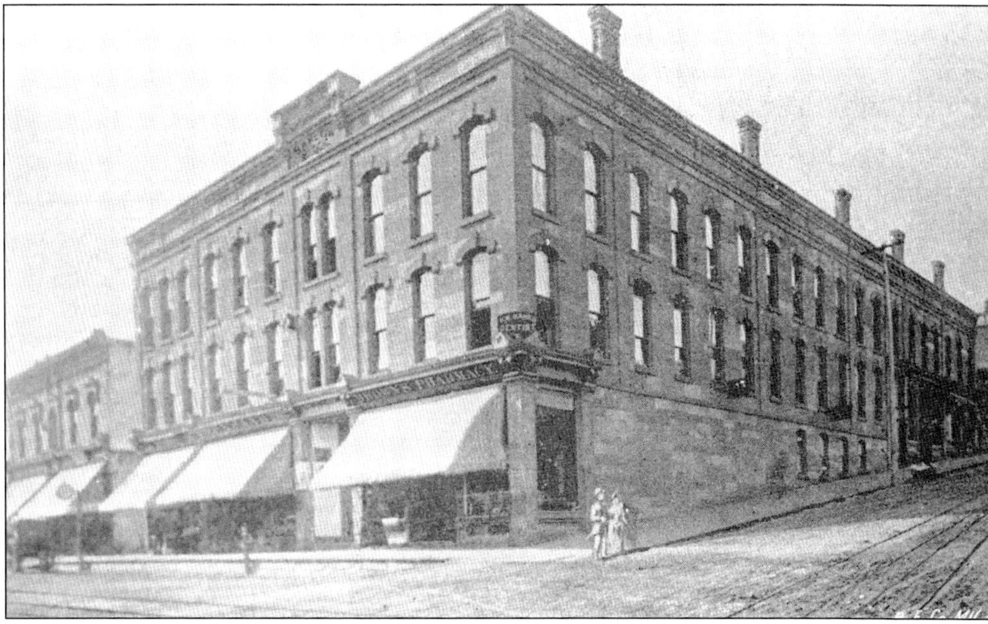

This photograph and its companion show the Harlow Block at different times in its history. This first image shows the Block in the 1890s, when it was still quite new. It was built as a speculative real estate investment in 1887, shortly before Amos Harlow died. With its central location and unadorned design, it offered both convenience and solid reassurance to its occupants and their patrons. (Courtesy Peter White Library.)

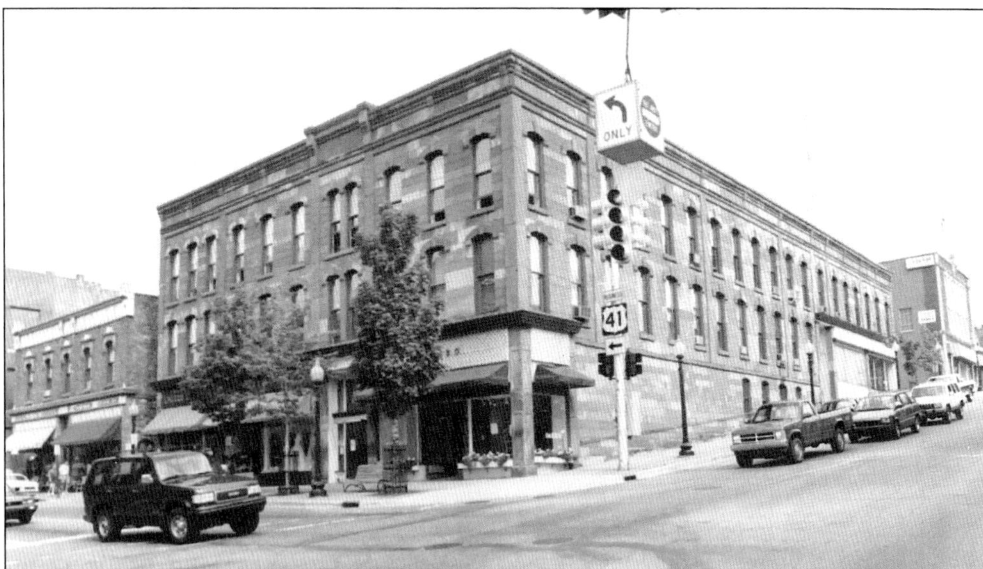

The Harlow Block is a commercial site that has held its value. Pictured here in 1998, it still bustles with business activity, and its blunt Italianate style has worn well. The businesses in the building are now more tourist oriented and upscale than the pharmacies and dentists of the 1890s, but the Block has successfully adapted to the area's changing commercial patterns. (Photo by G. Downs.)

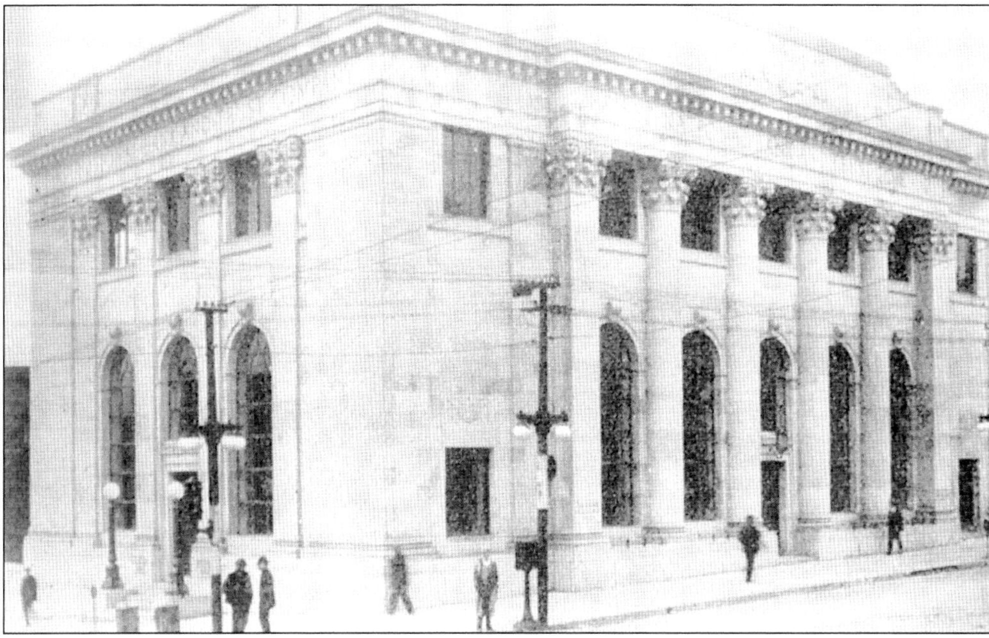

Louis G. Kaufman, president of the First National Bank in the 1920s, was primarily responsible for the construction of this handsome Beaux-Arts classical building in 1926. He wanted a dignified, architecturally distinguished and impressive edifice, and he got it. Instead of native brownstone, the architects used a lighter-colored, Indiana limestone. The contrast with the bank's neighbors is striking. (Courtesy Peter White Library.)

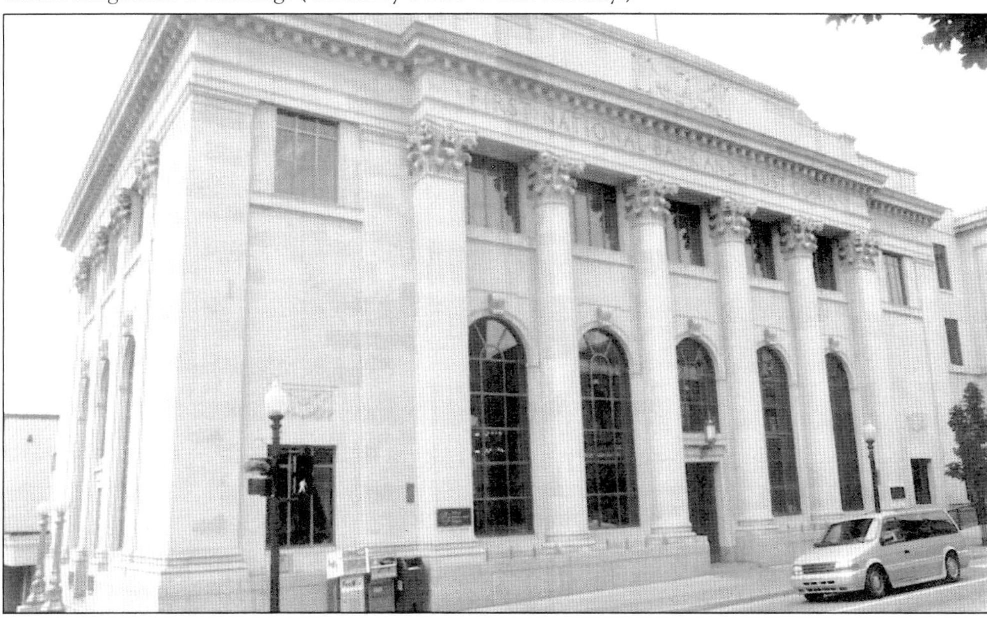

Seventy-one years after its opening, the First National Bank and Trust Company building still dominates the intersection of Washington and Front Streets. Its exterior remains unchanged, but the building's interior belies the bank's conservative image with its adaptation to contemporary needs. Its expansion, which is not seen in this picture, provides the convenience its patrons demand. (Photo by G. Downs.)

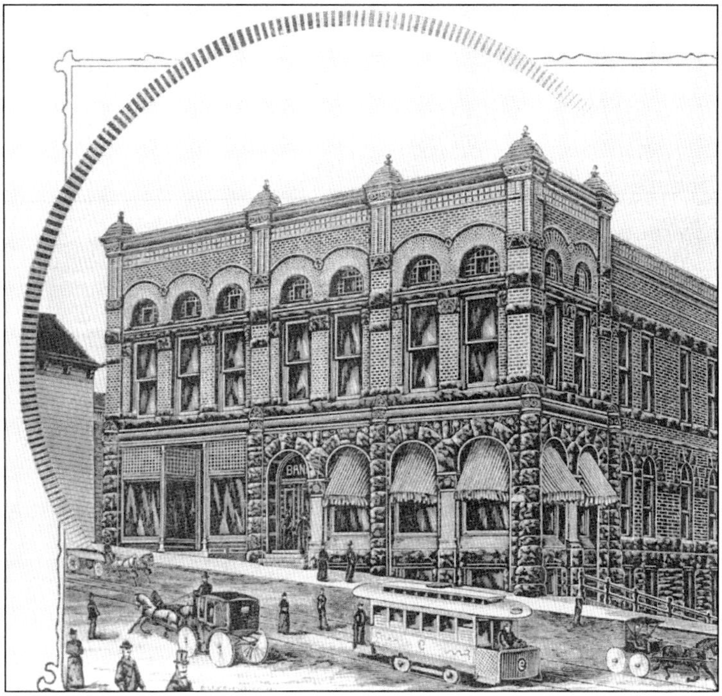

The Wilkinson Bank Building on the northeast corner of Washington and Front Streets appears in this engraving of an 1891 photograph. Interesting architectural details include the heavy, Richardsonian stone-arched windows and door at ground level and lighter, more ornate brickwork above. The engraver has obviously augmented the original image by adding some slightly out-of-proportion street traffic. (Courtesy Peter White Library.)

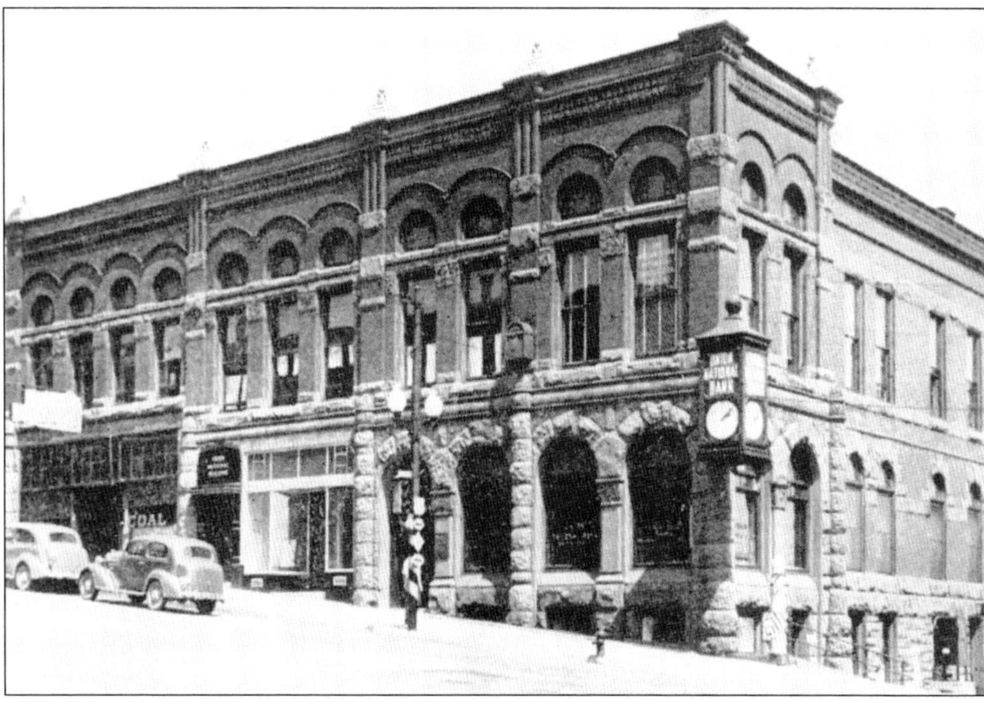

Fifty years later, the Wilkinson Bank became the Union National Bank. The building had been expanded, and the bank was sharing quarters with a coal company. The clock is a nice addition, and more modern cooling methods probably made the large window awnings unnecessary. The First Bank of America now occupies a modern building on the same corner. (Courtesy Peter White Library.)

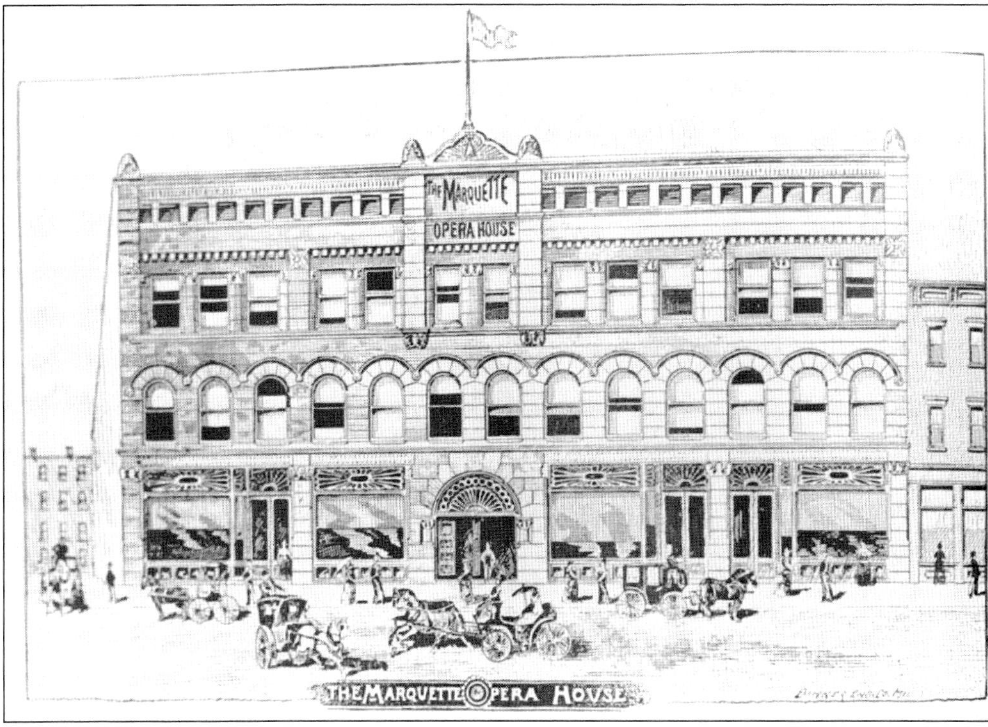

It was the "finest building of its kind north of Milwaukee and east of Duluth" and its projected cost was $75,000. Its opening on Monday evening, February 8, 1892, was the event of the year. Although the bustle on Washington Street in this 1900 lithograph was probably imaginary, the Opera House was a cultural center until it burned down in 1938 during a three-day blizzard. The Montgomery Ward store replaced it. (Courtesy Peter White Library.)

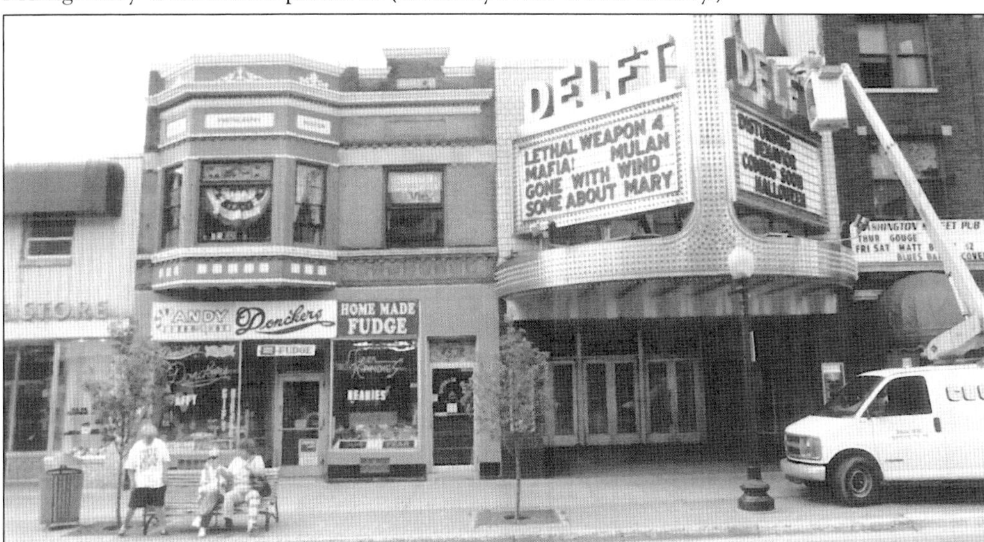

This contemporary photo shows how vital Marquette's downtown remains in the face of the commercial change that has gutted the central business core of many mid-sized American cities. The Delft Theater, in particular, which opened in 1919 and has overcome the competition of newer movie houses in local malls, is a noteworthy survivor. (Photo by G. Downs.)

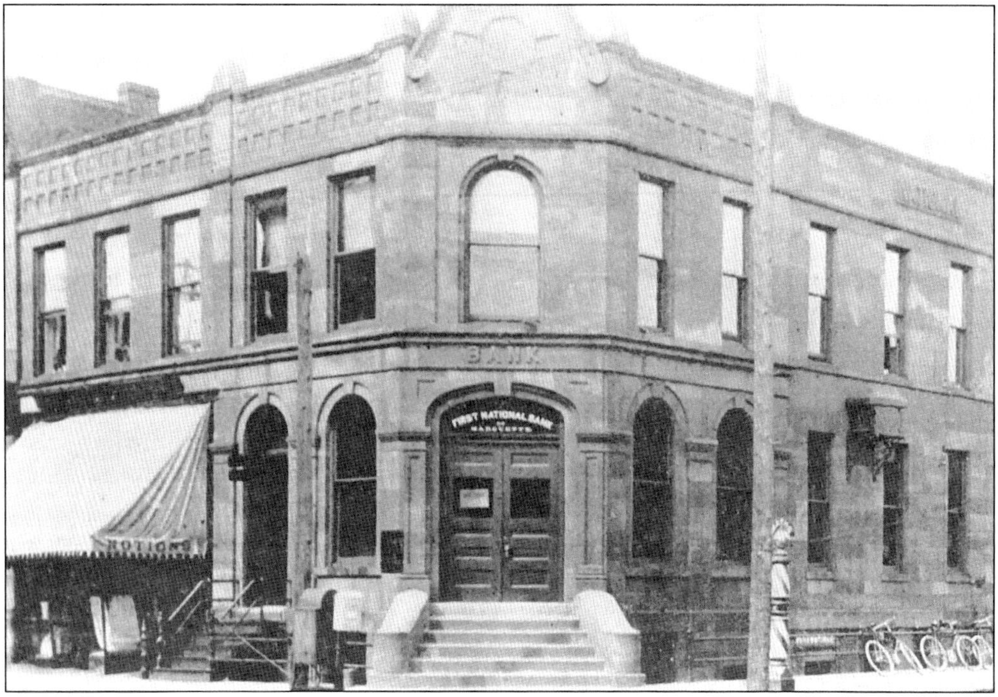

Pictured is a view of the First National Bank of Marquette, published by the Levytype Company of Chicago in 1900. First located on Front Street, the bank was founded in 1864 by Peter White. Currently the successor to this bank is located on the southwest corner of Front and Washington Streets and is called The First National Bank and Trust Company. (Courtesy Peter White Library.)

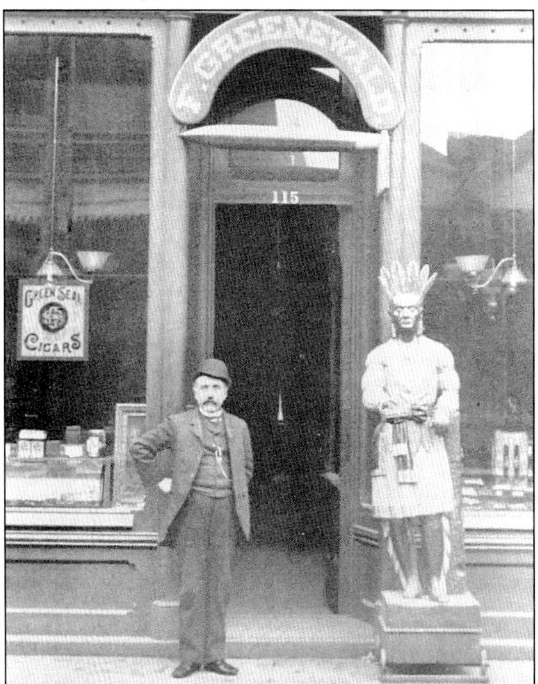

Certain symbols—a red and white striped pole, a large bicuspid or molar, or a wooden Indian holding a handful of cigars—indicated what lay within: a barbershop, a dentist, or a tobacconist. F. Greenewald was doing business as a tobacconist in Marquette in 1885 when these two icons, the Indian and the sturdy burgher, were snapped. (Courtesy Peter White Library.)

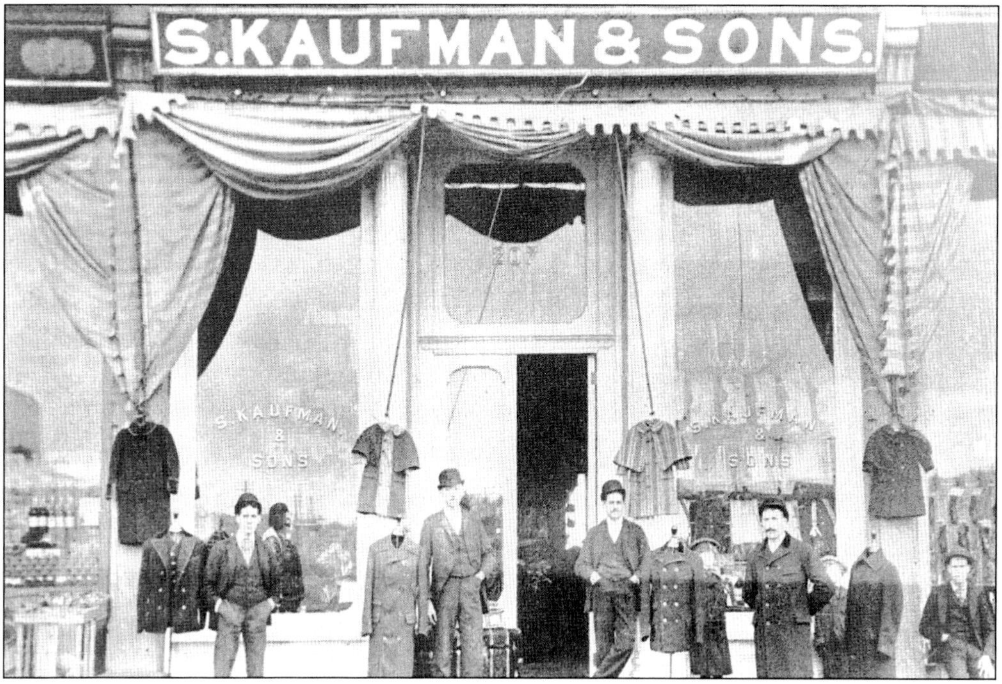

Shown in this 1885 view is Samuel Kaufman, the owner of Kaufman and Sons. He made and sold clothing in Marquette from 1853 until he retired in 1895. His store was located on Front Street, where the Rosewood Hotel is now, and he was one of the first clothiers in the Upper Peninsula to make custom suits and coats. There were seven other clothing stores competing with Kaufman and Sons in Marquette's early days. (Courtesy Peter White Library.)

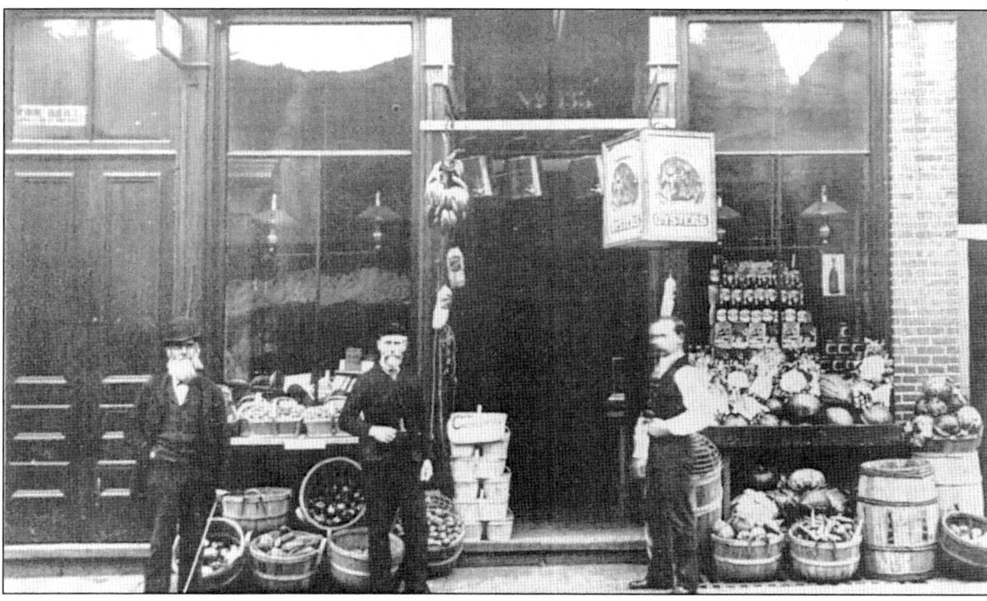

This is Delf's Grocery as it appeared in 1889. It was one of 20 groceries in Marquette at the time; there were also ten butcher shops. When Mr. Delf retired, his son continued the business at this address, 133 Washington Street, until 1936. A Piggly-Wiggly Market, part of a national chain, moved in when Delf's closed. (Courtesy Peter White Library.)

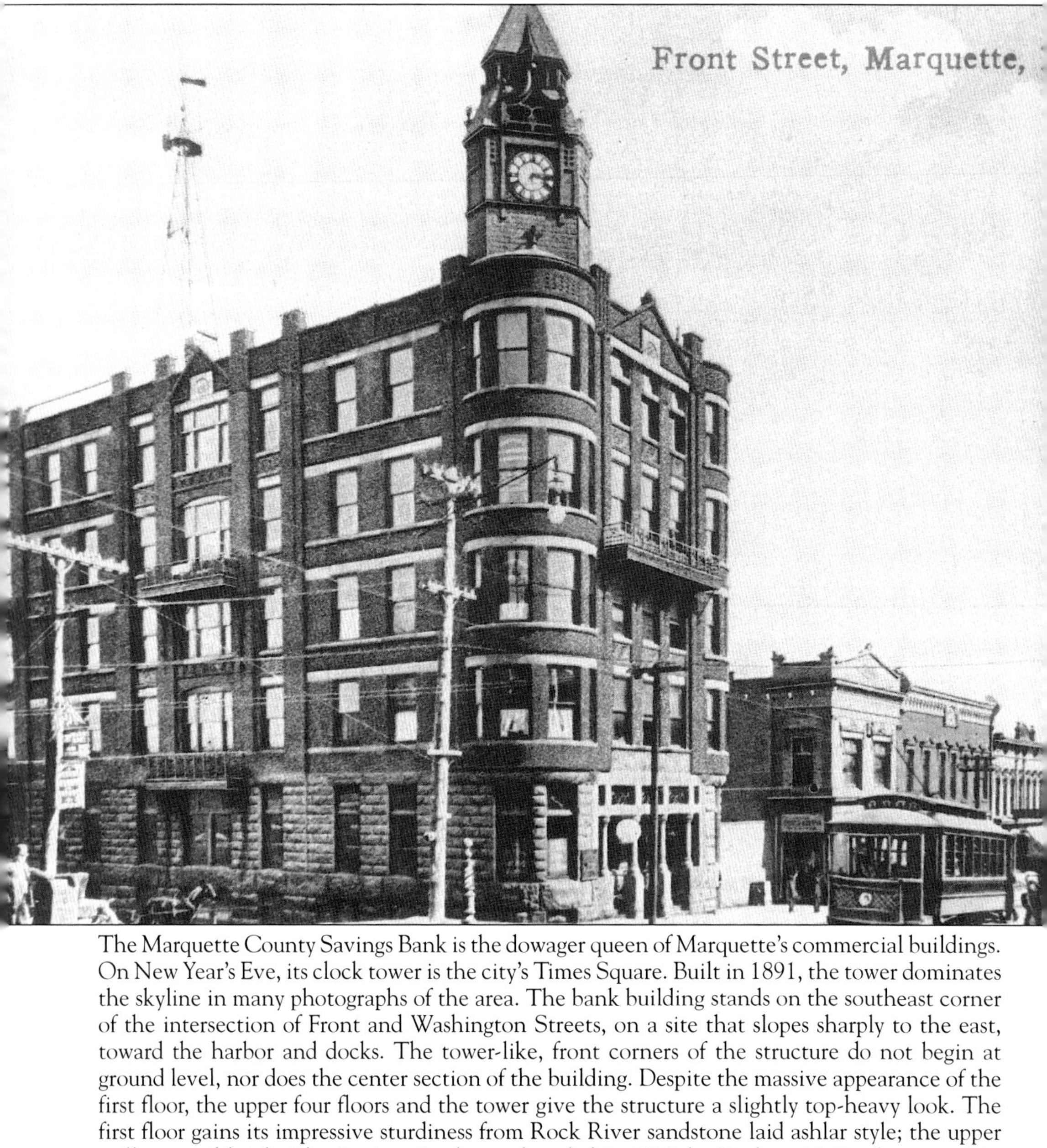

The Marquette County Savings Bank is the dowager queen of Marquette's commercial buildings. On New Year's Eve, its clock tower is the city's Times Square. Built in 1891, the tower dominates the skyline in many photographs of the area. The bank building stands on the southeast corner of the intersection of Front and Washington Streets, on a site that slopes sharply to the east, toward the harbor and docks. The tower-like, front corners of the structure do not begin at ground level, nor does the center section of the building. Despite the massive appearance of the first floor, the upper four floors and the tower give the structure a slightly top-heavy look. The first floor gains its impressive sturdiness from Rock River sandstone laid ashlar style; the upper walls are red brick. The Savings Bank was founded in 1890 by Nathan M. Kaufman, and its rapid growth made the construction of this "fascinating commercialized version of the Queen Ann style" possible. The building still stands, but the fussy balconies are gone. (Courtesy State Archives of Michigan.)

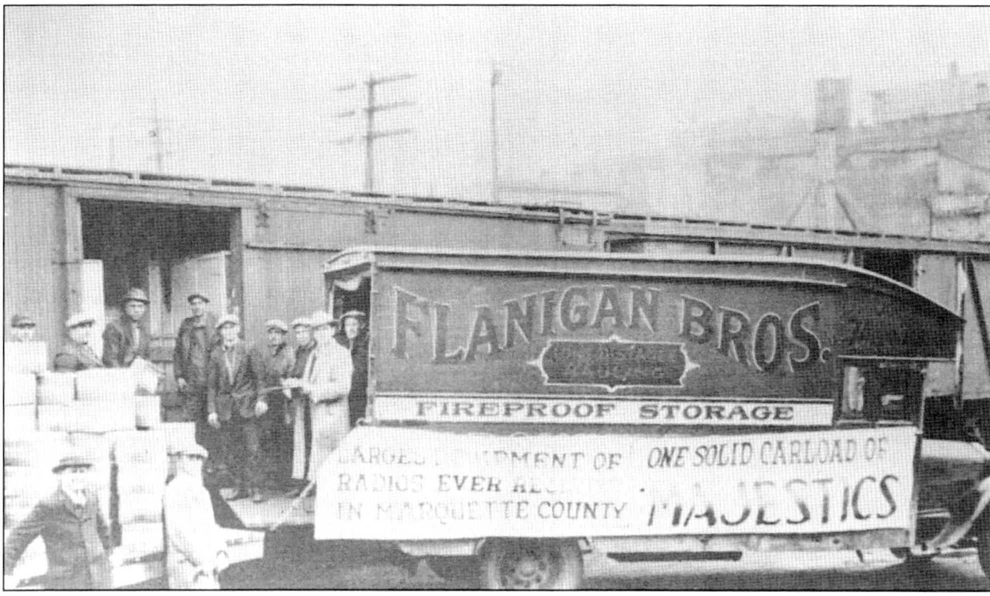

Flanagan Brothers, in the 1920s a dealer in fireproof storage and radios, is still in business after more than 100 years. The brothers sold a variety of household goods and assorted merchandise—the stuff that dreams are made of. Their warehouses were located in the vicinity of Lakeshore Boulevard and the docks. (Courtesy Peter White Library.)

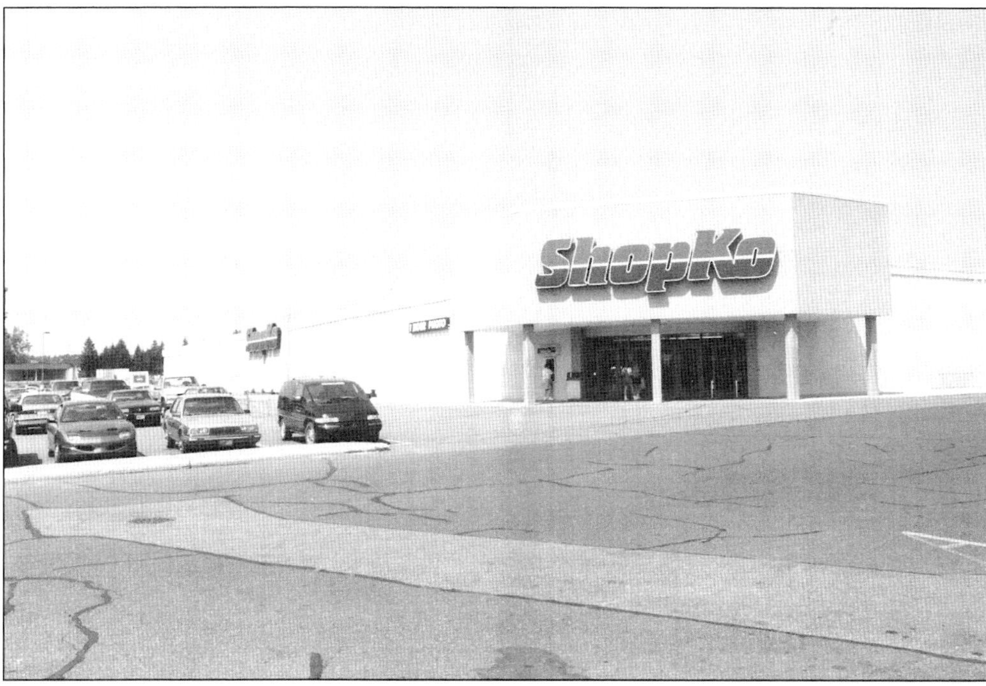

Shopko, located west of Marquette's downtown on U.S. 41, is an excellent example of recent trends in merchandising in Marquette and throughout the United States. Located inside are services and products that, in an earlier time, would have been spread over most of a downtown business district; outside are acres of parking for automobiles, built on the outskirts of the city on less expensive land. (Photo by G. Downs.)

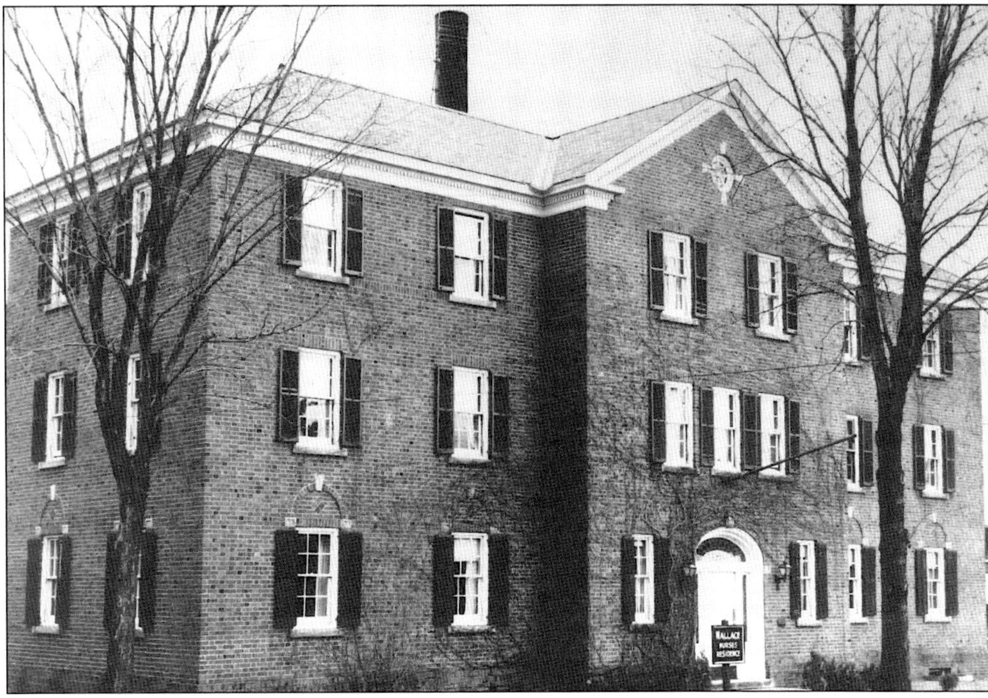

The Wallace Nurses Residence, shown here in the late 1950s, was a home away from home for student nurses at the St. Luke's School of Nursing. The nursing school was located at St. Luke's Hospital on Hebard Court. Marquette City Hospital was renamed St. Luke's when it moved in 1897. (Courtesy Marquette County Historical Society.)

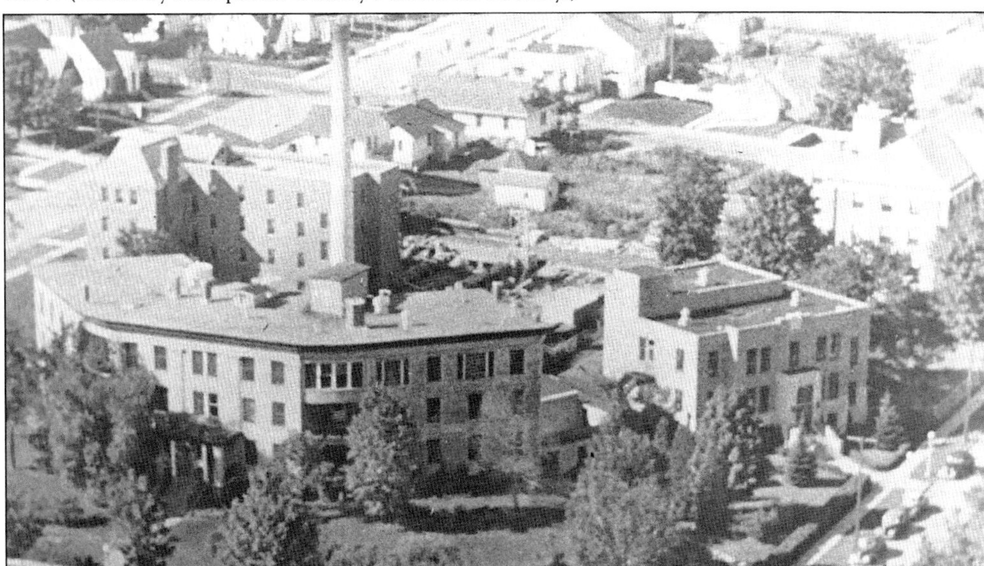

This is the old St. Luke's Hospital on Hebard Court in 1948. The three-story building was built in 1915 and is still in use. In 1954, St. Luke's acquired the Northern Michigan Children's Clinic, which had been established in 1934. The James Couzzens Memorial Building was added in 1938. St. Mary's, the Catholic Hospital, merged with St. Luke's to create Marquette General Hospital in 1973. (Courtesy Marquette County Historical Society.)

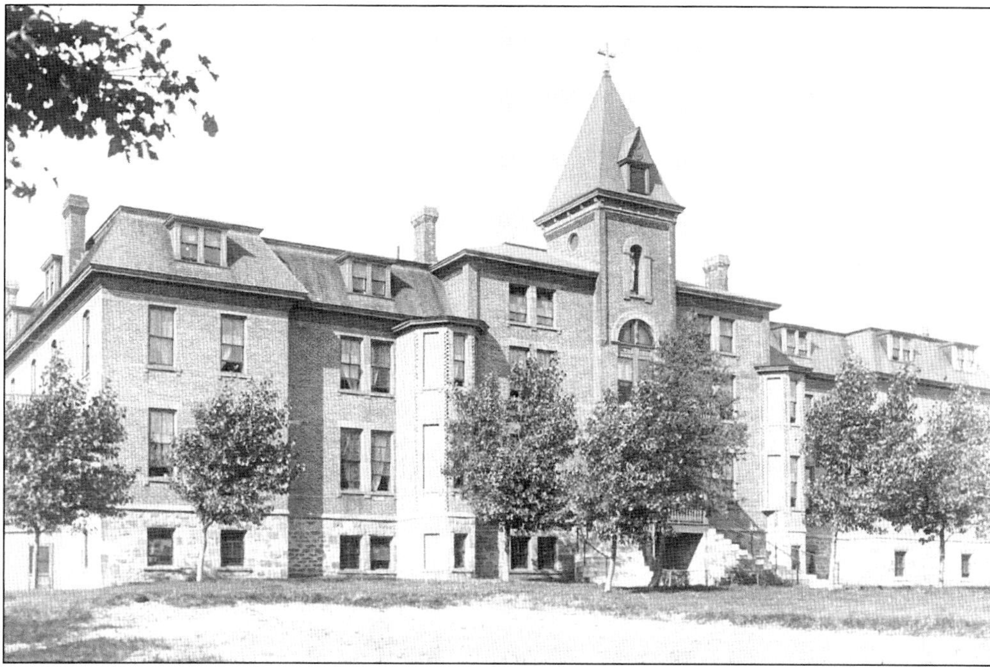

St. Mary's Hospital, Marquette's oldest, opened in 1891 under the direction of the Sisters of the Third Order of St. Francis. This impressive photographic view of the building was taken several years later. When Marquette's two hospitals faced financial problems in the 1970s, St. Mary's became Marquette General South in the consolidation and developed into the Upper Peninsula Rehabilitation Center. (Courtesy Marquette County Historical Society.)

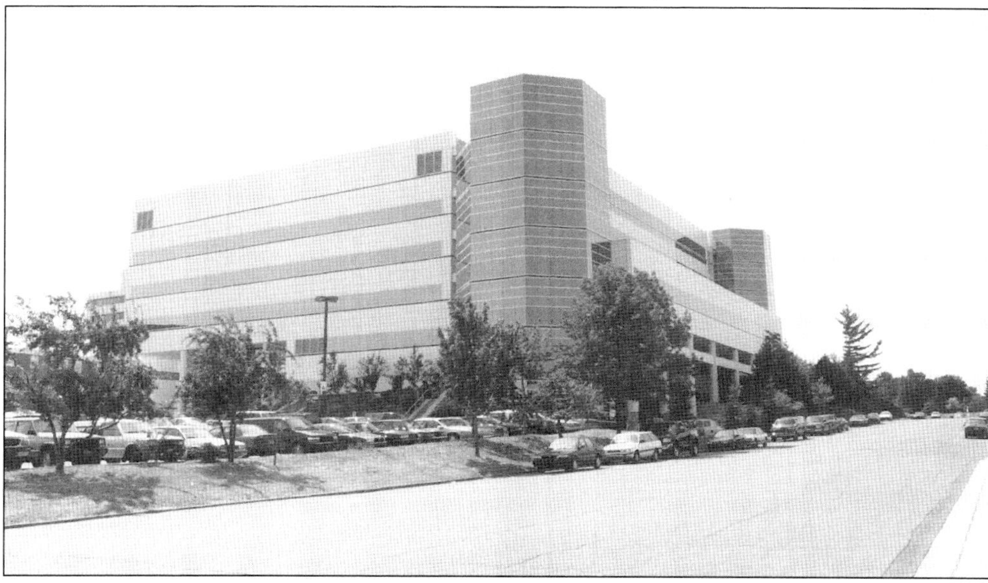

Marquette General Hospital had been serving residents and patients for 25 years when this picture was taken in 1998. This health-care institution got its start 103 years ago, when six local physicians established a small care center with 12 beds in what was formerly a private home at 152 East Prospect Street. The current facility has 400 beds and employs 2,400. (Photo by G. Downs.)

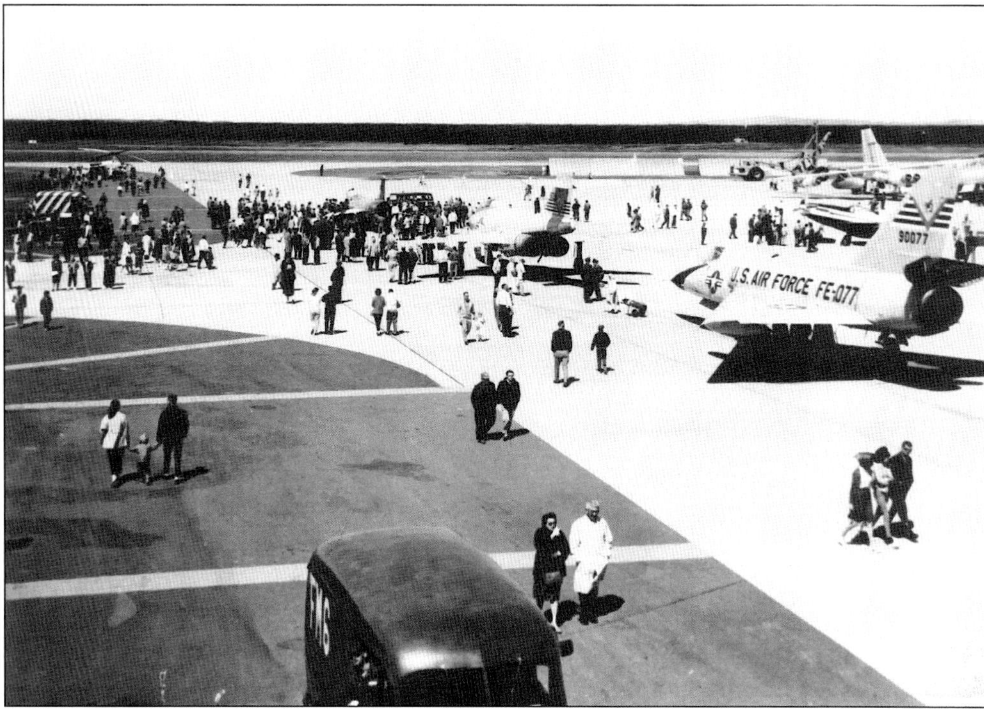

K.I. Sawyer Air Force Base was hosting an open house when this picture was taken in the 1970s. The interest in the base and its welfare was due in part to international political tensions as well as to the vital contribution the base and its personnel made to the economic, social, and political life of Marquette County. The base closed in 1995. (Courtesy Marquette County Historical Society.)

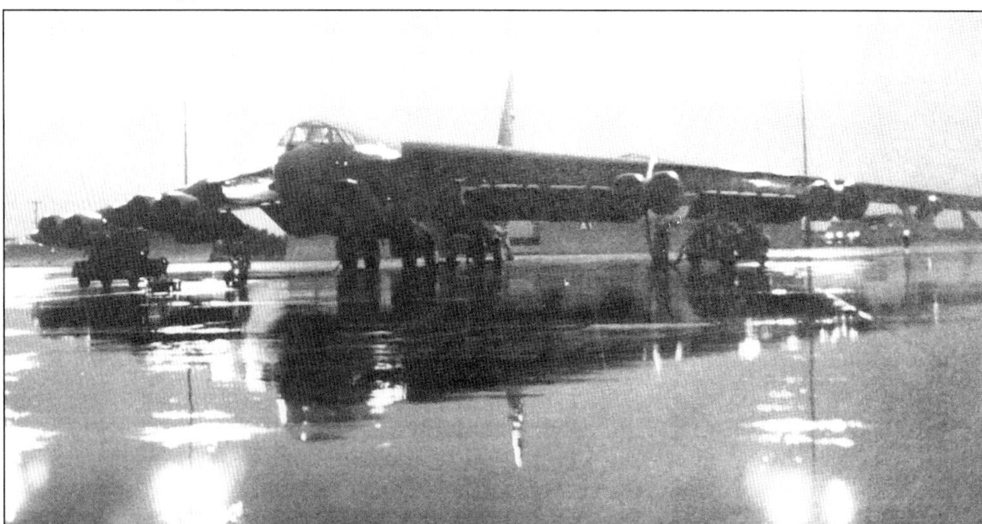

Despite the size of K.I. Sawyer's economic contribution to the Marquette community and the devastating loss its closing created, city and county leaders rebounded quickly. With the help of local government, they have tried to turn this disadvantage into leverage for a better future. This picture appears on a brochure that touts the industrial development potential of the base. (Courtesy Peter White Library.)

Four

Food, Drink, and Lodging

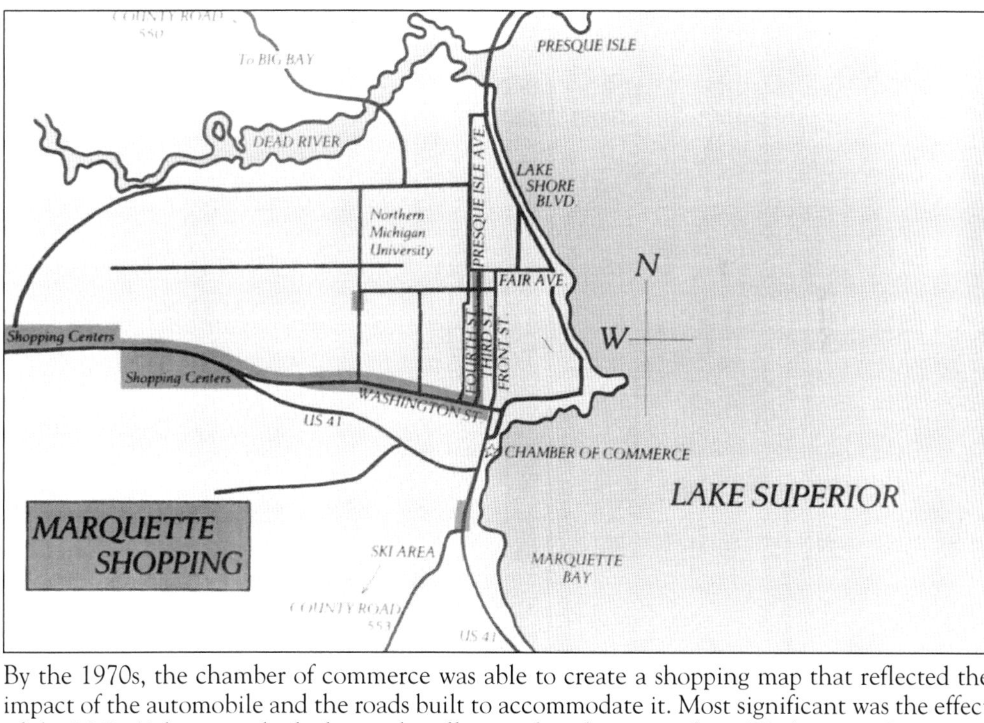

By the 1970s, the chamber of commerce was able to create a shopping map that reflected the impact of the automobile and the roads built to accommodate it. Most significant was the effect of the U.S. 41 bypass, which diverted traffic—and trade—away from Washington Street and made possible the construction of commercially attractive, large shopping centers along the highway west of the city. (Courtesy Peter White Library.)

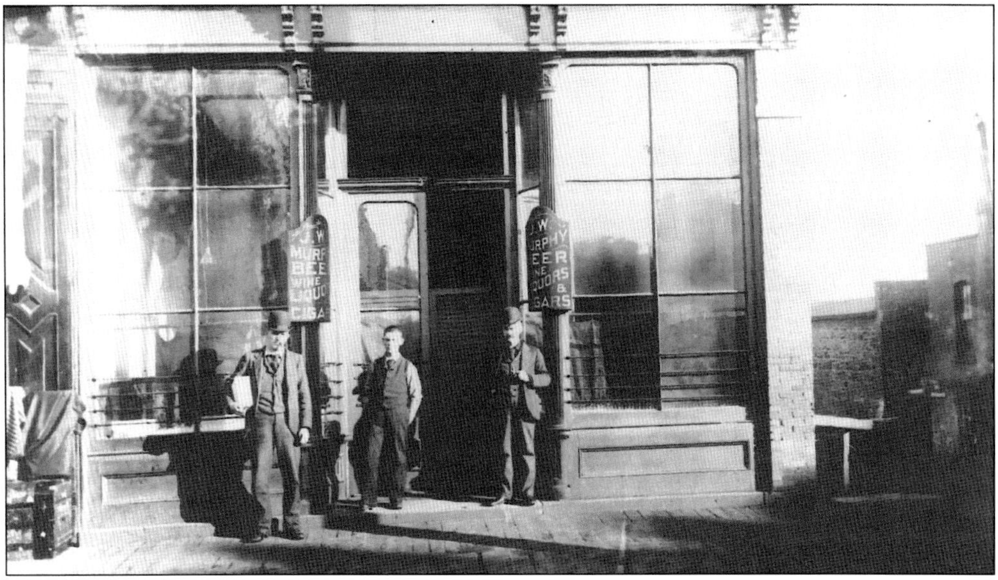

In 1890, the J.W. Murphy Saloon stocked and sold beer, liquor, and cigars—the staples of masculine society. One patron, seen here with a bundle under his arm, appears to be in the picture by accident and is perhaps just a passerby; a man wearing a hat and jacket poses just outside the door. (Courtesy Marquette County Historical Society.)

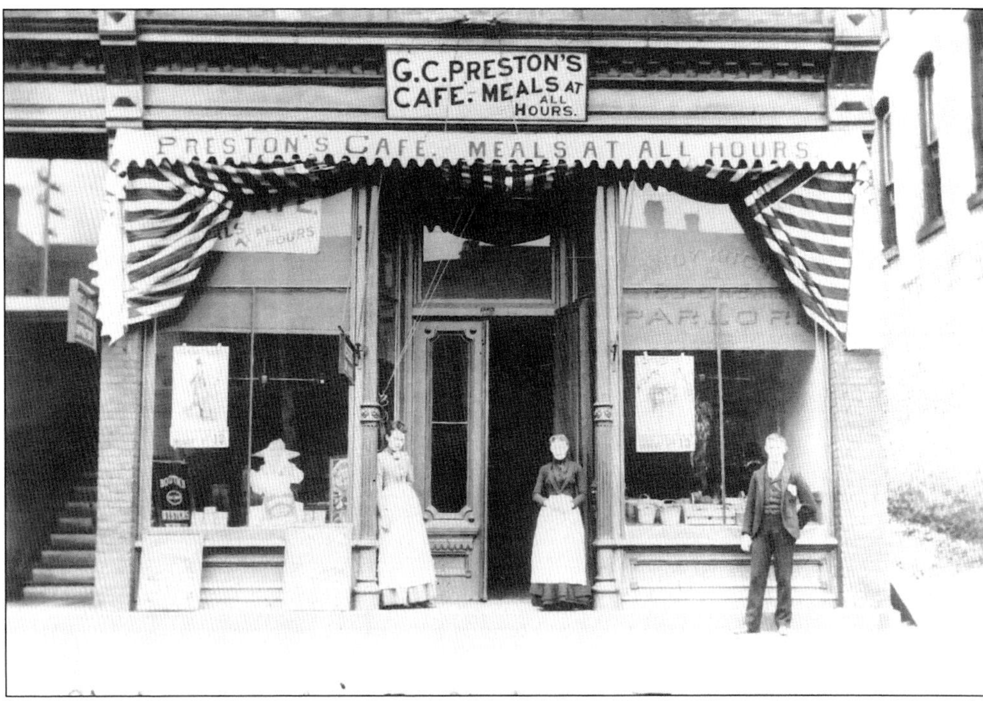

G.C. Preston's Café, located in the Harlow Block at 112 West Washington Street, was photographed at about the same time as The Louis Vierling Saloon (next page). Note the awning and the placards in the windows announcing the same coming attraction. In the Vierling picture, only the edge of the placard can be seen. (Courtesy Marquette County Historical Society.)

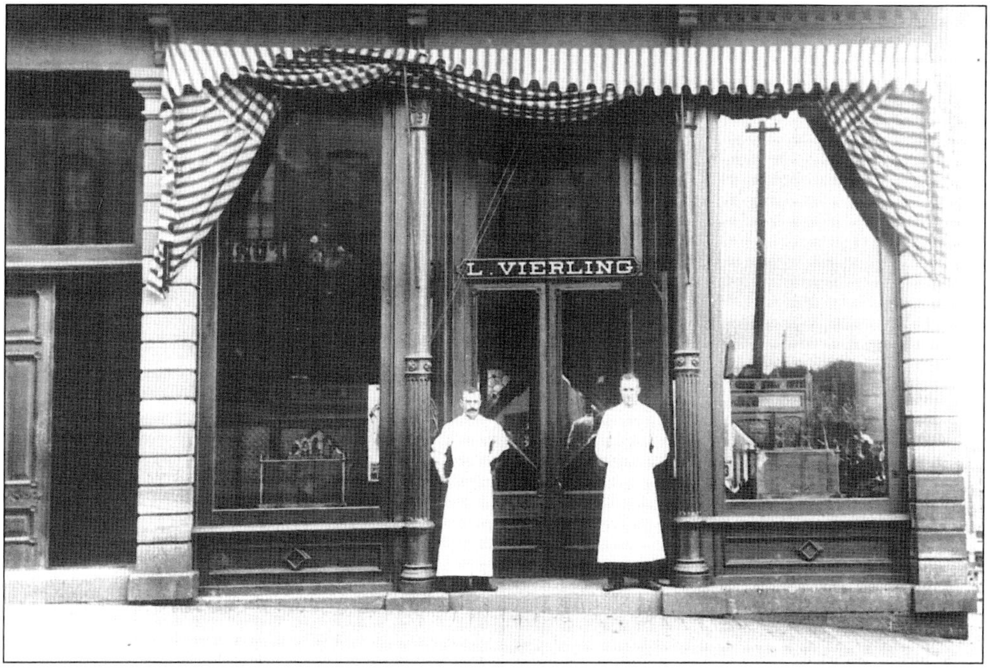

Shown here is the original Vierling on Front Street, The Louis Vierling Saloon, as it appeared in 1895. The awning indicates that the season is probably summer, and the fact that it is rolled up suggests that this picture was taken in the morning, before the rush of customers, or on an overcast day. It looks like a classy place; the aprons are clean. (Courtesy Marquette County Historical Society.)

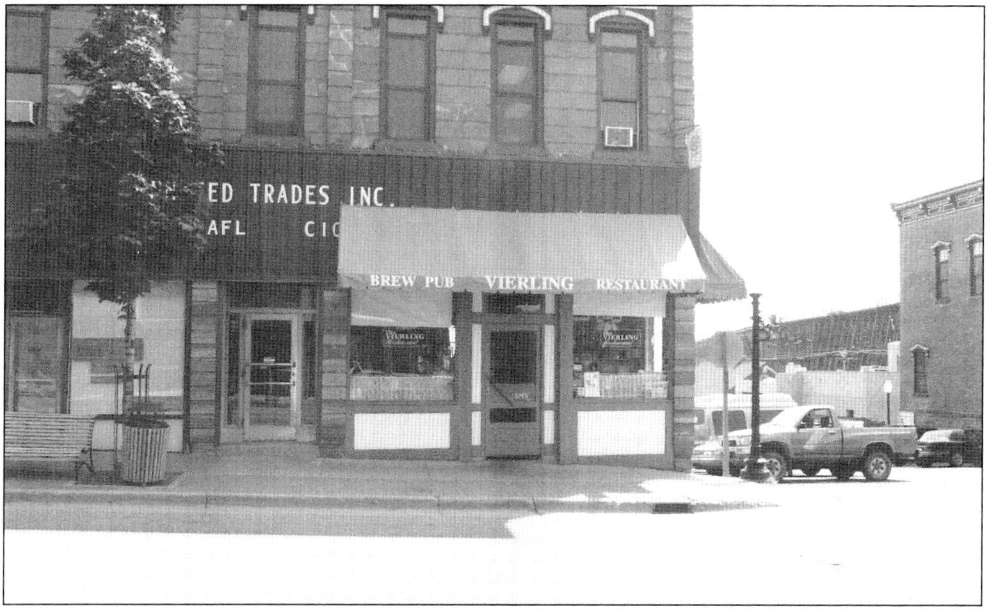

This version of the Vierling can be traced back in a not-quite-unbroken line to a much earlier establishment with the same name, at this address, in the same building. The D.S.S.&A. Ore Dock can be seen at the foot of Main Street (right). Across the street is the rear of the newly refurbished Rosewood Hotel. (Photo by G. Downs.)

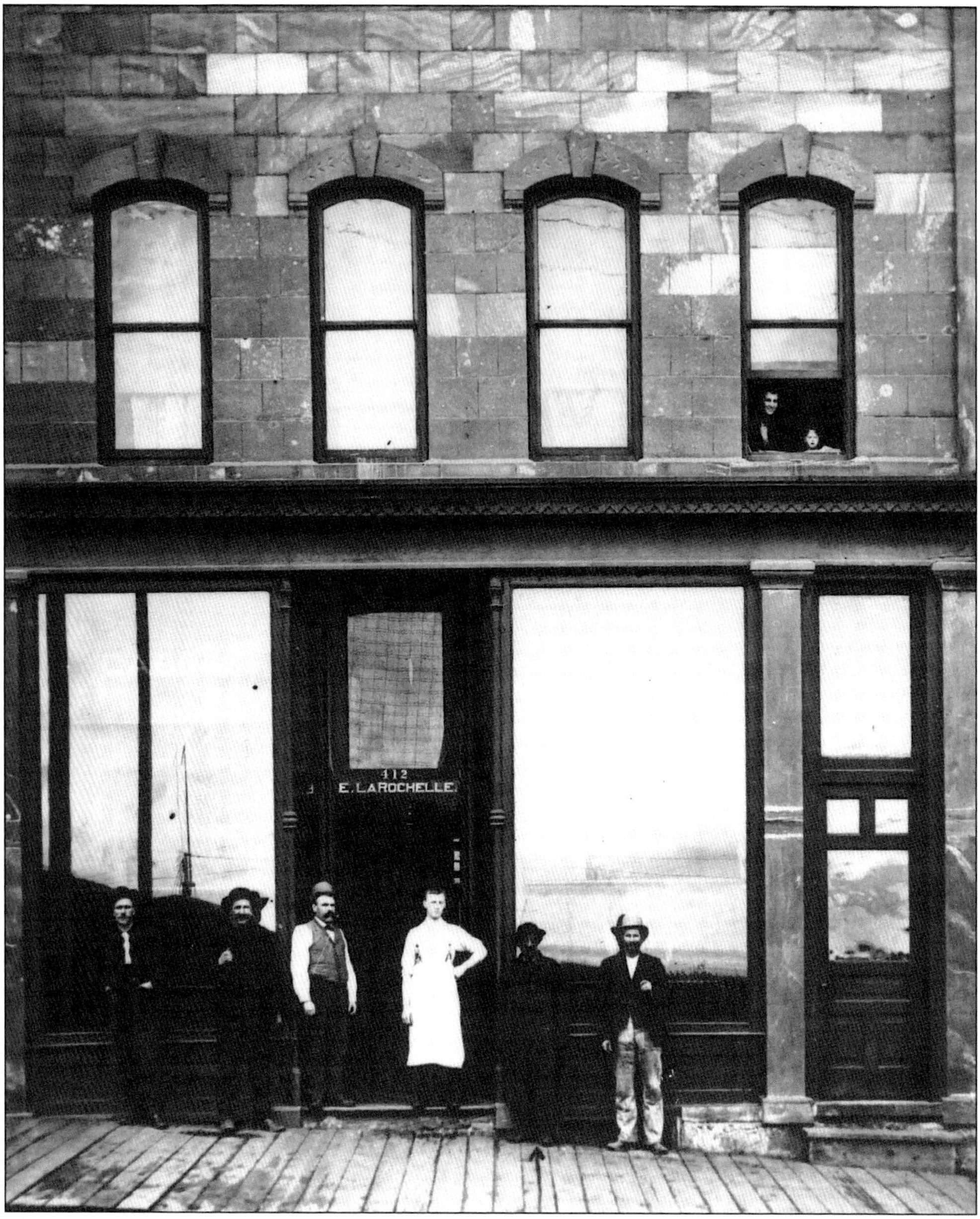

The La Rochelle, named after its proprietor, was located at 412 South Front Street when this picture was taken in the 1880s. The sidewalks were still boardwalks and the streets were unpaved, but plenty of plate glass and native sandstone were being used to good effect. The look of the place is still pretty raw and unfinished, but the arched windows, with their decorated lintels, large glass transoms in the entries, segmented glass-paneled doors, and ornate fascias indicate that a more refined environment was under construction. Then, as now, taverns were like social clubs, but the area's early taverns primarily served male clientele. Advertising and products associated with taverns—cigars, oysters, beer, and stronger spirits—were clearly aimed at men. These ads show up in most of the window displays in old pictures. The people pictured in this view outside the La Rochelle were not passers-by; they are typical of the crowd that could be found inside. (Courtesy Marquette County Historical Society.)

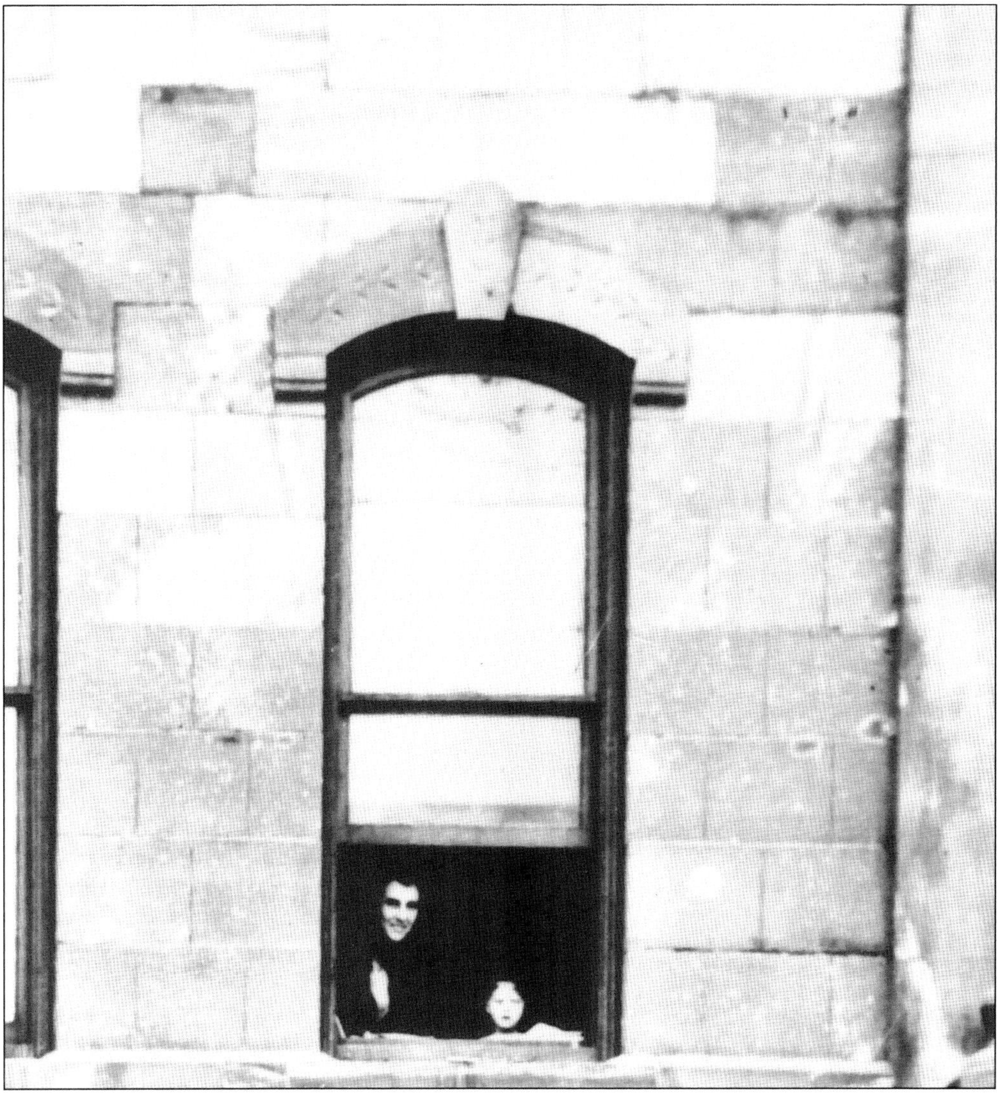

This is a detail of the picture on the facing page; the close-up view of the image contributes a great deal to its charm. The whole picture is one of the most arresting of the many considered for this publication. The woman in the open window is smiling, a rare sight in the photographs of that period. She was probably unaware that she was being included in the picture. The child beside her is solemn but unposed, coolly observant rather than awed by the photographer. Below them, on the street, the men are woodenly and conventionally posed, with legs apart and toes pointing outward. Notice the arrow drawn to focus our attention on the small, dark figure who is seen second from the right. (Courtesy Marquette County Historical Society.)

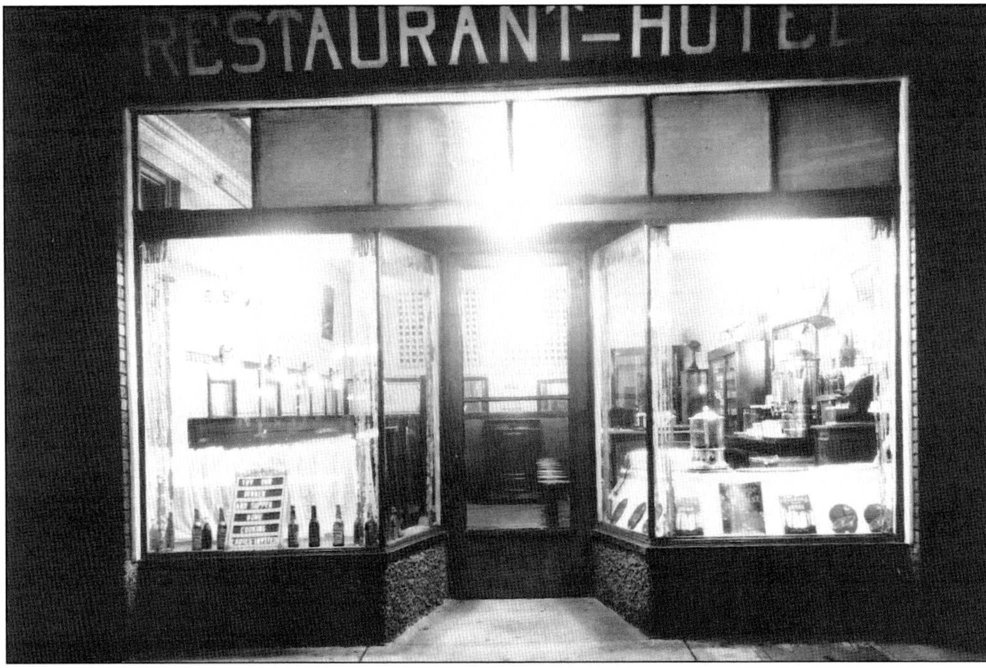

The Busy Bee Restaurant at 101 West Baraga Avenue was clean and well-lighted—but deserted—when this photograph was taken in the 1920s. The sign in the window reads "Ladies Invited." This Edward Hopper-like scene inspires all sorts of questions, but doesn't provide any answers. (Courtesy Marquette County Historical Society.)

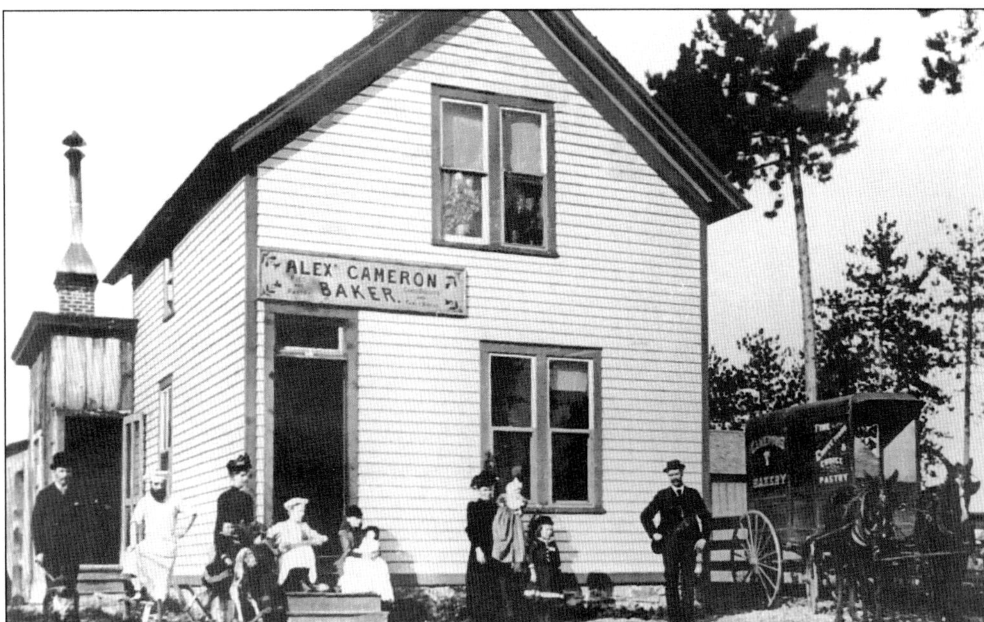

In 1888, Alex Cameron's Bakery was advertised as one of the four oldest bakeries in Marquette, specializing in confectioneries such as cakes and fancy breads. Here we can see Mr. Cameron's assets plainly presented: a premises at 128 West Ohio Street, a delivery truck and horses, a family, a rocking horse, and some hired help. (Courtesy Peter White Library.)

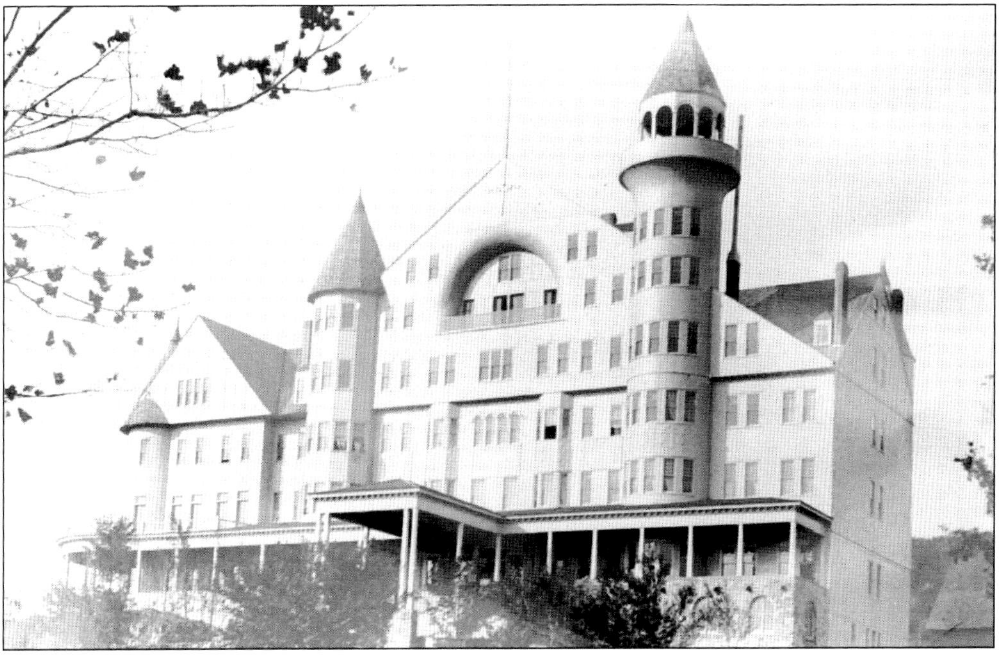

Opinions varied concerning the Superior Hotel; some referred to it as "glorious" while others called it "the biggest fire trap north of Chicago." Originally intended as a spa and sanatorium, the Superior opened in 1896 as a summer resort. Because the season was too short and the overhead too high, the venture never flourished. It was unoccupied for years and was torn down in 1929. (Courtesy Peter White Library.)

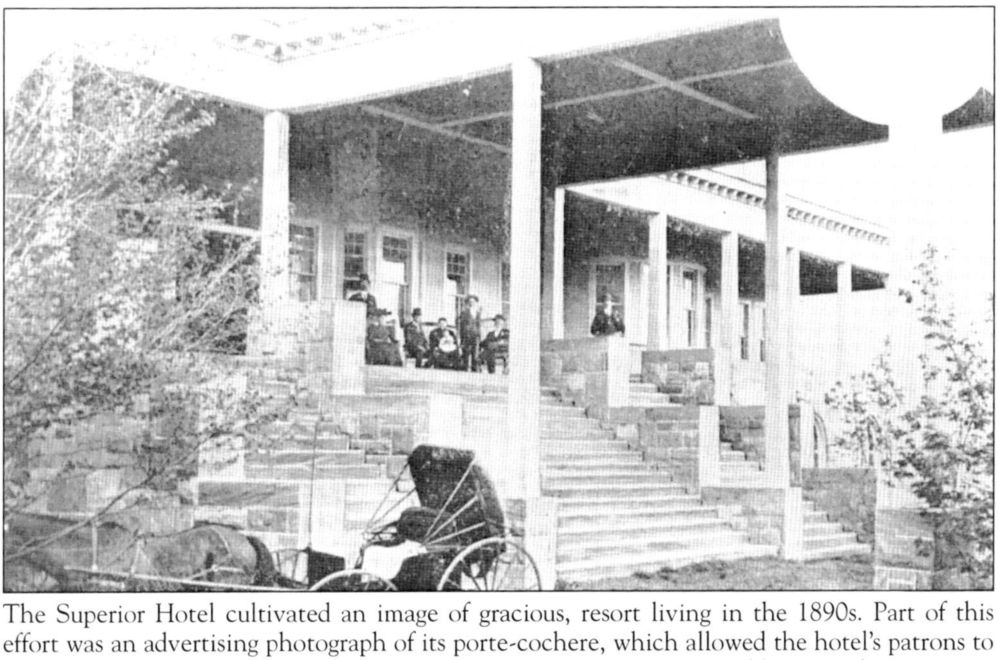

The Superior Hotel cultivated an image of gracious, resort living in the 1890s. Part of this effort was an advertising photograph of its porte-cochere, which allowed the hotel's patrons to dismount from their carriages without getting wet when it rained. In addition to this entrance, which was designed specifically for those arriving by buggy or carriage, there were others that were less grand. (Courtesy Peter White Library.)

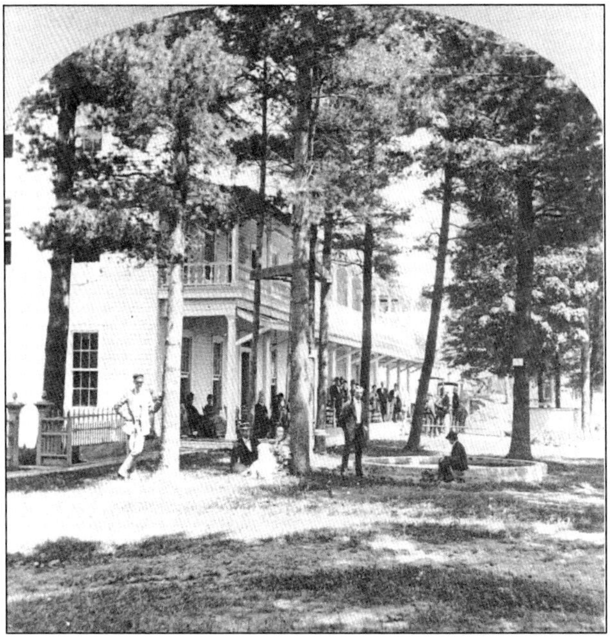

This image, taken from a stereopticon slide, shows the Northwestern Hotel at 423 West Washington Street on a high summer day in 1868. At the time, it was the largest and most popular tourist hotel in Marquette, and one of the first indications that tourism would develop into a profitable industry. (Courtesy State Archives of Michigan.)

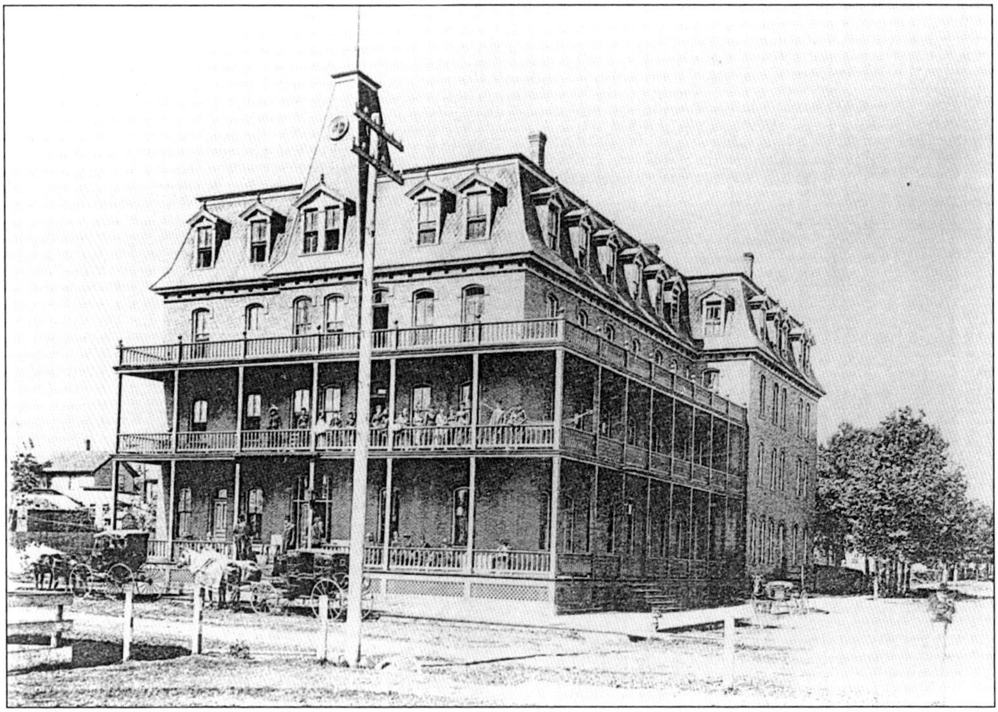

The Hotel Marquette, formally known as the Mesnard House, was built in 1883 and was advertised as "overlooking Lake Superior." It had 65 rooms, a dining room, and a staff of 30 employees. Its location on the southwest corner of Front and Rock Streets commanded a fantastic view of the ore docks. This 1891 view shows the additions that were built in 1888. The hotel burned in November 1930. (Courtesy Peter White Library.)

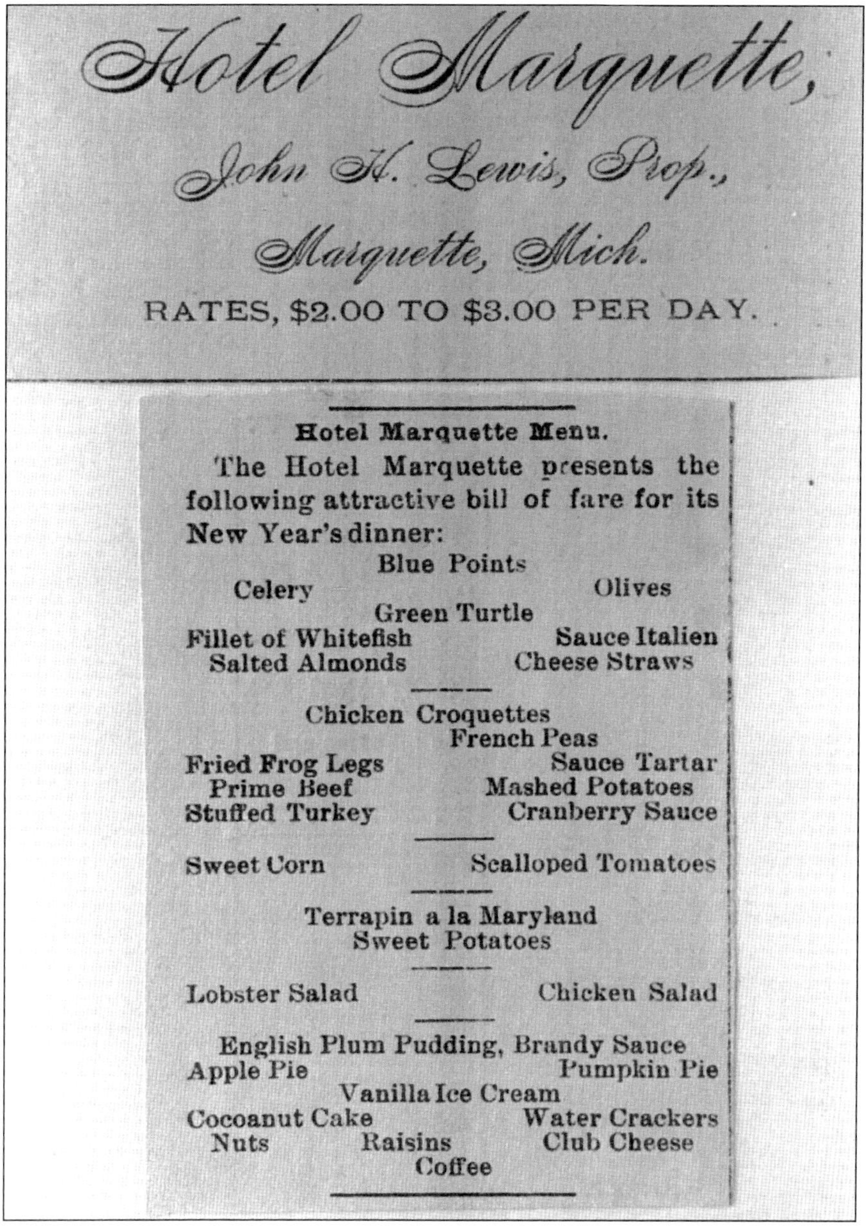

Hotel Marquette,

John H. Lewis, Prop.,

Marquette, Mich.

RATES, $2.00 TO $3.00 PER DAY.

Hotel Marquette Menu.

The Hotel Marquette presents the following attractive bill of fare for its New Year's dinner:

Blue Points

Celery — Olives

Green Turtle

Fillet of Whitefish — Sauce Italien

Salted Almonds — Cheese Straws

Chicken Croquettes

French Peas

Fried Frog Legs — Sauce Tartar

Prime Beef — Mashed Potatoes

Stuffed Turkey — Cranberry Sauce

Sweet Corn — Scalloped Tomatoes

Terrapin a la Maryland

Sweet Potatoes

Lobster Salad — Chicken Salad

English Plum Pudding, Brandy Sauce

Apple Pie — Pumpkin Pie

Vanilla Ice Cream

Cocoanut Cake — Water Crackers

Nuts — Raisins — Club Cheese

Coffee

This menu presents the bill of fare available at the Hotel Marquette on New Year's Day in 1897. During that time and season, Marquette lay at the far edge of the American transportation system, but the variety of exotic and perishable seafood featured—oysters, turtle, terrapin, lobster, frog legs, and whitefish—indicate that lake and rail connections were good and refrigeration was at least adequate. The canning industry probably made a contribution to the array of comestibles on the menu, too. The Marquette, which was situated on the southwest corner of Front and Rock Streets overlooking Lake Superior, was a good, moderately priced hotel with a clientele that included a large percentage of traveling salesmen. The proprietor, John H. "Cap" Lewis, concentrated on the essentials, especially the cuisine, going so far as establishing his own food supplier, The Honolulu Farm, on County Road 553, to provide fresh butter, eggs, and cream. (Courtesy Peter White Library.)

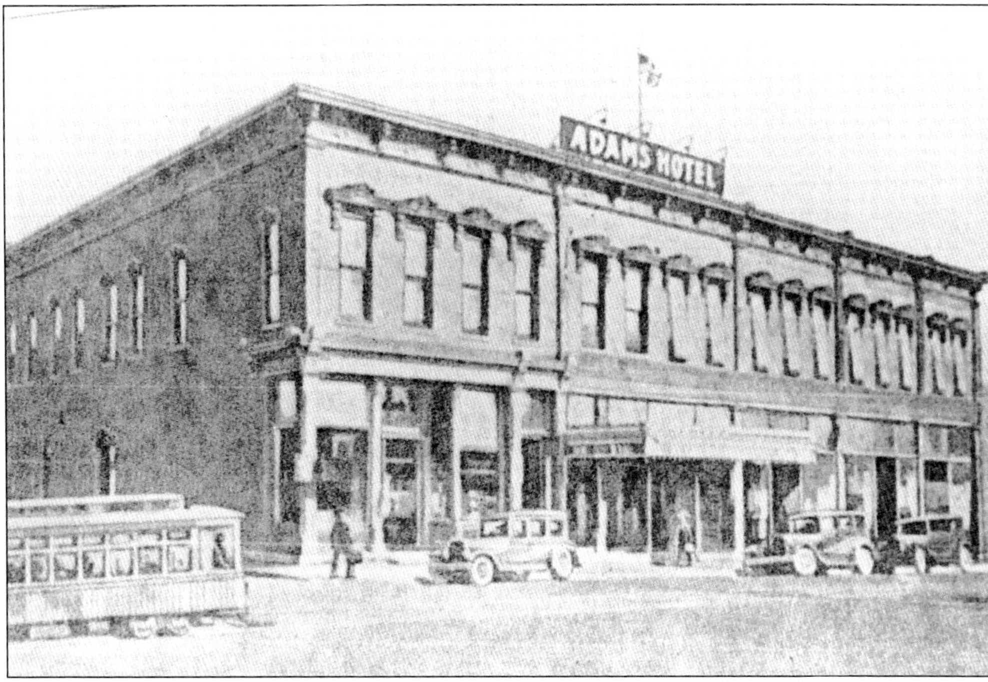

Seen here is the Adams Hotel on South Front Street as it looked in the heyday of its existence. The street railway car of the Marquette City Railway, the 1928 opening of the hotel, and the vintage automobiles parked in front suggest that the photograph was taken in the early 1930s. (Courtesy Peter White Library.)

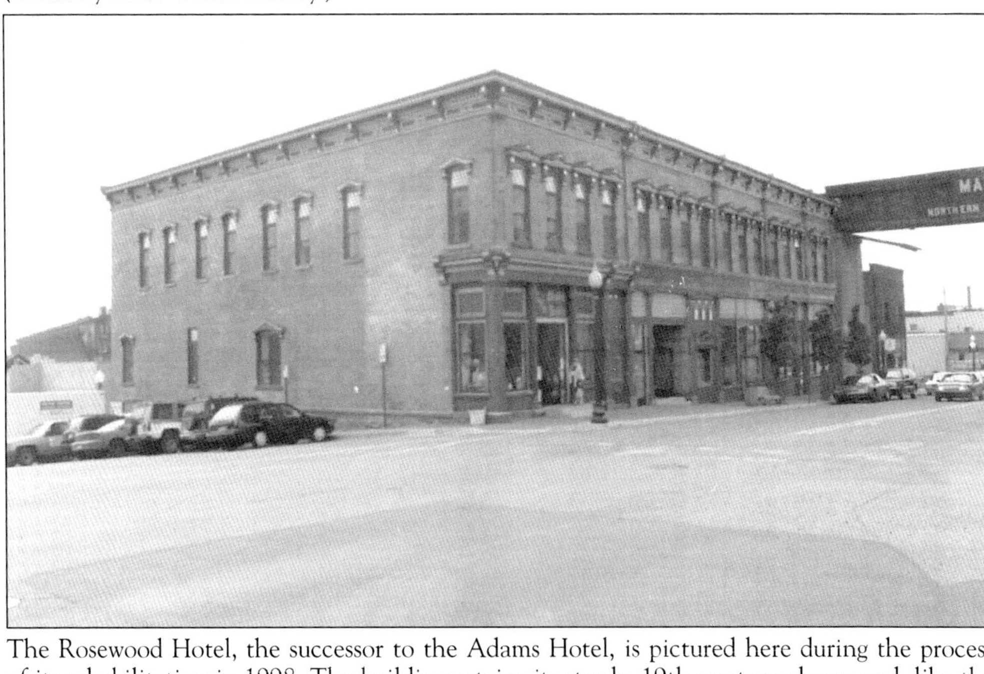

The Rosewood Hotel, the successor to the Adams Hotel, is pictured here during the process of its rehabilitation in 1998. The building retains its sturdy, 19th-century charm and, like the Adams, the Rosewood can claim to be "conveniently located to a number of restaurants." The railroad station, however, is no longer "just opposite." (Photo by G. Downs.)

When it was built in 1929, The Hotel Northland cost over $350,000 and represented a large, local investment in the future of the city and its growing tourist industry. The interior of the building was elegantly furnished. There were 100 guest rooms and nine apartments. This grand hotel's 1930 opening was ill-timed, however; it languished in the Depression era. (Courtesy State Archives of Michigan.)

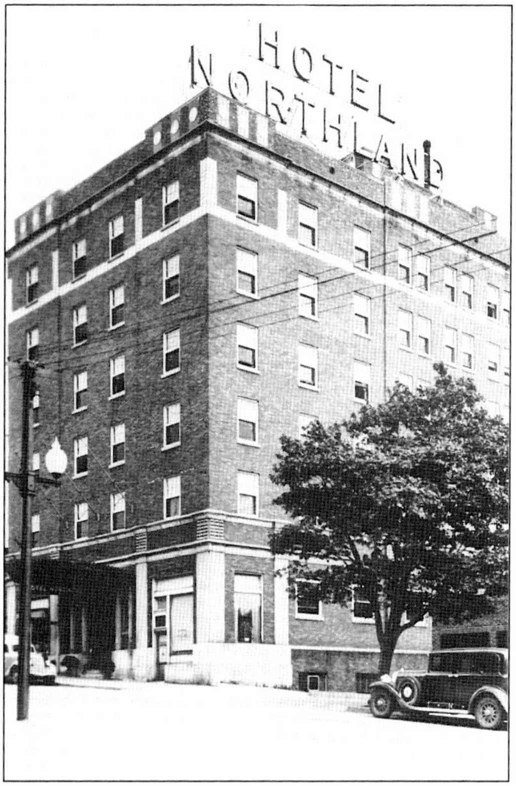

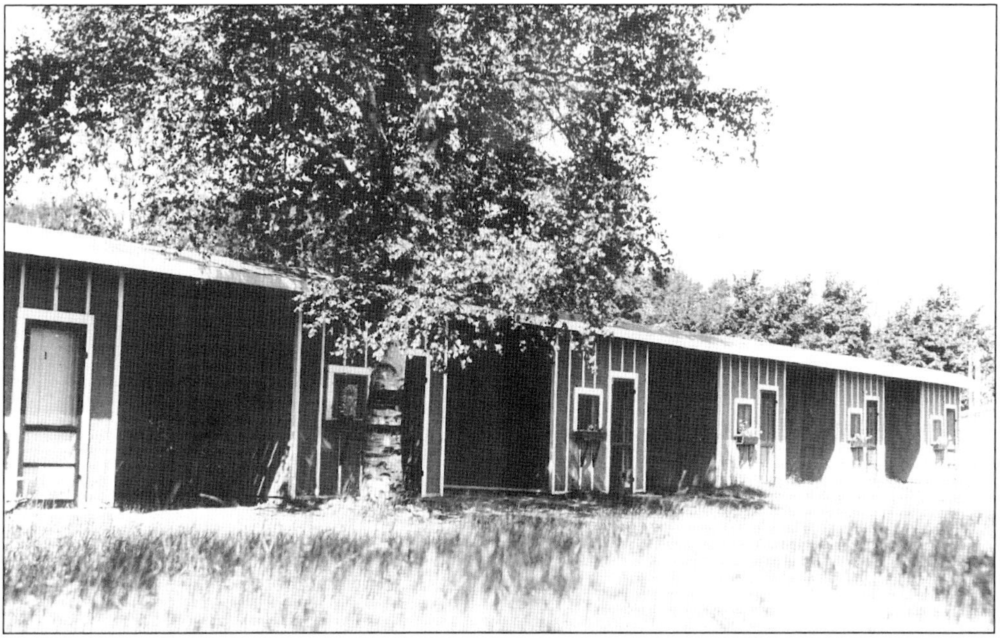

In the 1940s, the Birchmont Motel provided basic accommodations in an unpretentious building. By that time, travel for pleasure had been thoroughly democratized; tourists mandated that an urban area sized and situated like Marquette had to match the different incomes and tastes of these customers. (Courtesy State Archives of Michigan.)

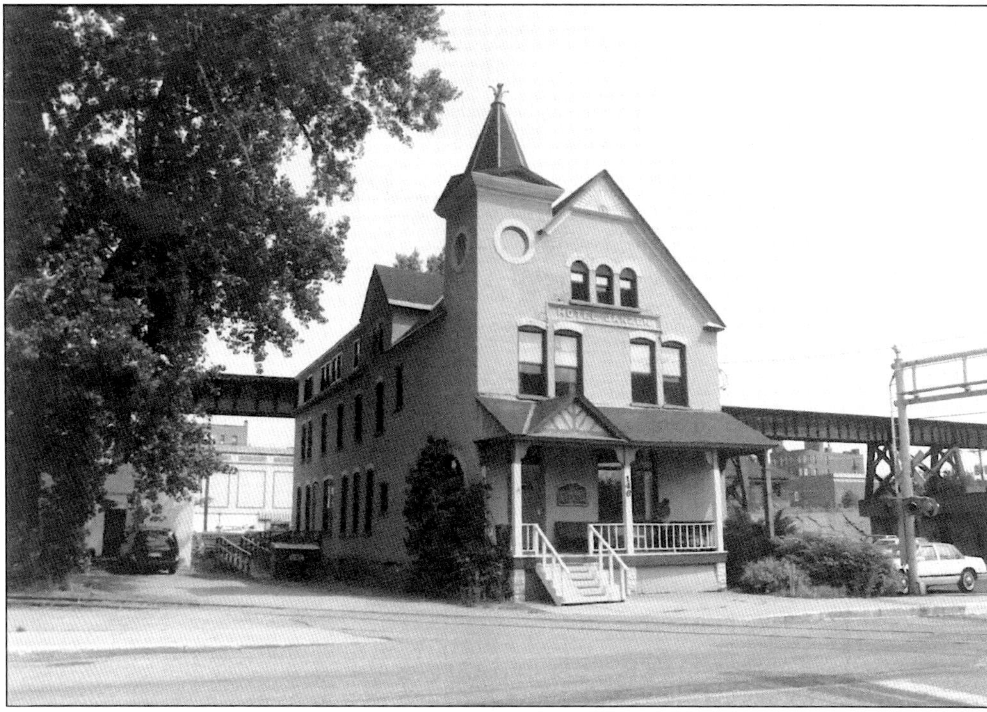

The Hotel Janzen opened in 1890, advertising 34 rooms and "hot and cold water." In those days, it operated under the American Plan, and its proximity to the D.S.S.&A. Depot made it handy for business travelers. After many trials, the Janzen still survives, more than 100 years after its beginning, as a low-income residence for the elderly. (Photo by G. Downs.)

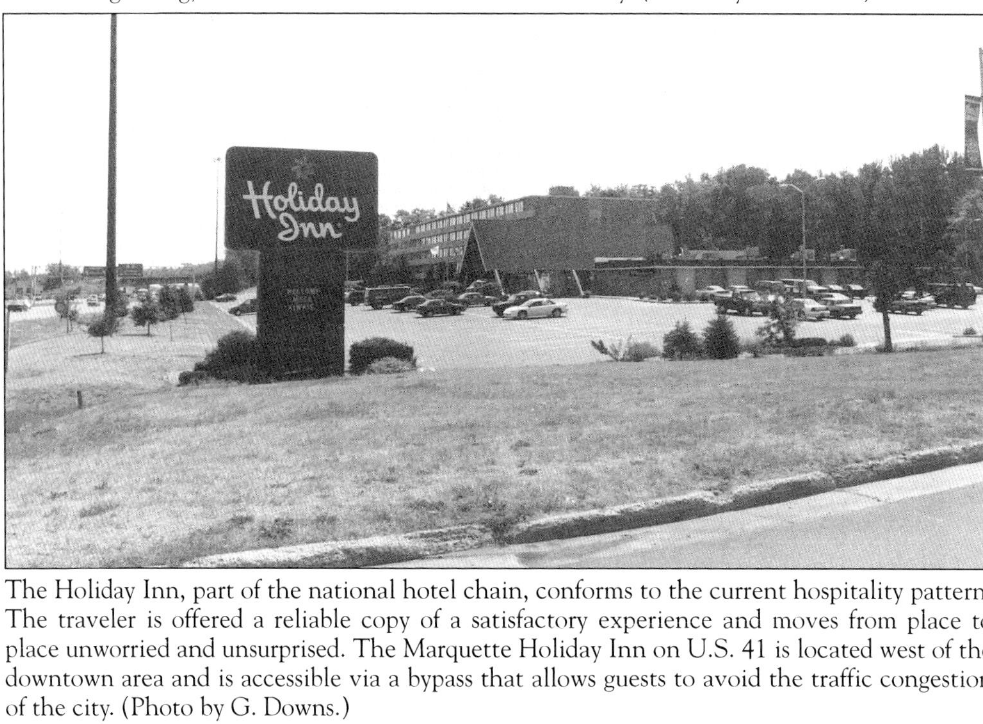

The Holiday Inn, part of the national hotel chain, conforms to the current hospitality pattern. The traveler is offered a reliable copy of a satisfactory experience and moves from place to place unworried and unsurprised. The Marquette Holiday Inn on U.S. 41 is located west of the downtown area and is accessible via a bypass that allows guests to avoid the traffic congestion of the city. (Photo by G. Downs.)

Five

GOING PLACES

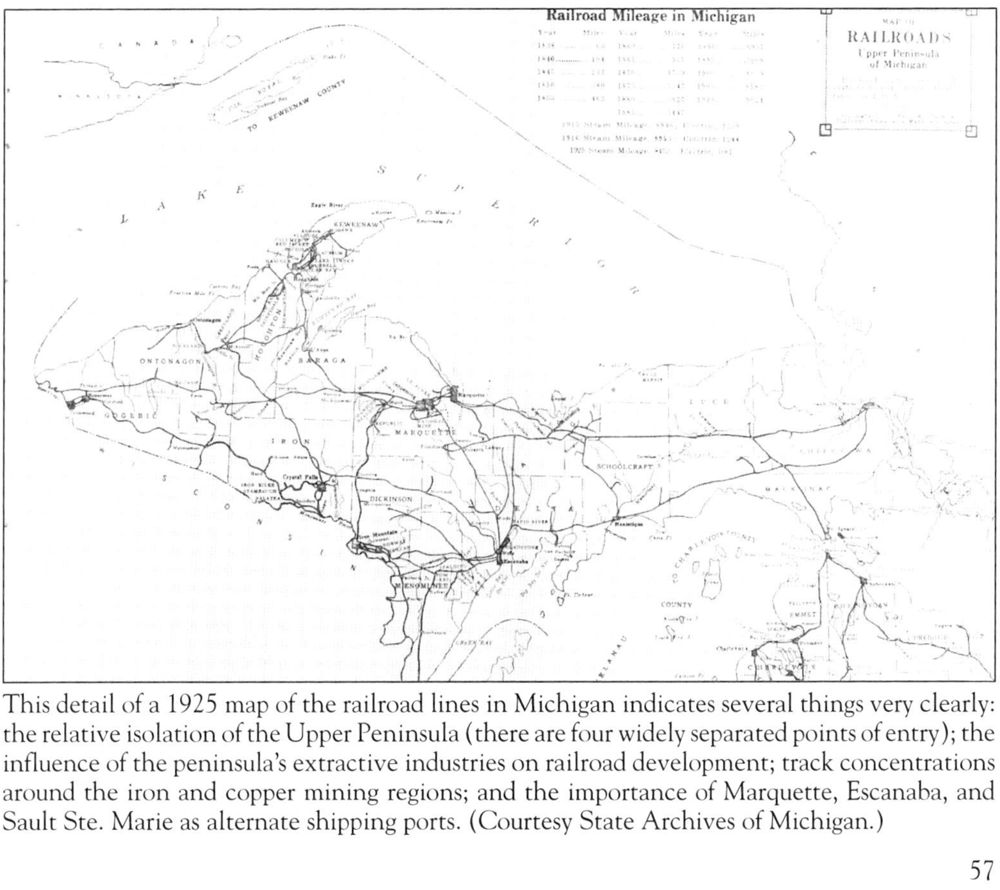

This detail of a 1925 map of the railroad lines in Michigan indicates several things very clearly: the relative isolation of the Upper Peninsula (there are four widely separated points of entry); the influence of the peninsula's extractive industries on railroad development; track concentrations around the iron and copper mining regions; and the importance of Marquette, Escanaba, and Sault Ste. Marie as alternate shipping ports. (Courtesy State Archives of Michigan.)

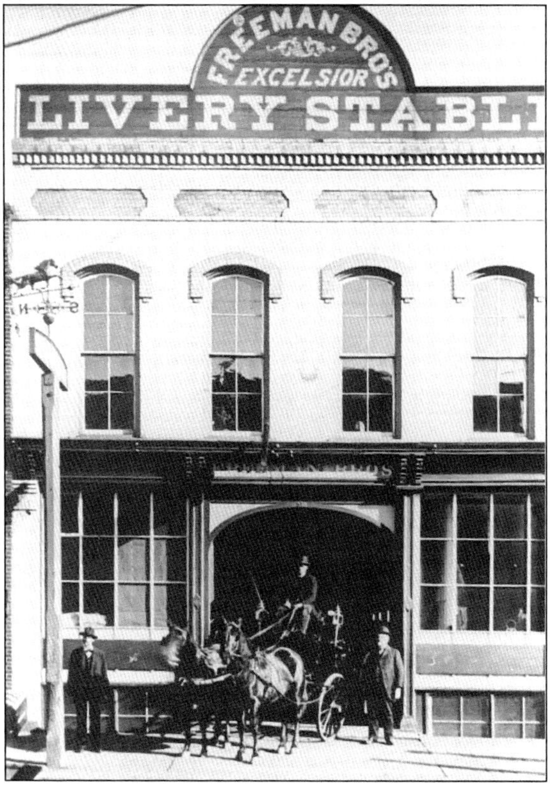

This beautiful image of Freeman Bros. Livery Stable at 315 Front Street dates to 1861. The Freeman motto, "Excelsior," which means "onward and upward," is as much about an American attitude as it is about a business that provided locomotion to its customers. It promised movement in the direction of something better. (Courtesy Peter White Library.)

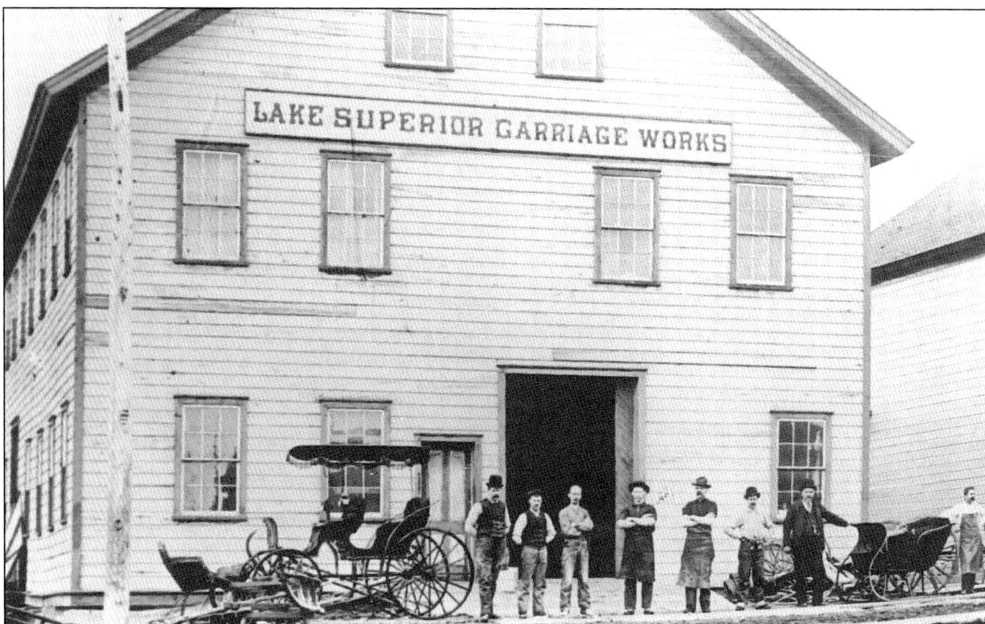

In this display of its products, including a surrey with a fringed top, a smaller carriage, and two sleighs, the Lake Superior Carriage Works tells us about local travel in the late 19th century, its dependence on the horse, the expedients forced on people by the weather, and the versatility of a skilled workforce able to produce elegant vehicles by hand. (Courtesy Peter White Library.)

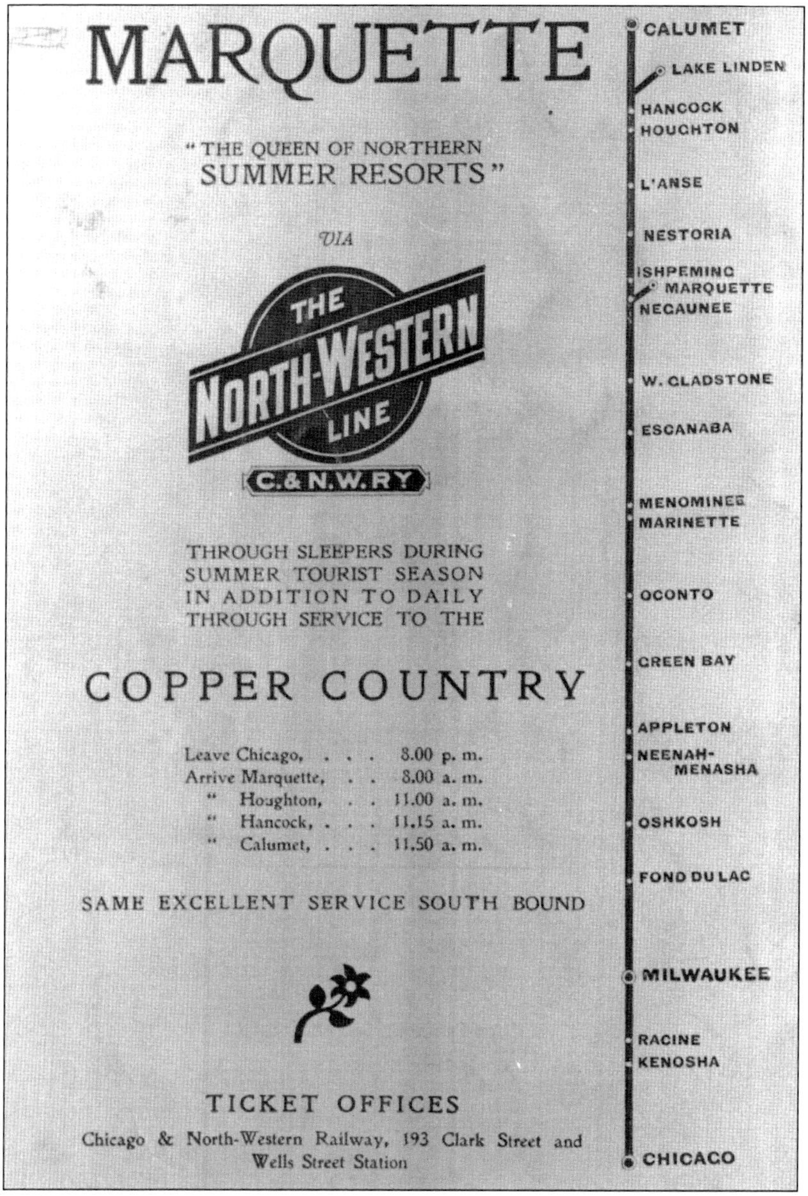

Marquette's first railroad link to Chicago was completed in 1872. It transformed the local economy, dependent until then on lake transport, and its commercial use broadened quickly to include tourism. Testifying to the symbiotic relationship that has always existed between railroads and their destinations, this brochure touts both Marquette, "the Queen of Northern Summer Resorts," and the Chicago and North Western Railway Company, with its "same excellent service southbound." In the 1930s, it took 12 hours to get from the "City with Broad Shoulders" to the "Queen City of Lake Superior," but if you could afford the sleeper car, the time probably passed more comfortably. A careful reader would note that the C&N.W.R.Y. required its Marquette passengers to detour slightly at Negaunee and wonder how that was accomplished. Part of the romance of train travel is the litany of place names—Fond Du Loc, Oshkosh, Neenah-Menasha, Ishpeming, Nestoria, L'Anse—and this route had an interesting one. (Courtesy Peter White Library.)

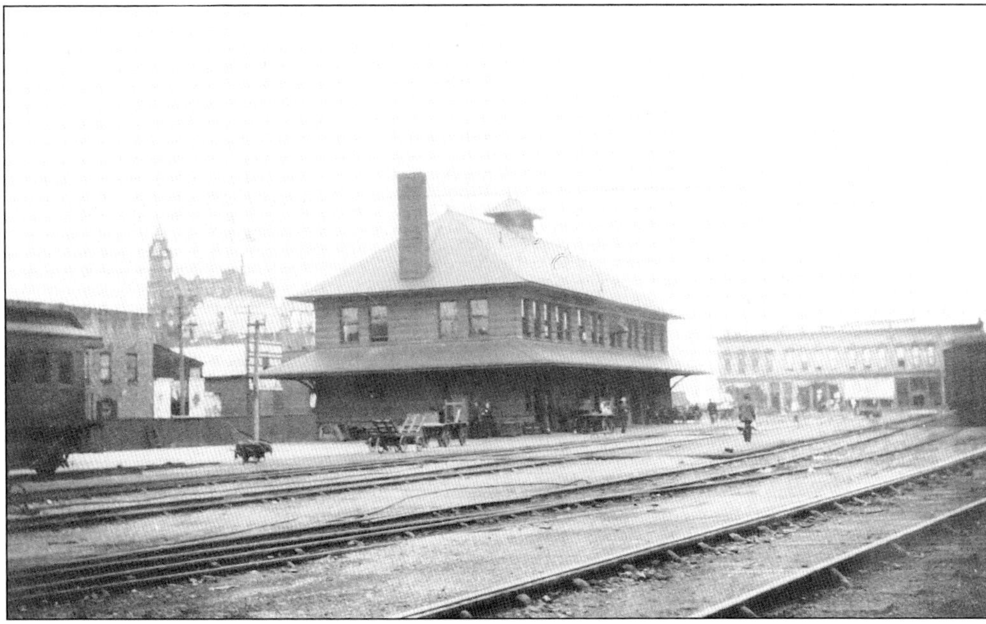

In this *c.* 1900 view of the D.S.S.&A. Depot, taken at the height of its usefulness, the Marquette County Savings Bank tower rises in the distant background, and the buildings of South Front Street appear in the right background. This solidly built passenger depot with baggage carts on its platform was a center of activity; it was the first impression that some train travelers had of the city. (Courtesy State Archives of Michigan.)

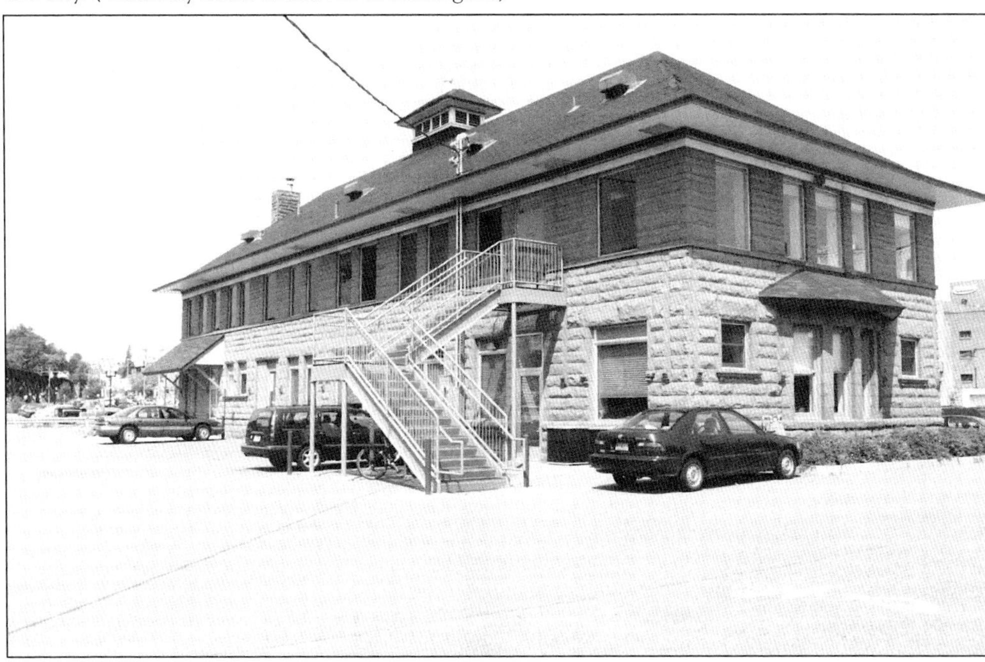

The old depot has been successfully recycled and now serves as an example of how buildings learn. New access to the second floor has been built, and attractive offices have taken over the interior. The building's durability, handsome exterior, and central location have given it new life. There is adequate parking as well. (Photo by G. Downs.)

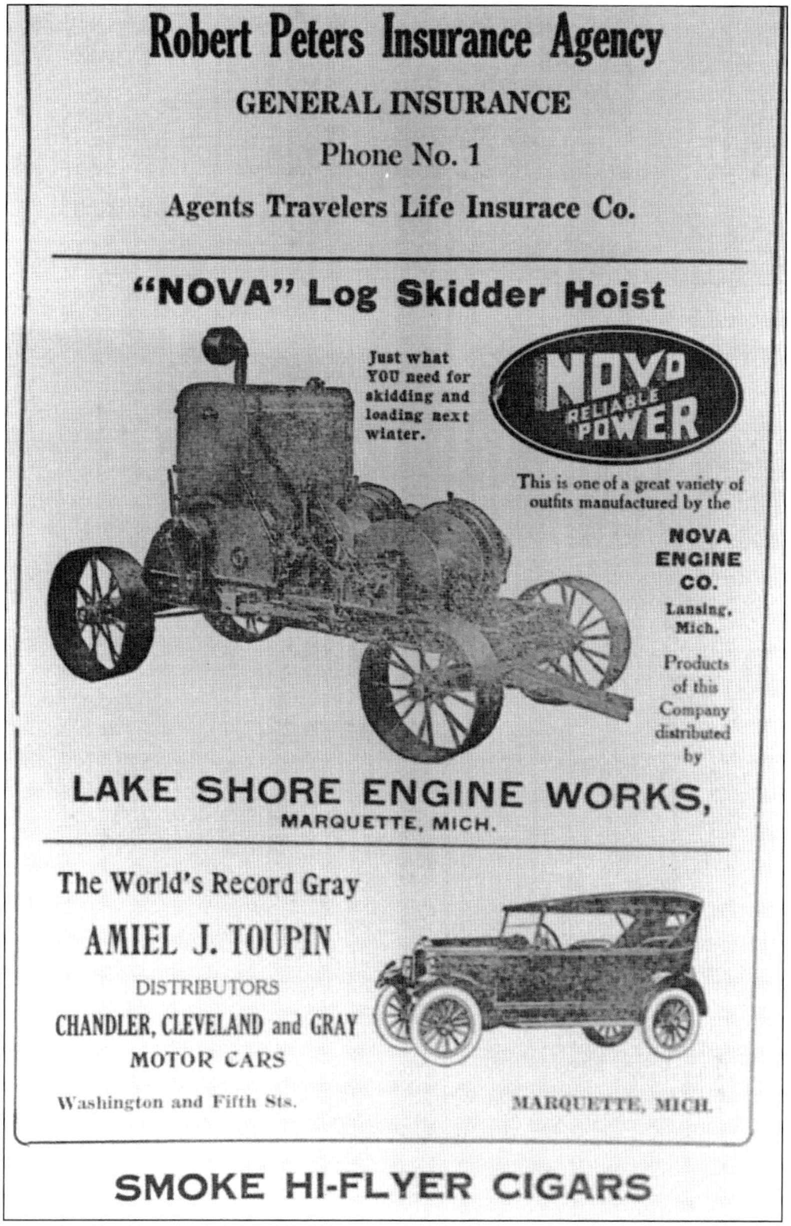

This page from the 1923 Marquette City Directory provides a little of the flavor of the time and place. It was a time when someone could actually have "Phone No. 1," an easy number to remember, and much shorter than what the customers of the Travelers Life Insurance Company contend with today. Automobile dealerships "distributed" makes that seem to have disappeared without a trace, such as Chandlers, Clevelands, and Grays. Most interesting, though, and clearly related to a local industry, is the advertisement for the "Nova" Log Skidder Hoist. Although the machine looks primitive and complicated in the way that Rube Goldberg's inventions did, it and others like it made a big difference in the woods. The Skidder Hoist used energy that was plentiful and cheap; when loggers began using it and the rest of the "great variety of outfits" manufactured by Nova, the Upper Peninsula's old growth forests disappeared even more quickly. (Courtesy Peter White Library.)

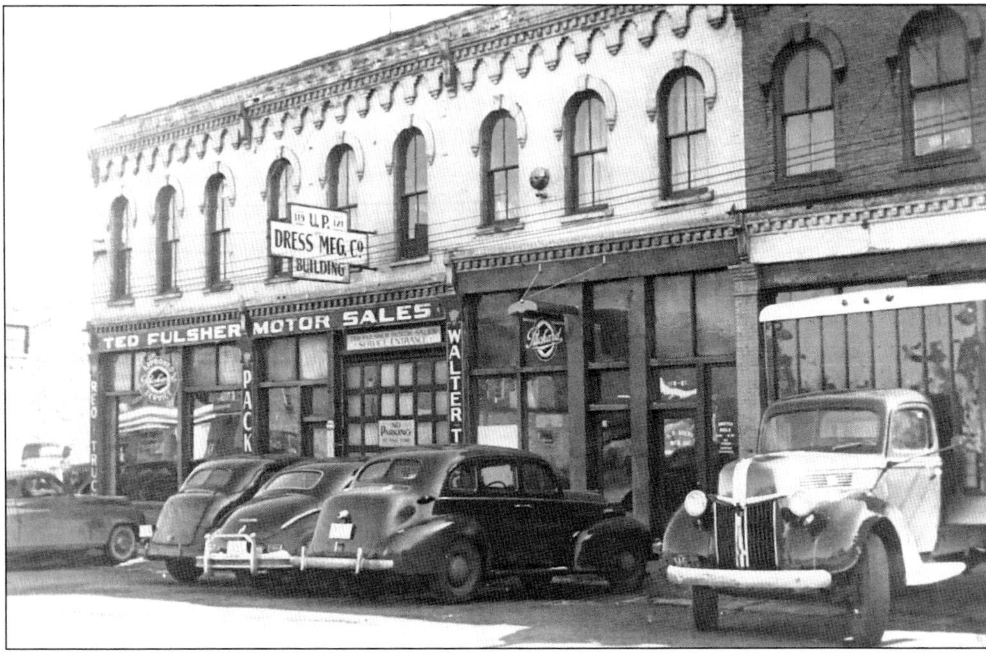

When this picture was taken in 1948, the Ted Fulsher Motor Sales Packard agency was located on Baraga Street. The Packard, nearly a luxury car, didn't survive the 1950s. Fulsher Motor Sales was a typical automobile sales outlet of the time: small, low overhead, a downtown location, and a dependence on the sale of a variety of automobile-related products. (Courtesy Marquette County Historical Society.)

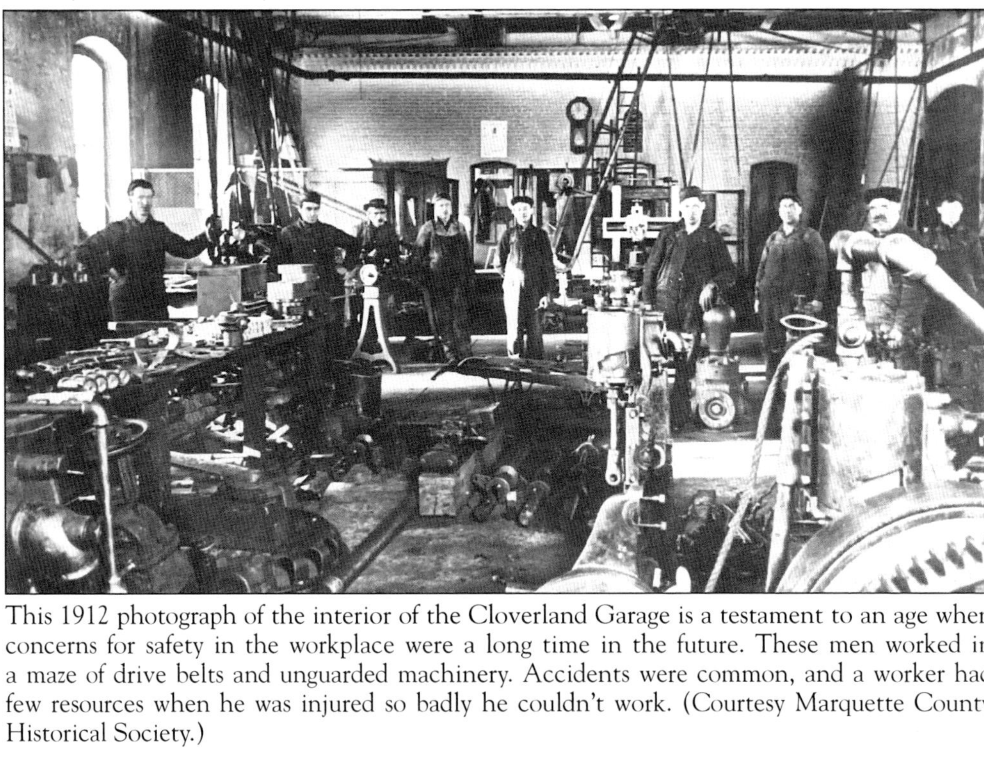

This 1912 photograph of the interior of the Cloverland Garage is a testament to an age when concerns for safety in the workplace were a long time in the future. These men worked in a maze of drive belts and unguarded machinery. Accidents were common, and a worker had few resources when he was injured so badly he couldn't work. (Courtesy Marquette County Historical Society.)

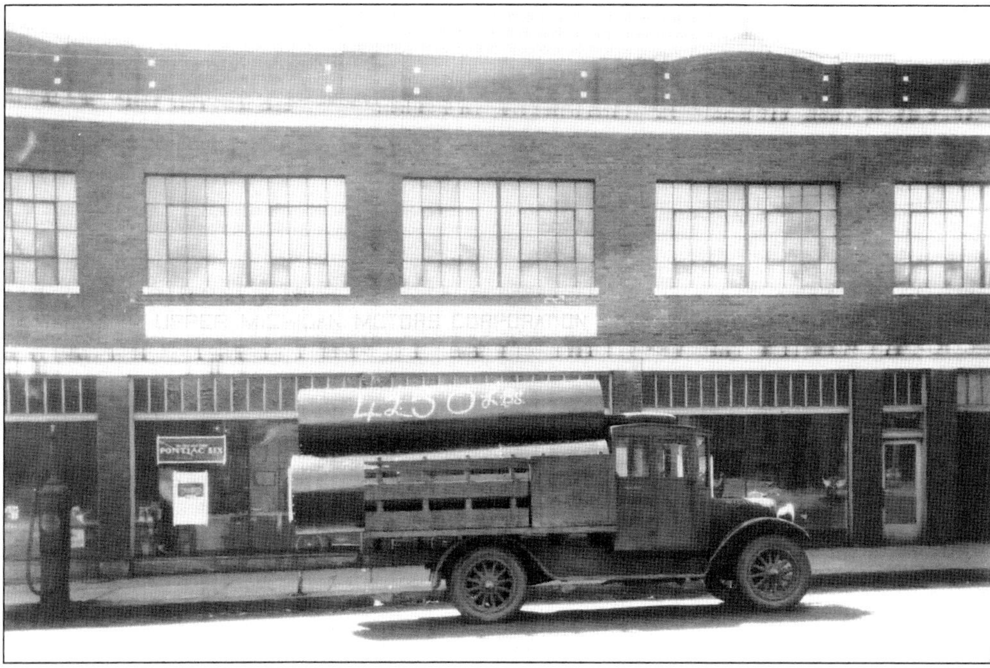

This truck, proudly advertising its load-carrying capacity, is parked in front of the Upper Michigan Motors Corporation. In 1925, U.P. Motors was Marquette's Pontiac dealer, but there was a gas pump out front for customers who just needed fuel. (Courtesy Marquette County Historical Society.)

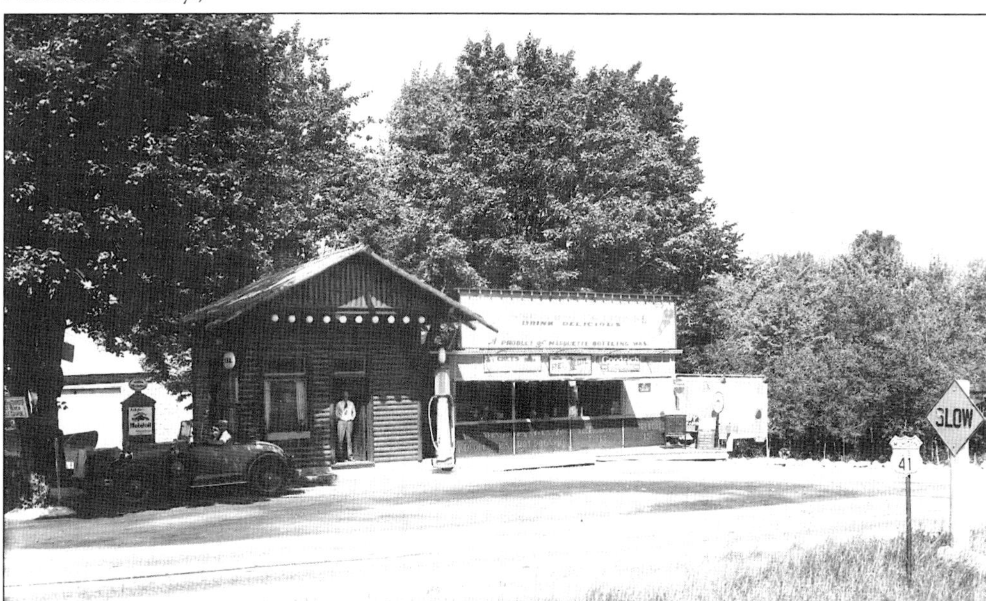

Pictured is Chet's Log Cabin Service Station in 1925. Chet Young, the proprietor, provided his customers with a range of services that went beyond selling gasoline. To the right is an open-air lunch counter where food items served were either red hot or ice cold. A garage was located in back. The roadster seen in the shade by the pump was the classic sports car of the 1920s. (Courtesy Marquette County Historical Society.)

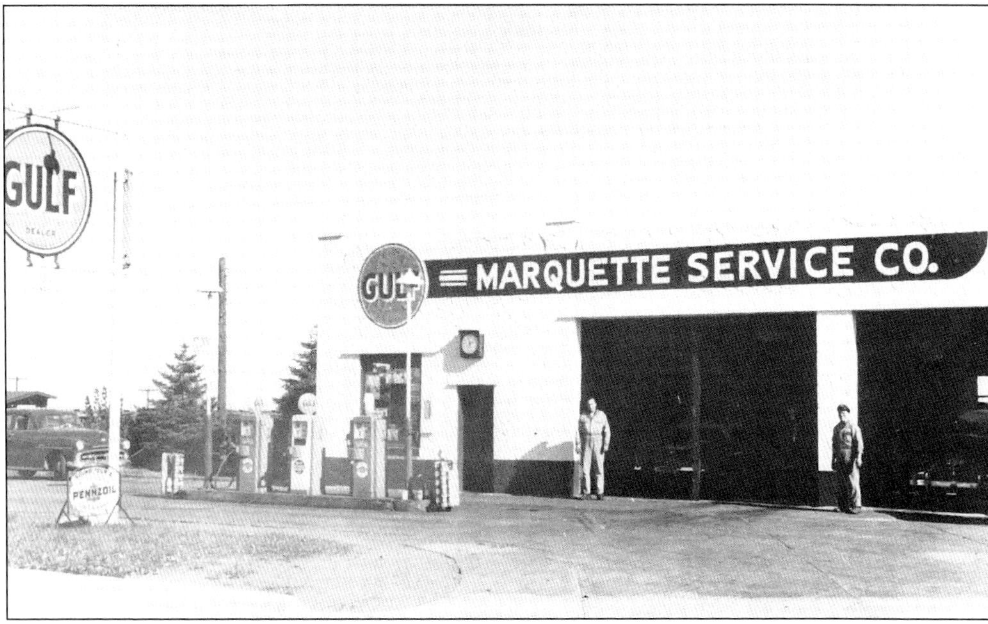

Until the late 1960s and the oil embargo of the early 1970s, locally owned franchises of major oil companies made much of their profit by providing automotive service to their customers. Gas stations doubled as garages. The Marquette Service Company sold Gulf oil products at this station in the 1940s and 1950s; you could get an oil change and an engine tune-up there, too. (Courtesy State Archives of Michigan.)

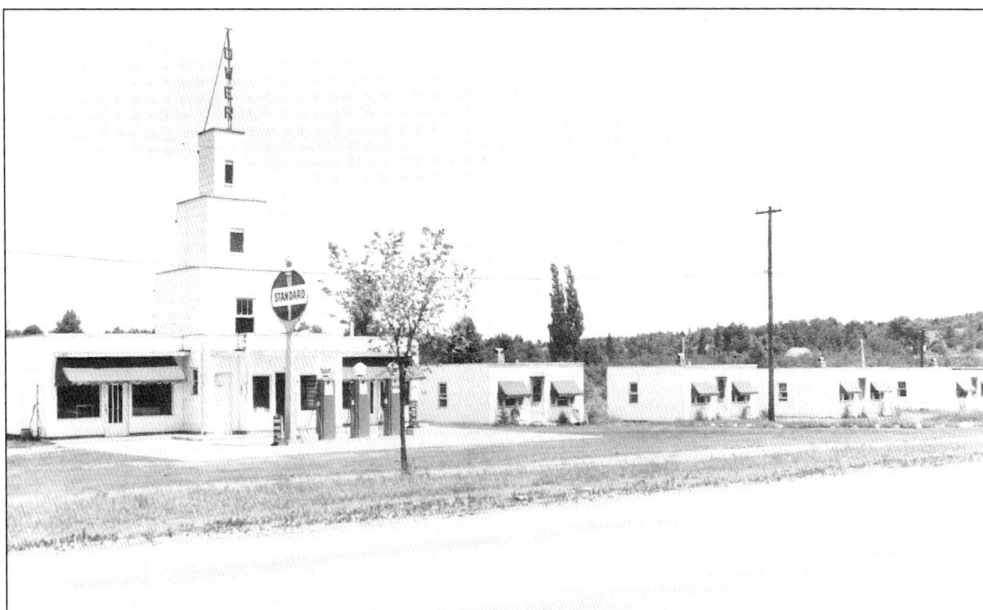

The Tower Standard gasoline station with its utilitarian modern-style motel and attached restaurant offered one-stop service to motorists in the 1940s. It was a step up from the Birchmont (see page 55). Its architectural unity gives the impression that it was purpose-built and depended on some rudimentary market research for its presentation. (Courtesy State Archives of Michigan.)

Six

Schools and Education

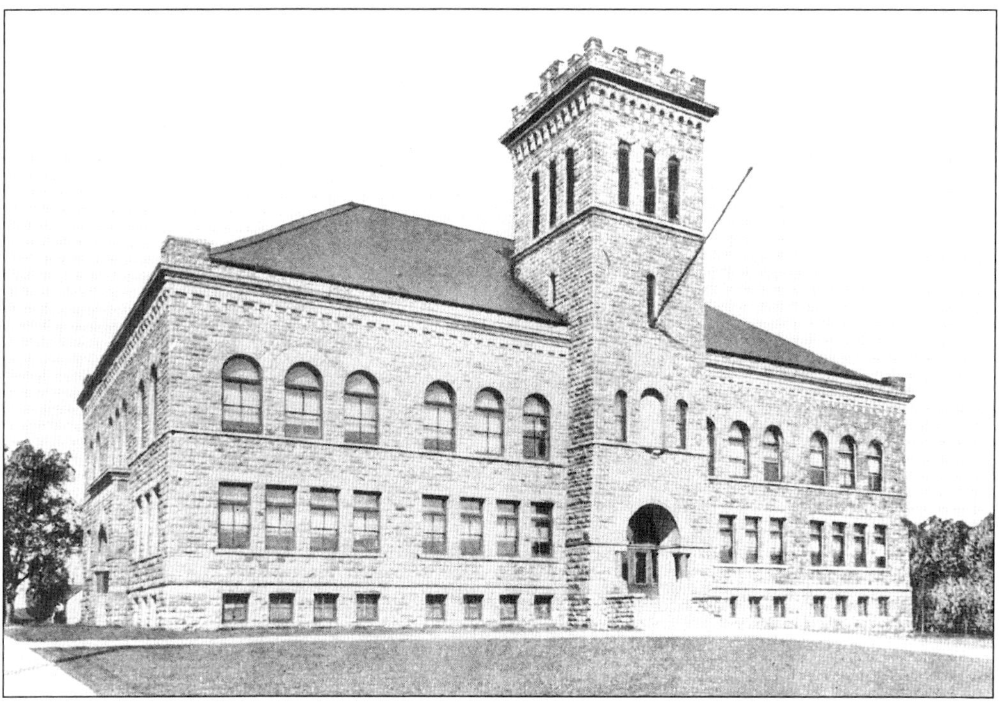

Bishop Frederick Baraga, the first bishop of the Catholic Diocese, was instrumental in the development of the Catholic Church and its infrastructure in the city's early days. His name appears on plat maps dating back to 1855, a city street, and on this early parochial school building, which was built in 1903. An Upper Peninsula county and a city also bear the Bishop's name. (Courtesy State Archives of Michigan.)

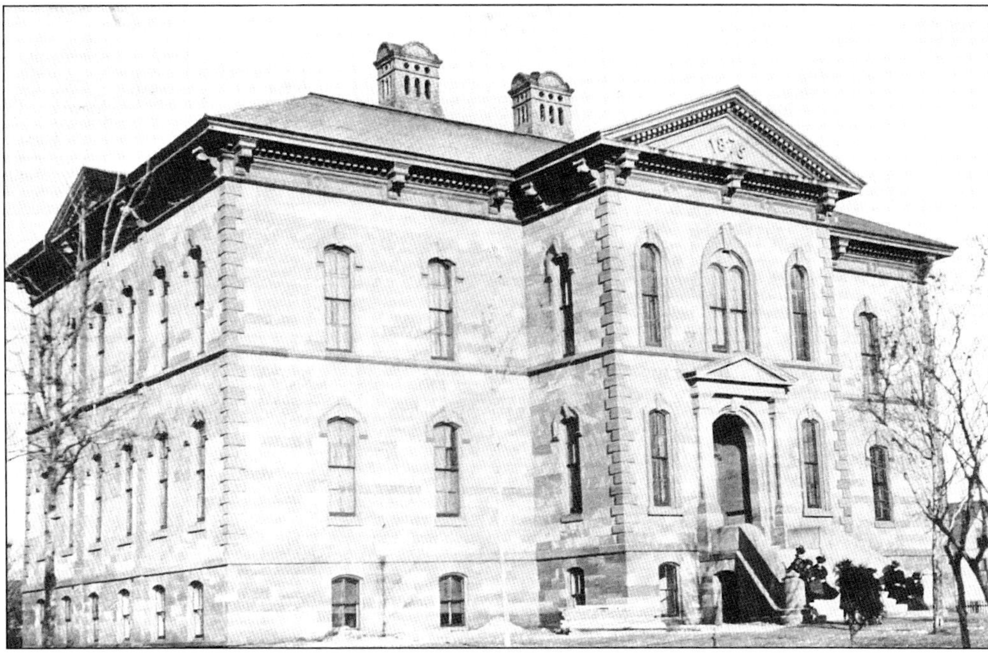

This picture of the old Ridge Street School was taken shortly after it was built in 1875. It was an imposing public building for its time, with heavy reinforced corners, massive columns at the entrance, and an ornate cornice surmounting the walls. The stairway to the entrance held enough heat from the sun on this early spring day to provide comfortable seating for several teachers or patrons. (Courtesy Peter White Library.)

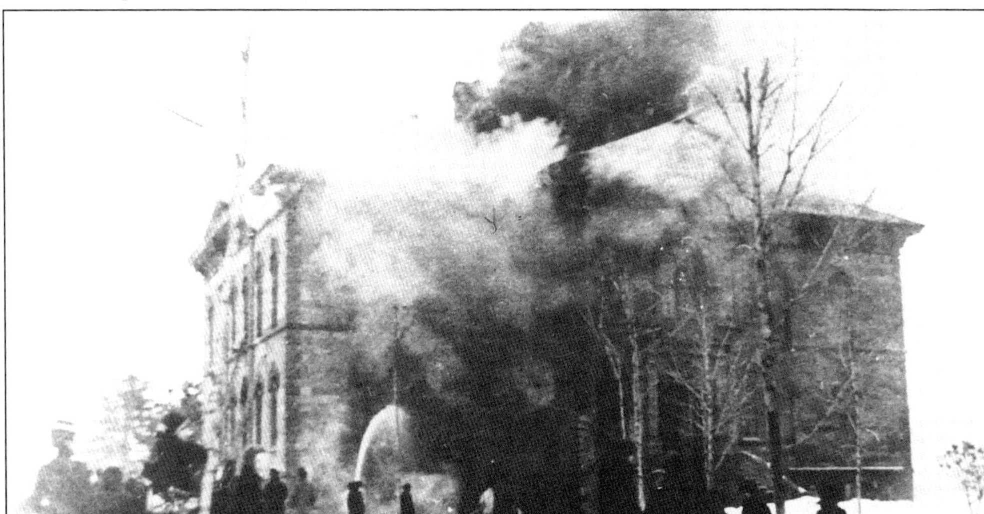

Buildings from the 19th century, despite their appearance of great strength and permanence, were extremely vulnerable to fire. Although built with stone or masonry walls, their interiors made lavish use of wood, varnish, and paint. Other combustible products were used for cleaning and maintenance. When these materials burned, the destruction was devastating. The Ridge School succumbed to this scourge at the turn of the century. (Courtesy Peter White Library.)

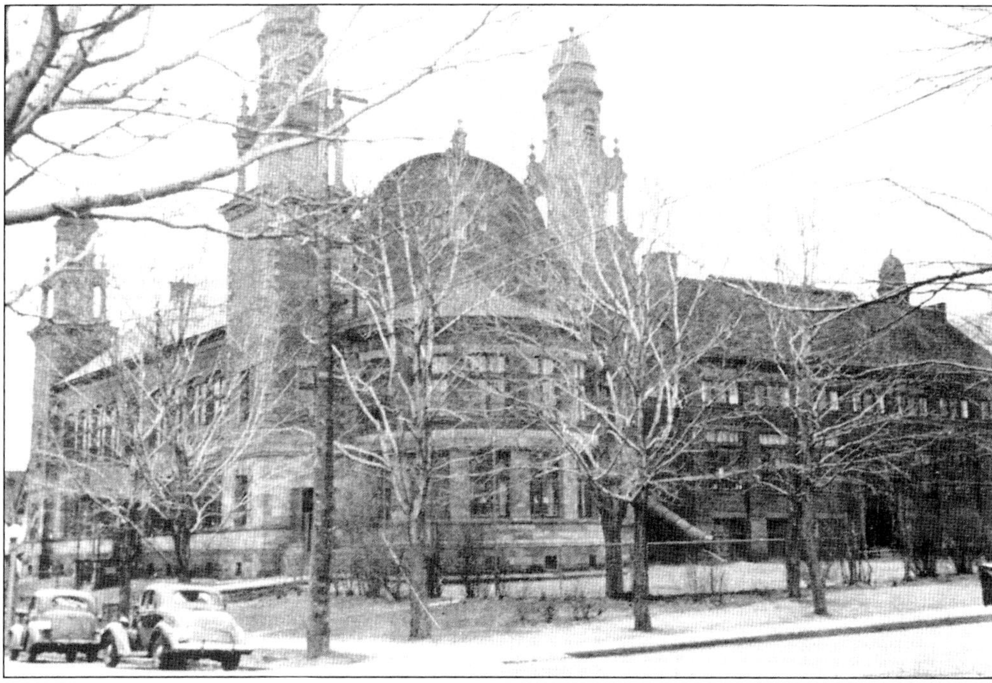

The Froebel-Howard School, later the Froebel School, was built in 1900 according to a complicated design with much more fanciful ornamentation than was usual in Marquette. This postcard picture, which was taken on an autumn day in the 1930s, shows the contrast between the building's almost delicate towers and its heavily browed windows and stone accents. (Courtesy Peter White Library.)

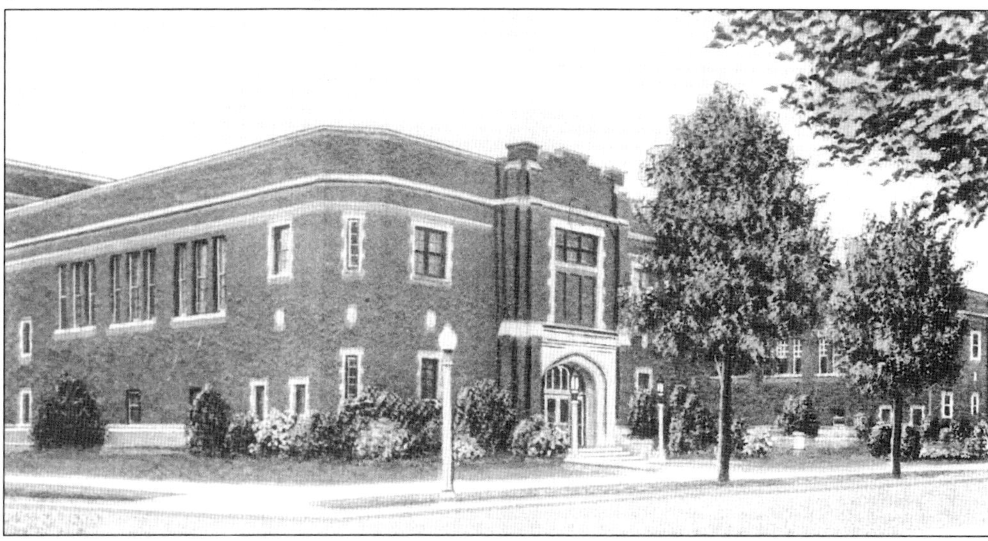

Graveraet High School was built in 1937 in an architectural style common to public buildings of the period. It differed greatly from the earlier sandstone or limestone-clad structures that dotted the city prior to that time. The part of the school that dominates this picture is the Kaufman Auditorium. These two men thus immortalized, Robert Graveraet and L.G. Kaufman, were important figures in Marquette's early settlement and financial history. (Courtesy State Archives of Michigan.)

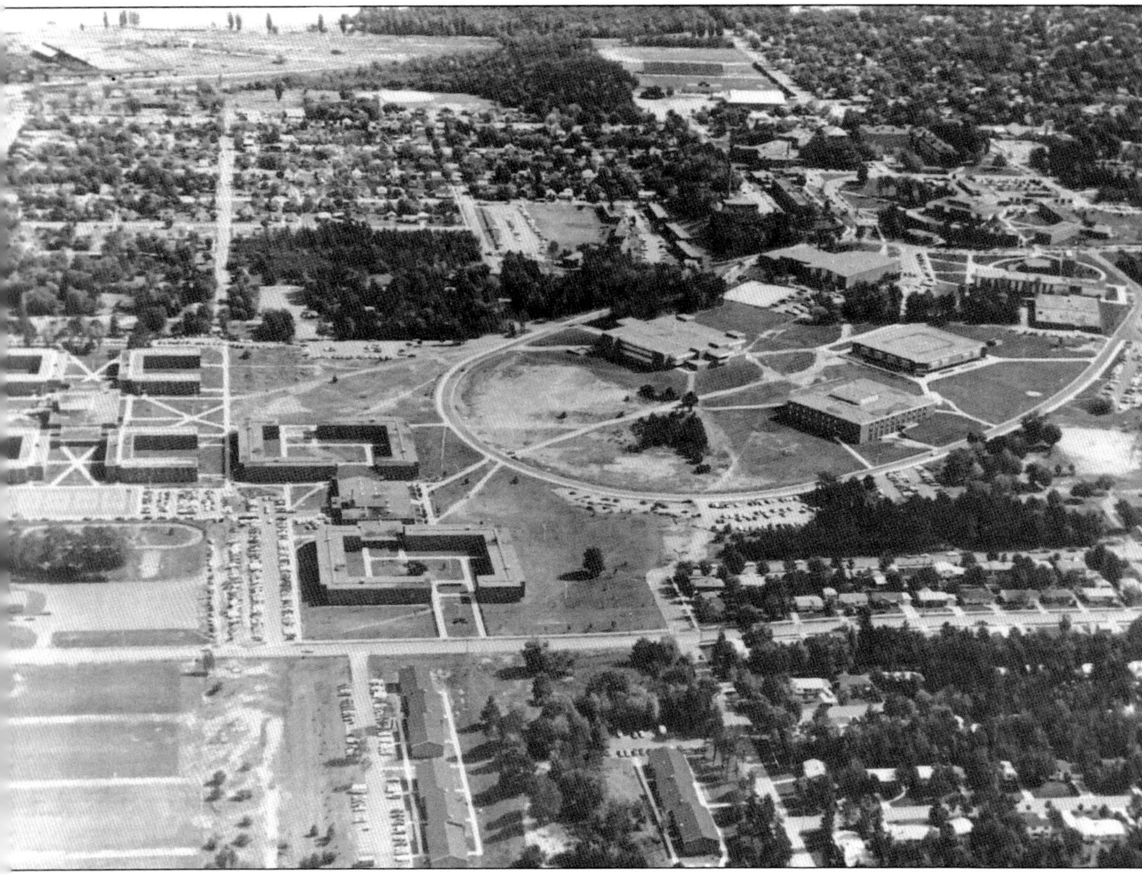

The campus of Northern Michigan University was beginning to bloom when this aerial photograph was taken in the 1960s. In 1963, the college was given university status by the state legislature and Gov. George Romney; by 1967, its enrollment reached 7,000. This picture was taken looking east across the developing campus. To the left, dormitories are filling up the empty space to the north and west of the old main campus and, although there are nearly a half dozen new buildings within the oval, there will soon be more. Like all American public colleges and universities, Northern benefited from population growth, increased government support of higher education, and the rising educational expectations of the post-war generation. Northern also had solid academic leadership, and its location and potential attracted quality faculty and so it was able to maximize its opportunities for development. (Courtesy Marquette County Historical Society.)

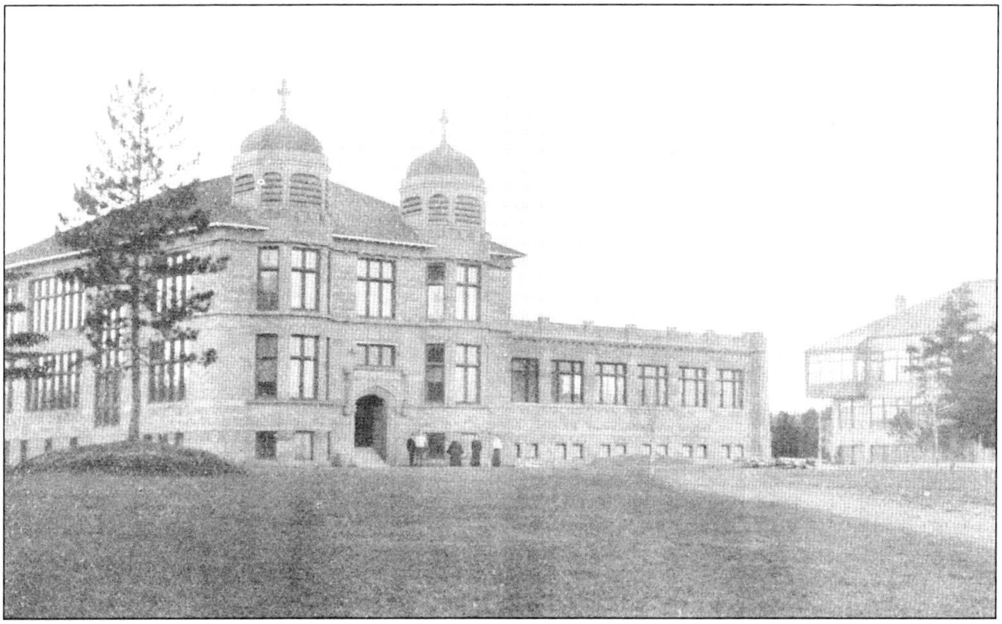

Five years after its first class had matriculated, the Northern Normal School had its first large building, and additional construction was under way. Until the post–World War II period, the school's growth was steady and undramatic. By 1939, its average enrollment was 900. Additions included the Peter White Science Hall, Longyear Hall, and the Pierce Training School. There were also three gymnasiums and an auditorium. (Courtesy State Archives of Michigan.)

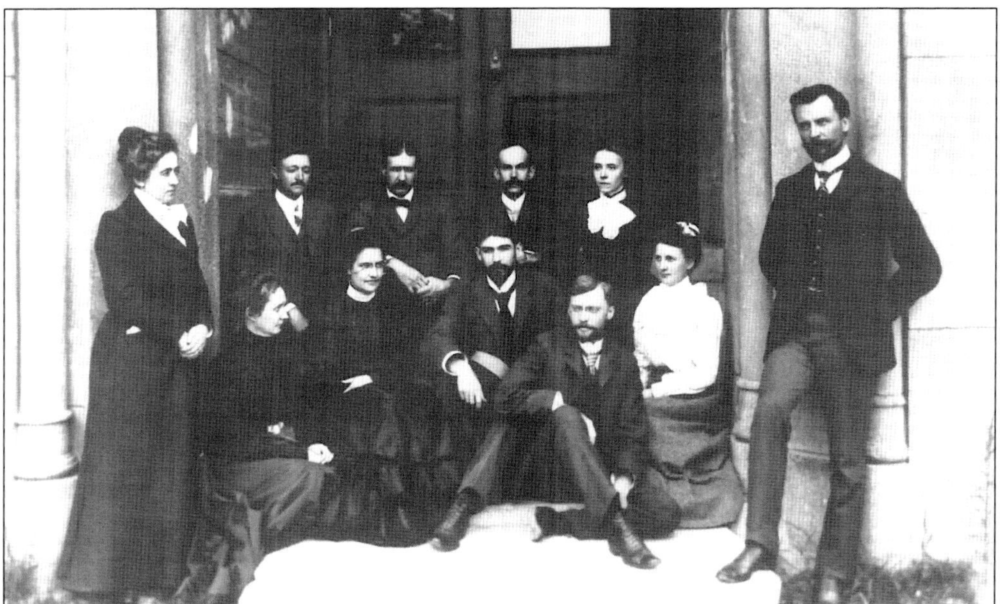

Pictured is the administrative and instructional staff of Northern Michigan in its first year of operation as the Northern Normal School in 1899–1900. From small beginnings, the School has grown into a respected regional university with graduate programs, a diversified academic program, and a distinguished faculty. Since its earliest days, women have played a major role in the institution's development. (Courtesy Marquette County Historical Society.)

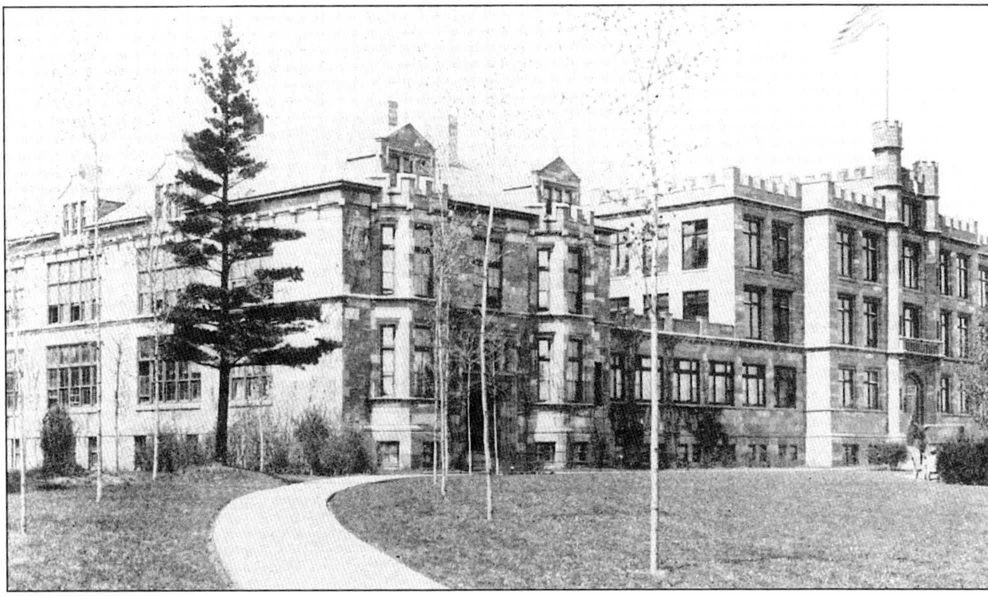

This 1917 photo of the old administration building on the Northern Michigan campus shows a growing campus with new construction and landscaping. The architectural design is ornate, even fussy, but the materials are typical of Marquette construction. The building on the left has undergone some radical rearrangement. As a result of a fire, the cupolas are gone, and the roof line has been changed. (Courtesy State Archives of Michigan.)

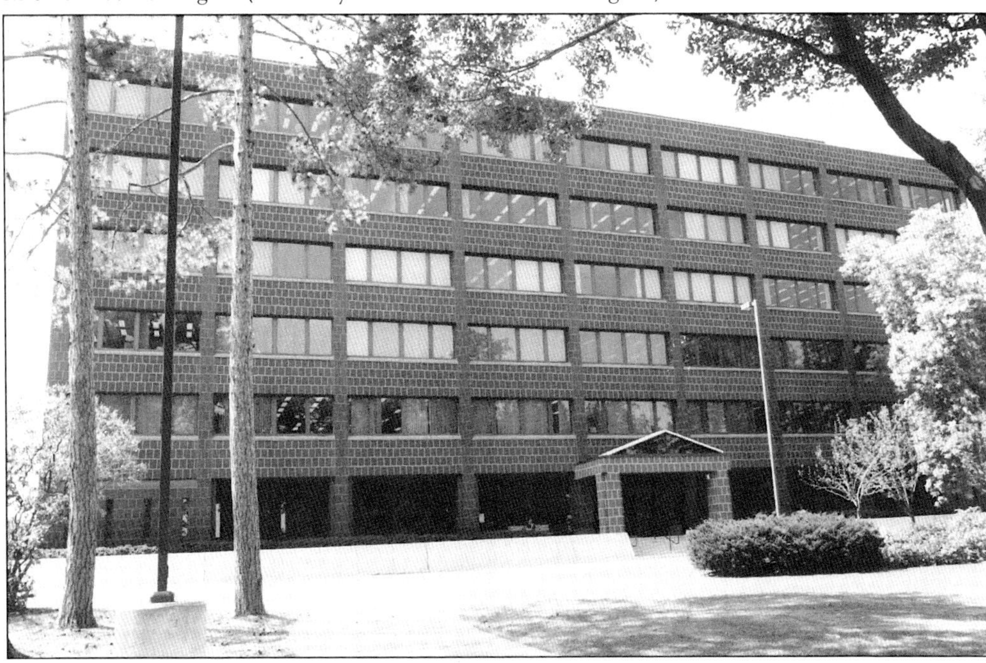

The Sam M. Cohodus Administrative Services Center on the Northern Michigan University campus, pictured here in the summer of 1998, was completed in 1975. It is named for a banker-philanthropist and longtime friend of the University. His gift of $250,000 endowed the Cohodus Professorship in Banking at Northern. The dramatic, contrasting stone facing of the structure and its strongly square and rectilinear lines are eye catching. (Photo by G. Downs.)

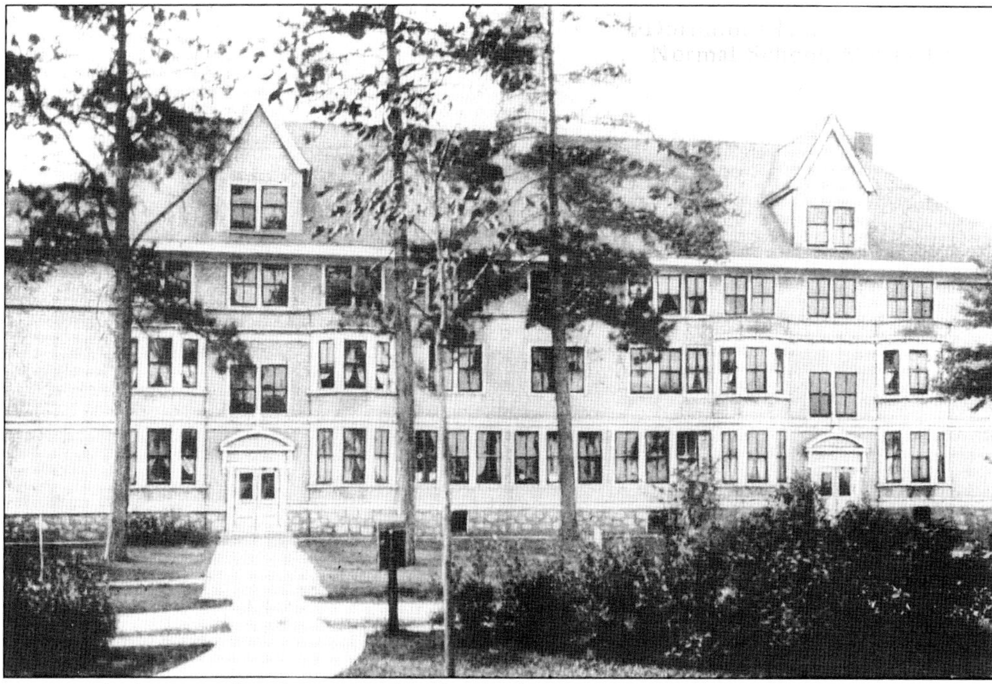

To provide housing for the Normal School's first students, local entrepreneurs built this semi-replica of a resort hotel. The project was not a financial success and, after a short time, the state arranged for it to be taken over and used as a dormitory. It was the first of many different kinds of student housing on the campus. (Courtesy State Archives of Michigan.)

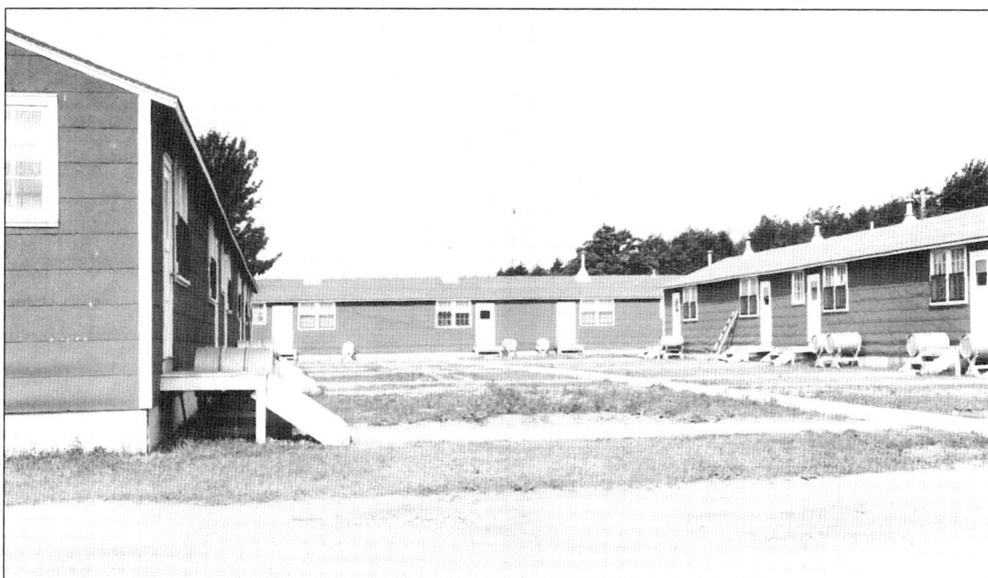

In 1947, when American colleges and universities were still hard pressed to accommodate WW II veterans, many of whom had married and begun their families, Northern Michigan housed this new generation of students and their families in these temporary quarters. They were not air-conditioned and were heated by unreliable oil stoves. "You had to be young," one resident said, remembering what it was like to live there. (Courtesy State Archives of Michigan.)

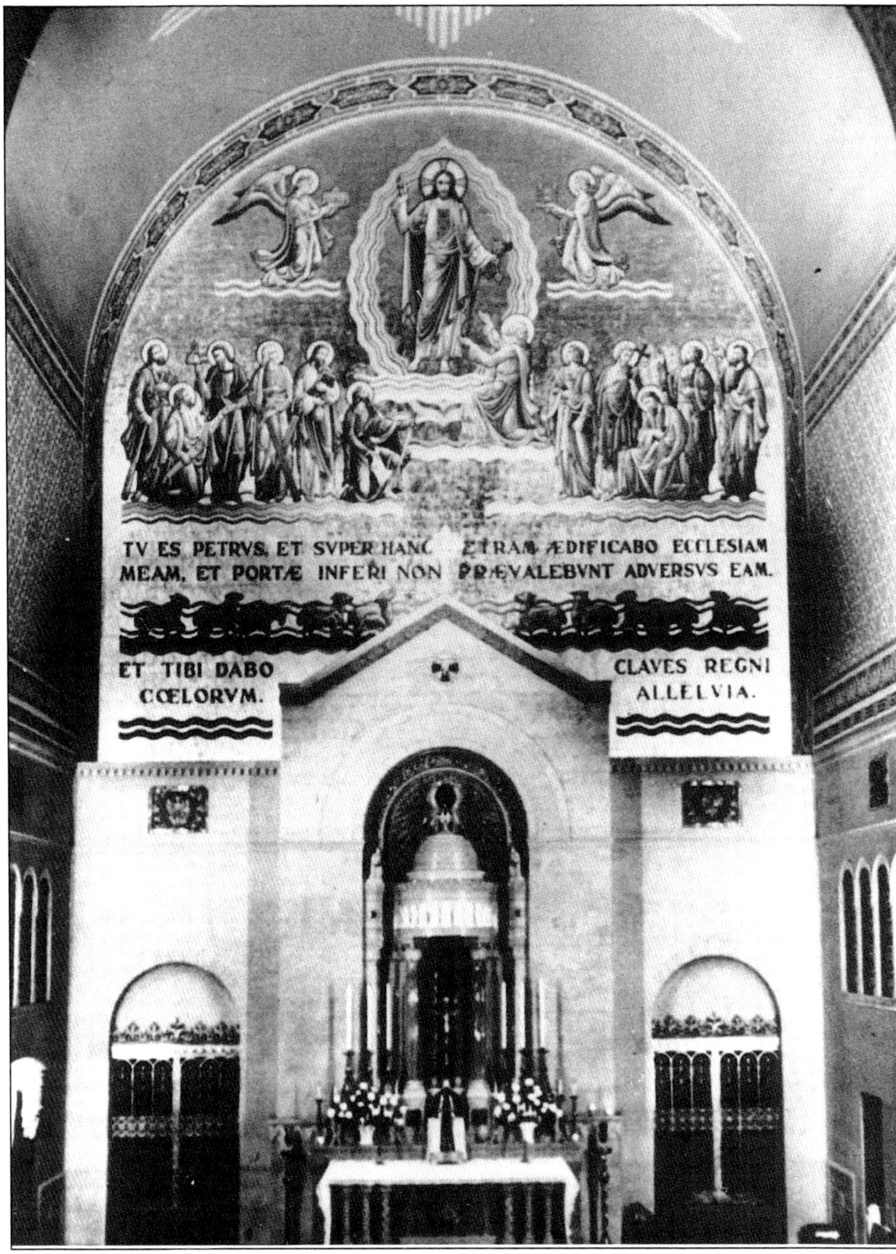

This picture of the main altar in St. Peter's Cathedral dates to a time when Latin was still the only official language of the Catholic Church, and the priest celebrated Mass with his back to the congregation. The Romanesque arch of the structure, the ornate style of the altar and its accouterments, and the somewhat dimly lighted interior are all very representative of that time and place. Many of the styles and rituals have changed. A new cathedral might be more open, airy, and spacious. It may look less like a church and more like an auditorium or amphitheater. Today, the legend over the altar is usually in English, but the meaning and spirit of the words has not changed: "You are Peter and upon this rock I will build my church and the gates of Hell shall not prevail against it. And to you I give the keys to the kingdom of heaven. Alleluia." (Courtesy State Archives of Michigan.)

Seven

CHURCHES

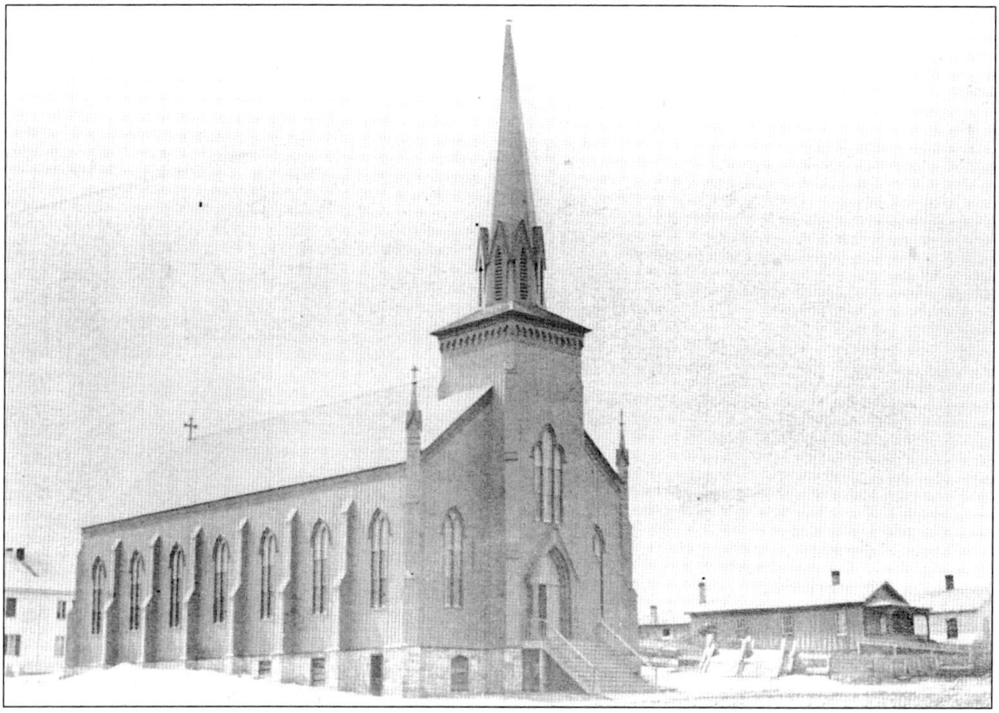

Shown in this 1865 view is the first St. Peter's Cathedral at West Baraga and Fourth Streets as it appeared one year after it was built by Bishop Baraga. Notice that the neighborhood still has the curious, unzoned look of new towns in America with humble, sometimes ramshackle, houses located next to much grander structures. The church burned down in 1879. (Courtesy State Archives of Michigan.)

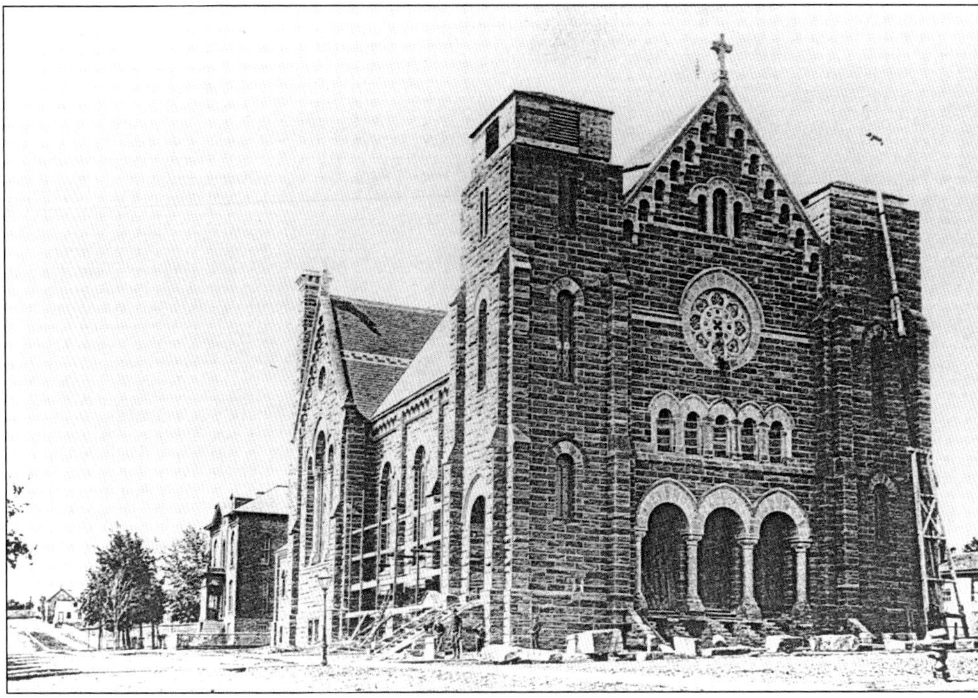

The second St. Peter's Cathedral was still under construction when this picture was taken in 1890. This Romanesque-style building, which was the same style as the first St. Peter's, was much grander than its predecessor, and the surrounding neighborhood had improved. The substantial diocesan building in its rear is evidence of that transition and the growing prosperity of the Church. (Courtesy Peter White Library.)

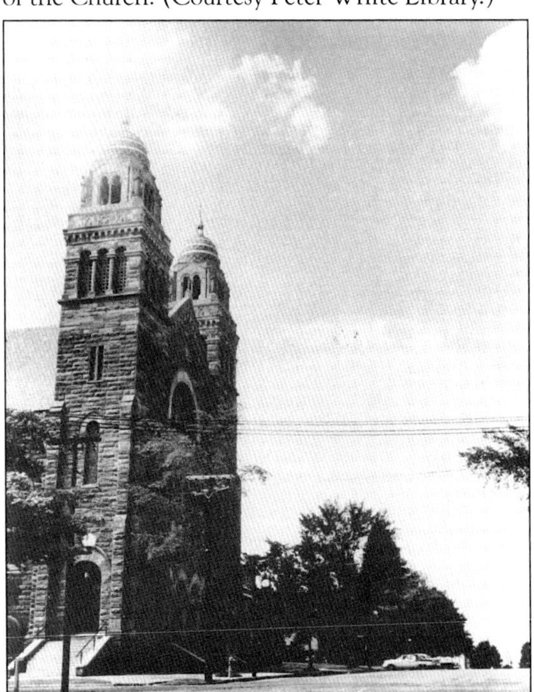

Today's St. Peter's monumental façade and twin towers can be seen from blocks away in Marquette. Its brownstone facing, triple arches at the main entryway, and large arched windows add a heavy dignity to the structure. Within, colorful stained-glass windows and elaborate woodwork lighten the characteristic darkness of Romanesque churches. The present church has undergone two renovations since it was damaged by fire in 1935. (Courtesy State Archives of Michigan.)

St. Paul's Episcopal is also a strong presence in the city. The parish complex with its three handsome structures, elegant architecture, magnificent stained glass, and brown-and-variegated sandstone walls is the most significant concentration of beautiful designs and skillful construction in the Upper Peninsula. Even the modern addition is a unique contribution to the city's culture. (Photo by G. Downs.)

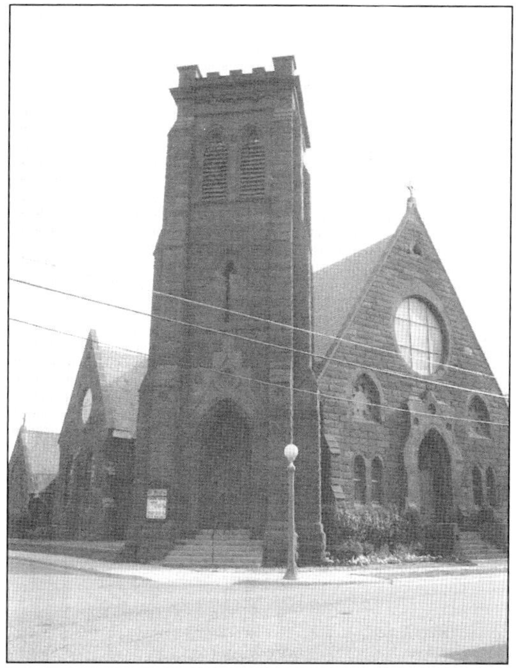

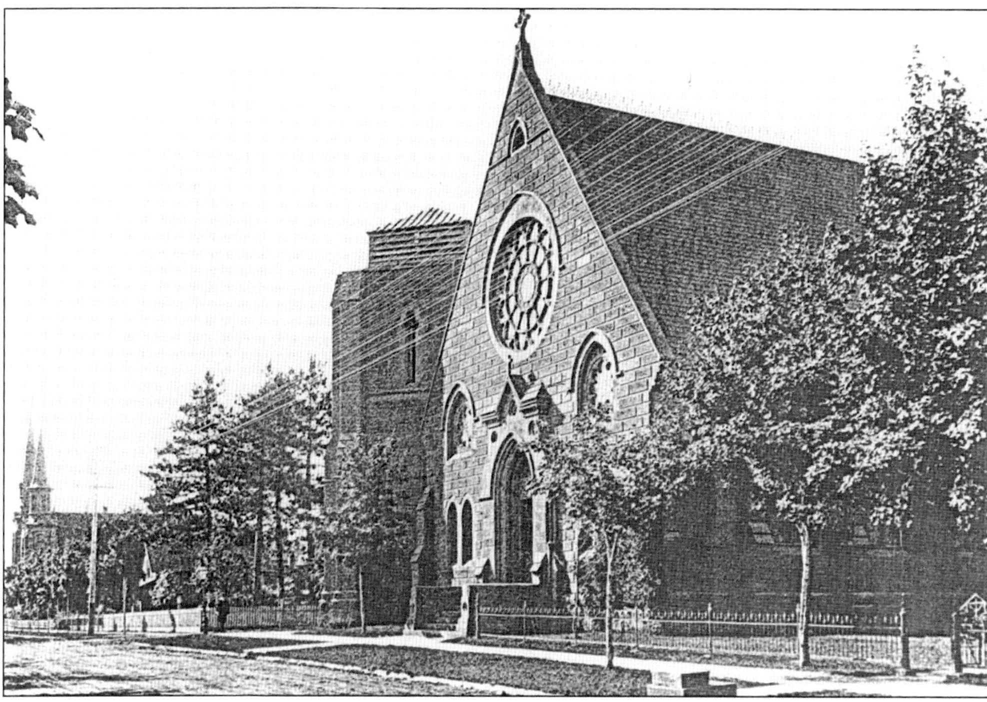

The most distinguished church in Marquette, St. Paul's Episcopal, is located at the northeast corner of Ridge and High Streets. This 1891 picture clearly shows the asymmetrical design of the structure with its exotic entry tower set at an angle to the southwest corner of the church. St. Paul's was built in 1874–1876 to replace an older wooden structure. The twin spires of the First United Methodist Church can be seen on the left, one block to the west. (Courtesy Peter White Library.)

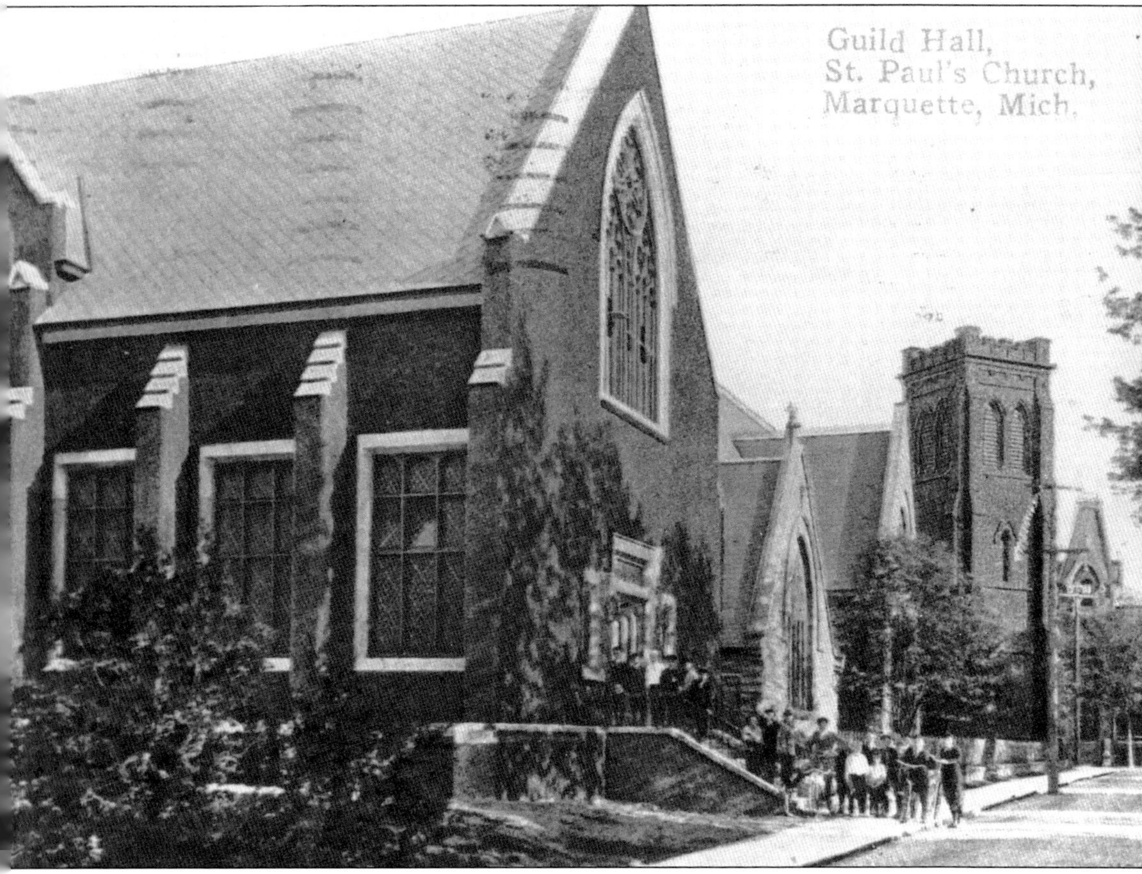

This postcard photo from 1920 shows the St. Paul's Guildhall in the foreground, the smaller Morgan Memorial Chapel beyond it, and in the middle distance, the church itself. A group has gathered, either just before or after some Guildhall activity, on the steps at the entry on a sunny, summer afternoon. The Episcopal congregation of St. Paul's is one of the oldest in Marquette, and its properties appear on the earliest city plat maps. The church tower is somewhat altered from its appearance in earlier pictures. The tower's top was redesigned, and the crenelations were added in 1903. The result enhances the structure's gothic appearance and adds force and drama to the church's presentation when it is approached from the north. The consistency with which the building's architects have carried out the neogothic motif as the complex grew is a large part of its visual appeal. (Courtesy State Archives of Michigan.)

This picture of the First Presbyterian Church was taken in 1891. Located on the southeast corner of Front and Bluff Streets, the church had a commanding position on the crest of the hill. Its spire can be seen in many early photographic views looking north on Front Street. The church was built in 1868 and served its congregation until 1931, when it was destroyed by fire in August of that year. (Courtesy Peter White Library.)

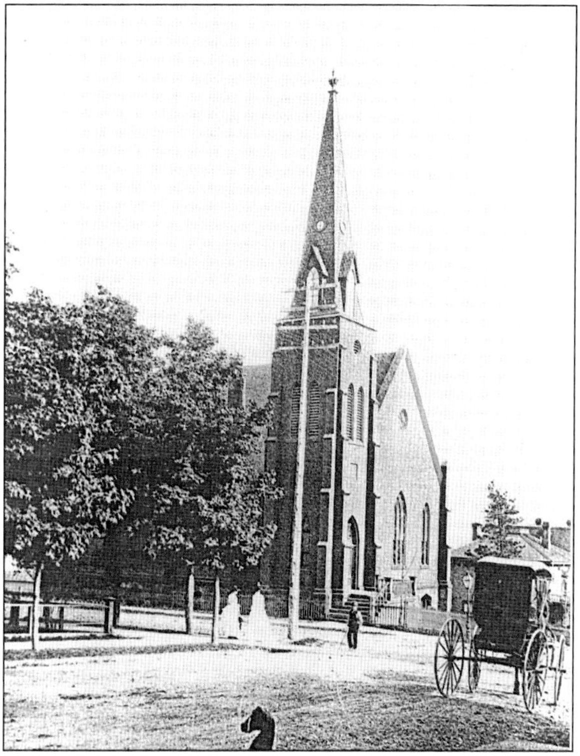

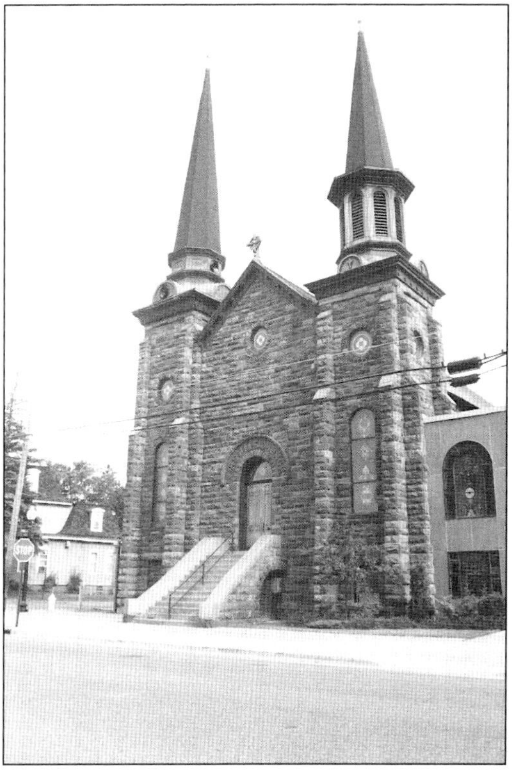

This contemporary photograph of the First United Methodist Church includes the modern (and somewhat incongruous) addition on its right. Situated at the corner of Ridge and Front Streets, this church was built in 1871 with uneven towers; the tower on the left was later shortened. (Photo by G. Downs.)

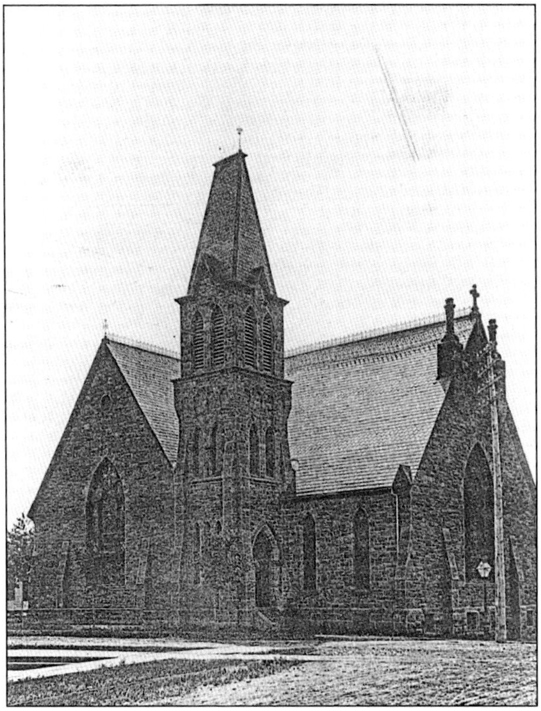

In 1890, the First Baptist Church, located on the southeast corner of Front and Ridge Streets, was still very new. Built in 1886 of local sandstone, its late Gothic revival design gave it an imposing and solid appearance. First Baptist was destroyed by fire in 1965, and the congregation, like so many, moved from this central location to a site closer to the homes of its members. (Courtesy Peter White Library.)

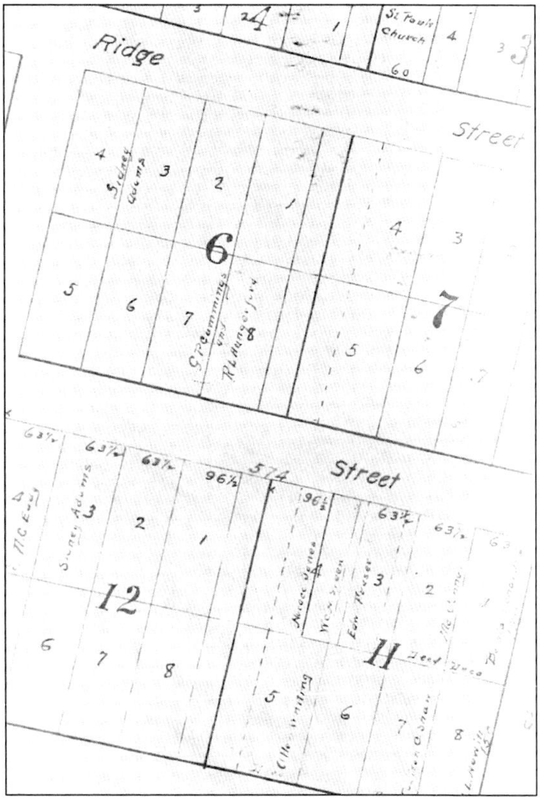

Early plat maps help us recover the early thinking and intentions regarding the shape of the city. This detail from an 1855 map shows the early design of what was one of Marquette's oldest and most attractive residential areas: Arch, Ridge, and Bluff Streets (between Third and Fourth). St. Paul's is now located at the corner of Ridge and High Streets, two blocks east of the site on the map. (Courtesy Peter White Library.)

Eight

NEIGHBORHOODS

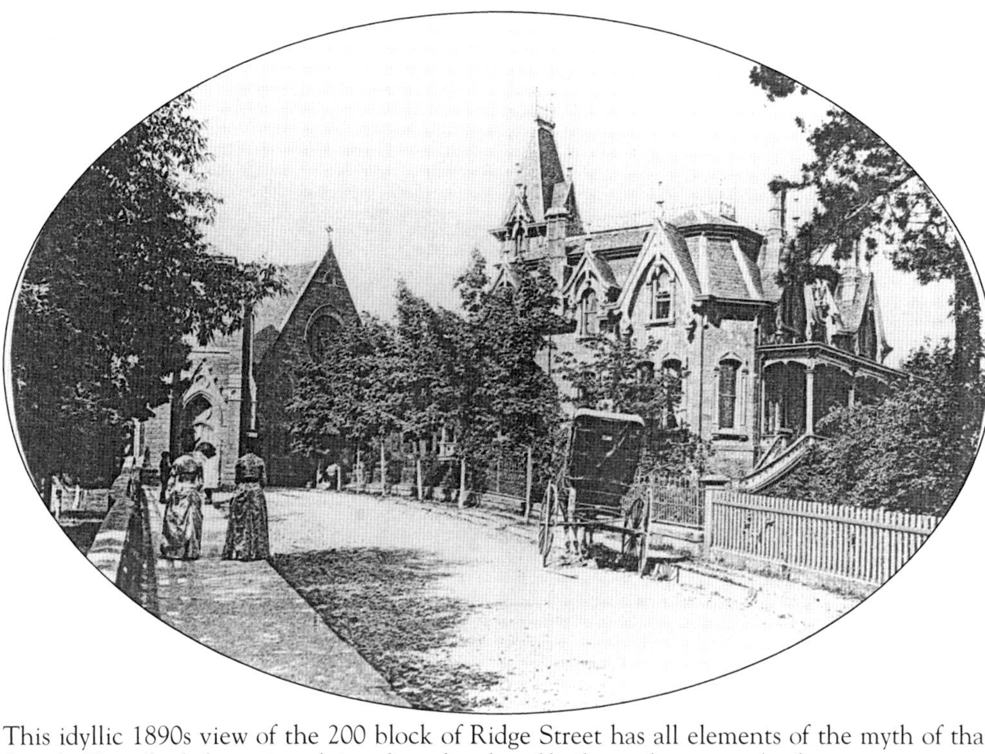

This idyllic 1890s view of the 200 block of Ridge Street has all elements of the myth of that decade. Tree-shaded, gracious, leisurely, ordered, and built on a human scale, the scene represents the nostalgia of years past. (Courtesy Peter White Library.)

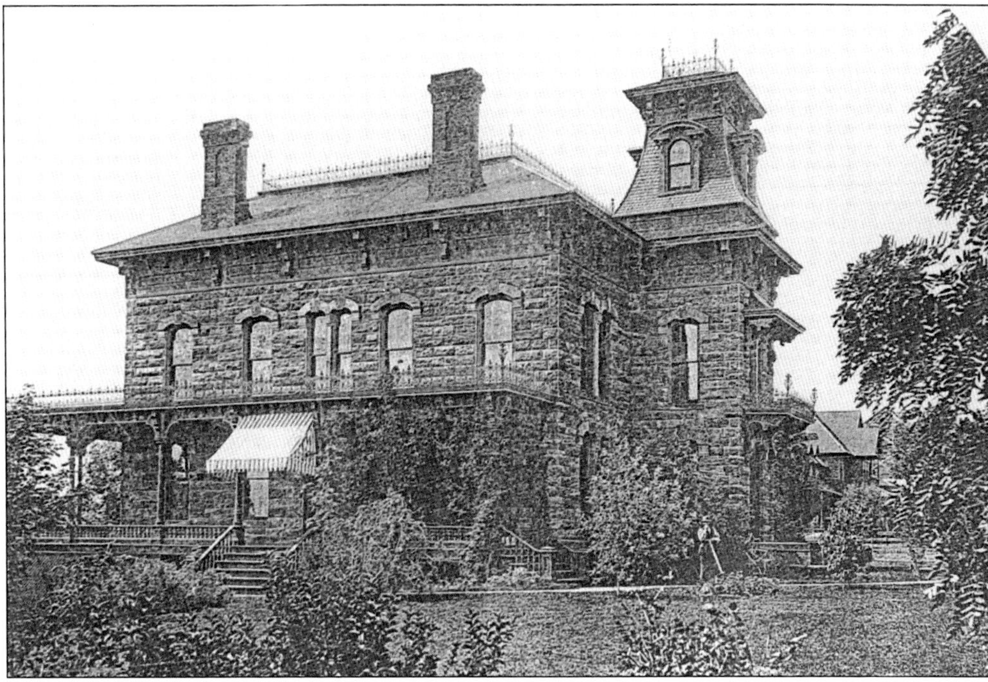

Shown here is an 1891 photograph of the Daniel H. Merritt residence at 410 East Ridge Street. Built in 1880, the house's west lawn was the site of one of Marquette's few tennis courts. Merritt served as president of the Iron Bay Manufacturing Company; the size and solidity of his estate are evidence of his success and standing in the community. (Courtesy Peter White Library.)

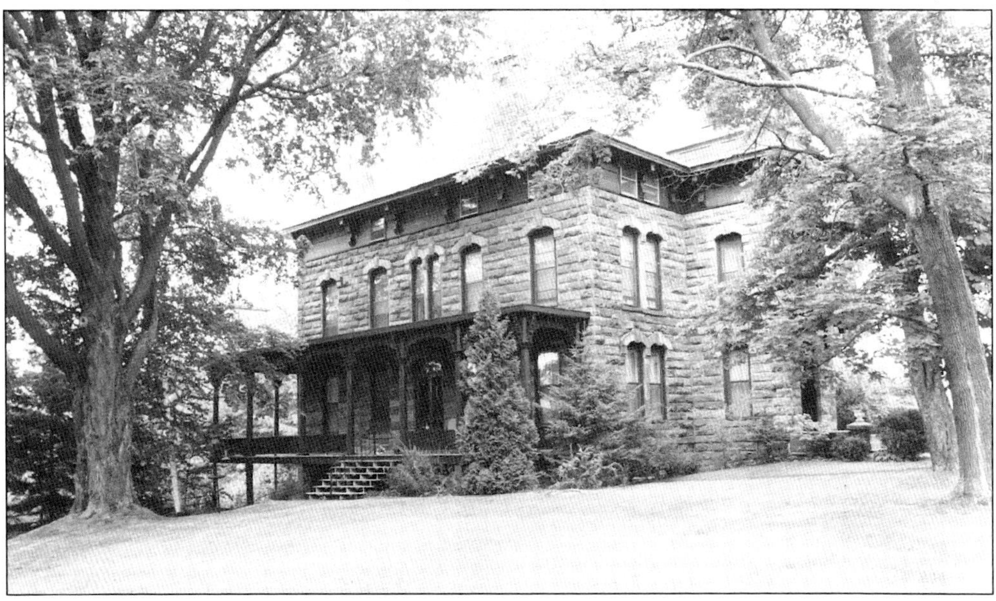

Shown here is the Merritt House, 118 years after its construction. It has been wonderfully maintained. The angle from which this photograph was taken differs from that of the earlier shot, and the landscaping, now mature, obscures some of the structure's details. The power of the rough, stone siding and the gracious proportions of its porch entry are still compelling and inviting. (Photo by G. Downs.)

Shown in this view is 461 East Ridge, the northwest corner of Ridge and Cedar, and the home of Alfred Kidder. He was an agent for the Champion Iron Company, the Pittsburgh and Lake Angeline Iron Company, and the Milwaukee Iron Company. His house is unabashedly Victorian and a fine example of Carpenter's Gothic. The horse and buggy and the ornate hitching post in the foreground are interesting accents. (Courtesy Peter White Library.)

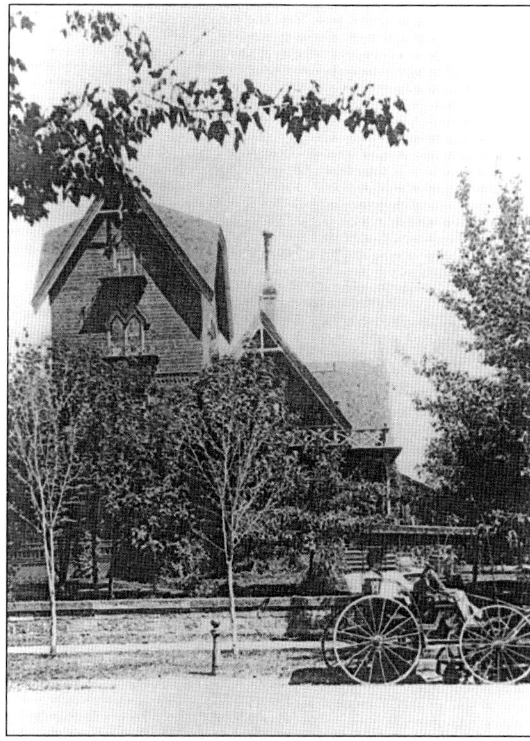

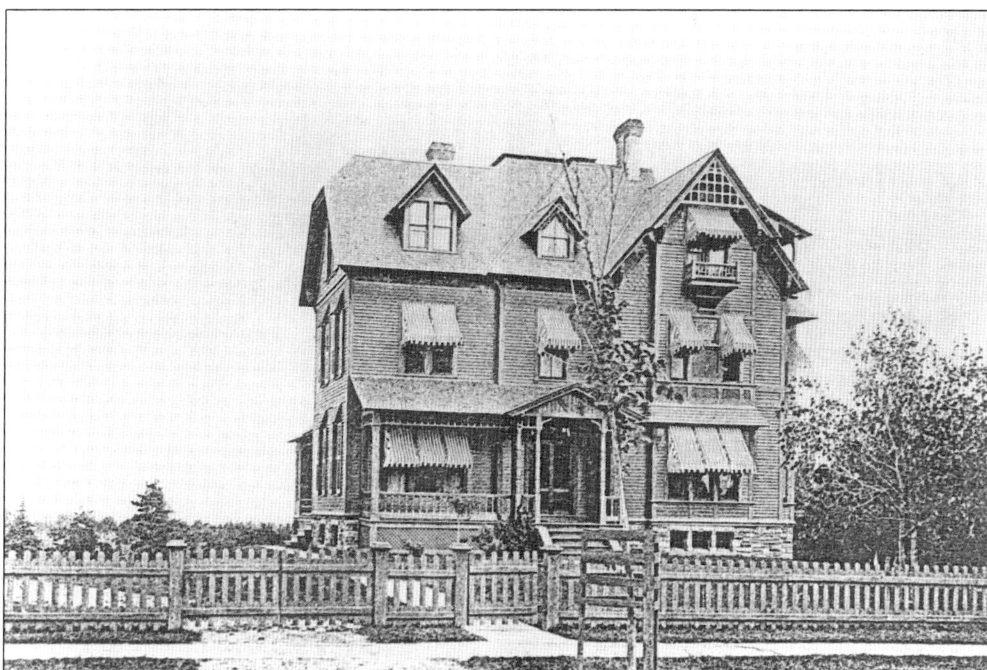

In the days before electric fans, when air conditioning wasn't even a dream, window awnings on the sunny side of houses and stores were an important climate-control device. This large house, the home of William W. Manning, an estate agent in the 1890s, is carrying more canvas than a good-sized sailing ship; even the porch windows have awnings. (Courtesy Peter White Library.)

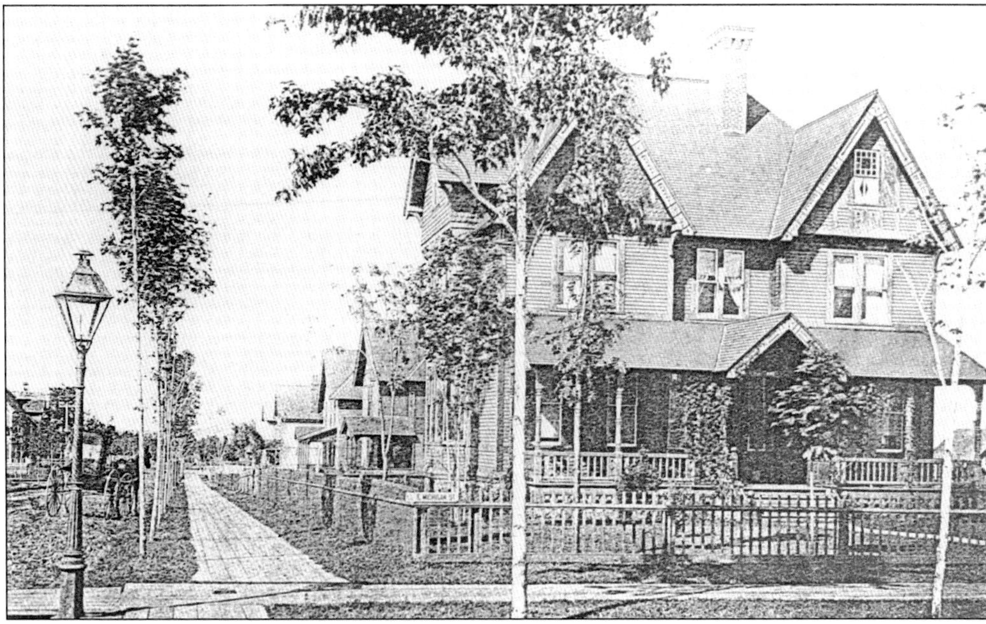

In 1891, this large, wooden house at the corner of Michigan and Spruce Streets was the home of John Wallace, superintendent of the local powder mill. Mining was of great economical importance in Marquette, and the mill was an essential service industry. There were still boardwalks in the late 1800s, and the trees were hardly more than new plantings. (Courtesy Peter White Library.)

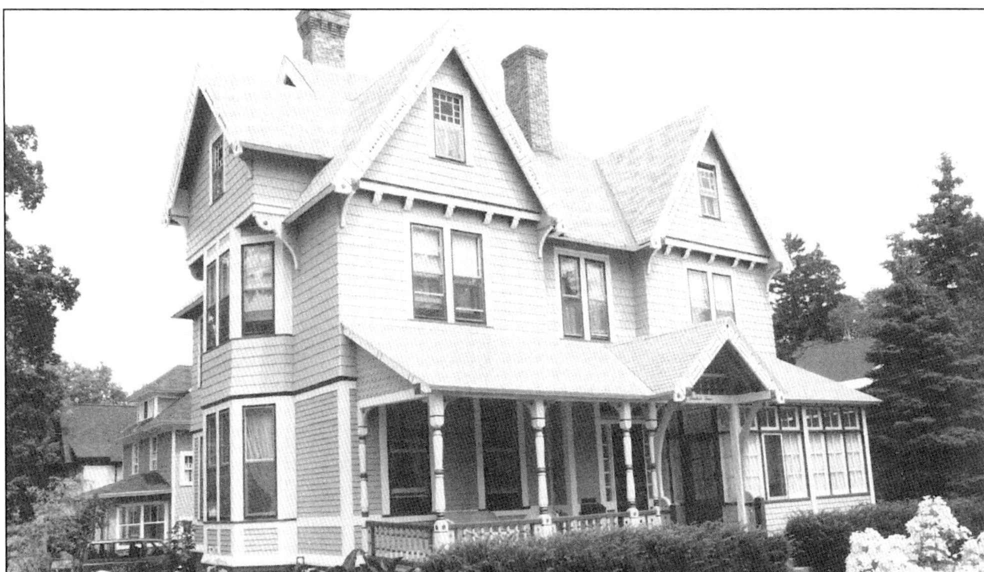

This 1998 photograph of the Wallace House is a much clearer view. Part of the front porch has been enclosed, and the yard is no longer fenced in to keep out wandering horses and other strays. Unfortunately, the attractive shingle accents of the original structure are gone, but the porch still provides a comfortable place from which to watch the passersby. (Photo by G. Downs.)

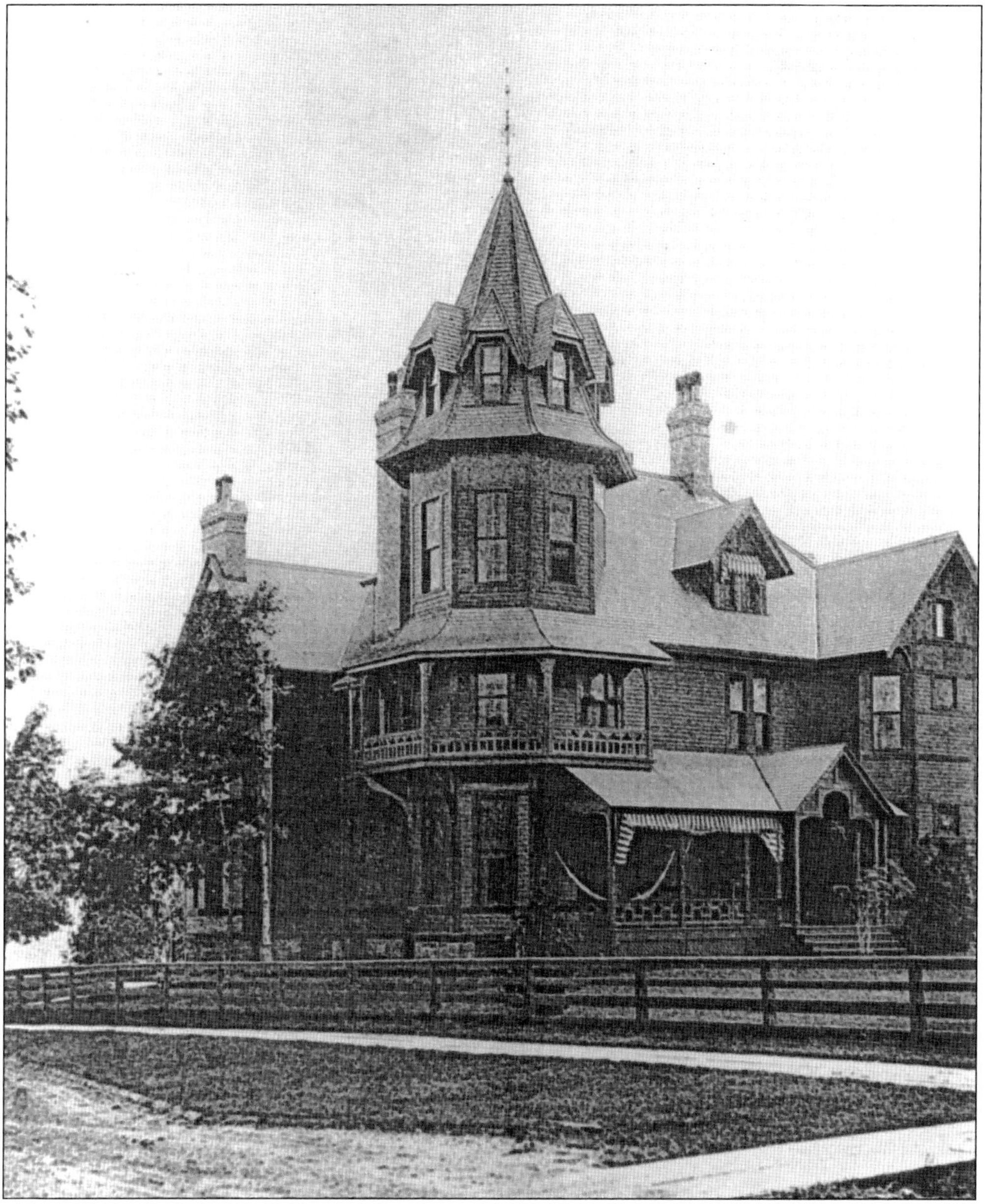

Of the houses owned by John Munro Longyear, the one pictured here is not exactly the most impressive. Taken without comparisons, however, this is a good example of what carpenters can do when wood is plentiful and labor is cheap. The corner tower itself, with its peak and heavily protected six windows four floors above the ground, is a designer's dream made real. The ornate railings and the scrolled wood frame under the gabled front entrance are interesting touches. It was built in 1883, about seven years before this picture was taken, for Nellie and Edward Stofford by Alfred Swineford, Nellie's father. The Longyears did not live at this Cedar Street address for long. They had a 66-room mansion built on the 500 block of Ridge Street, which they lived in for less than ten years. Emotionally devastated by the accidental death of a son and upset over a dispute with the city, Mr. Longyear had the house disassembled, shipped to Brookline, Massachusetts, and rebuilt. (Courtesy Peter White Library.)

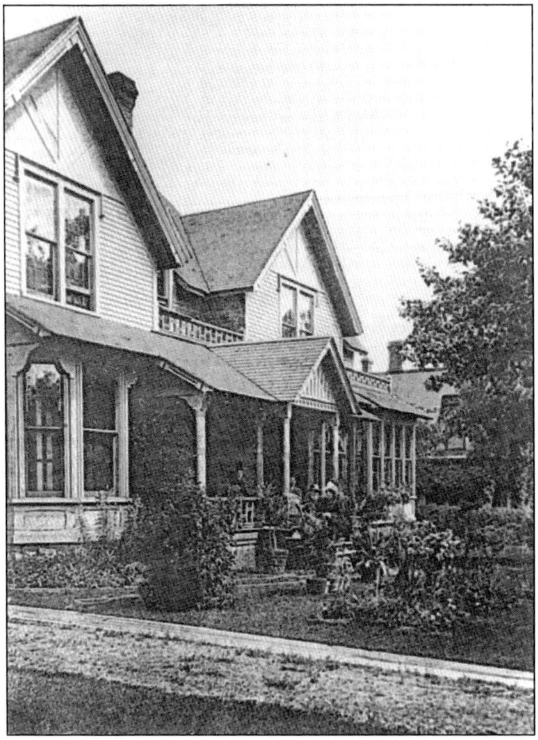

Attorney Daniel H. Ball, a partner at Ball and Hanscom, lived in this house at 411 East Ridge when this picture was taken in 1891. The front porch was an important architectural feature of comfortable houses in substantial neighborhoods, and Mr. Ball's house had an ample one. Several people can be seen enjoying it on this summer day. (Courtesy Peter White Library.)

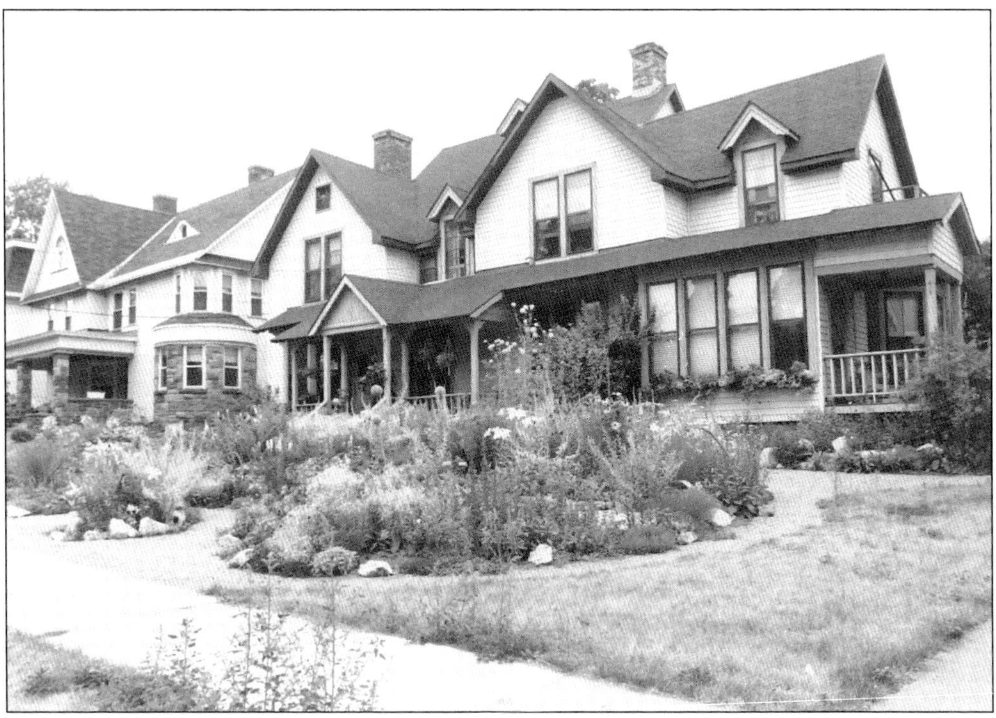

The full glory of Mr. Ball's porches emerges in this recent photograph. Across the front of the house, there is a large entry porch with three bays, a row of windows for a room under the porch roof, and a smaller entry porch for side-street traffic at the corner. (Photo by G. Downs.)

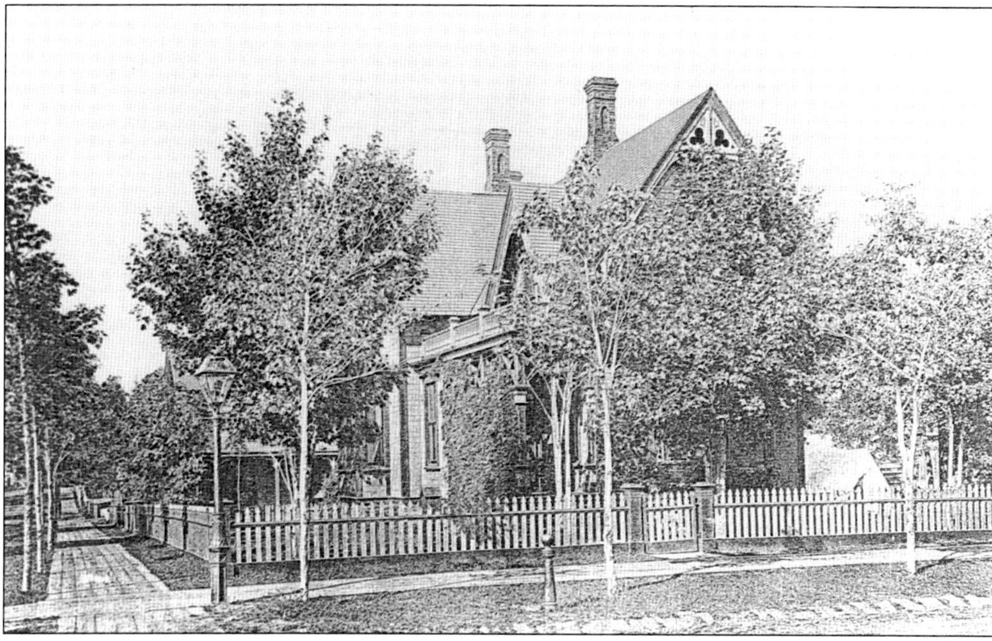

John H. Gillett lived at 203 East Arch Street in another Carpenter's Gothic house. The ornate, wooden scroll work at the front gable peak is typical of this 19th-century style. There is a gas light, a hitching post, and a picket fence to round off this conventional image. Mr. Gillett was a lumber manufacturer and the owner of a tugboat line. (Courtesy Peter White Library.)

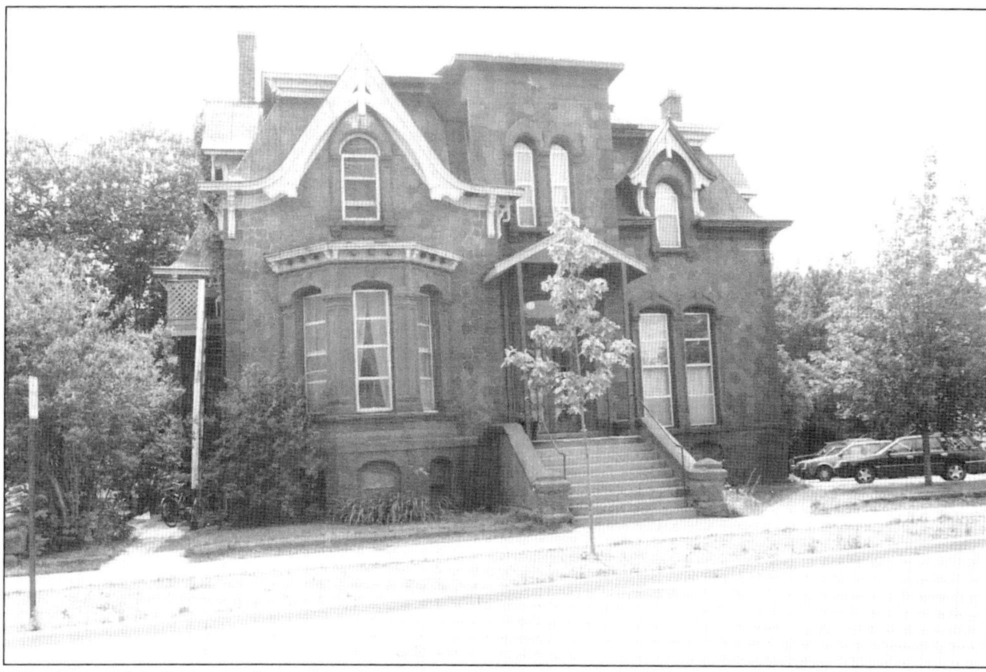

The demands of the city have begun to encroach on this fine, old building. The parking lot (once the side yard) is a jarring modernism juxtaposed with this 19th-century collection of architectural fancies; even the basement windows have arches. Other features include lattice work, a tower, a massive stairway to the entrance, and a variety of gables. (Photo by G. Downs.)

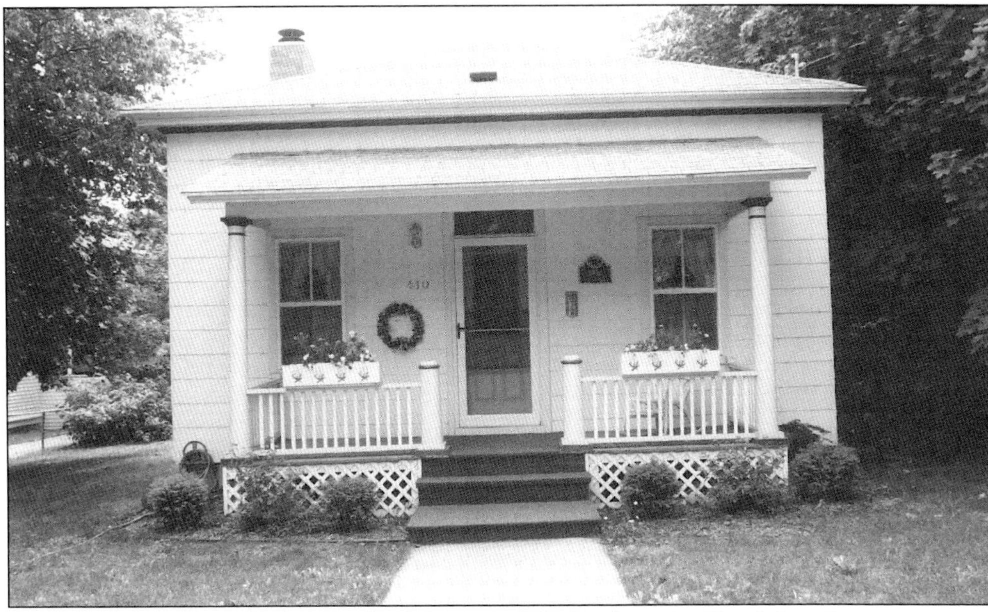

The title of a perennially favorite book by Carrol W. Rankin, the Dandelion Cottage is a real place, located at 440 East Ridge in Marquette. The story is about five self-sufficient young women who are allowed to live in the cottage in return for keeping the lawn free of dandelions. But that's only the beginning. Their adventures and their ability to cope with them are what make the book appealing. (Photo by G. Downs.)

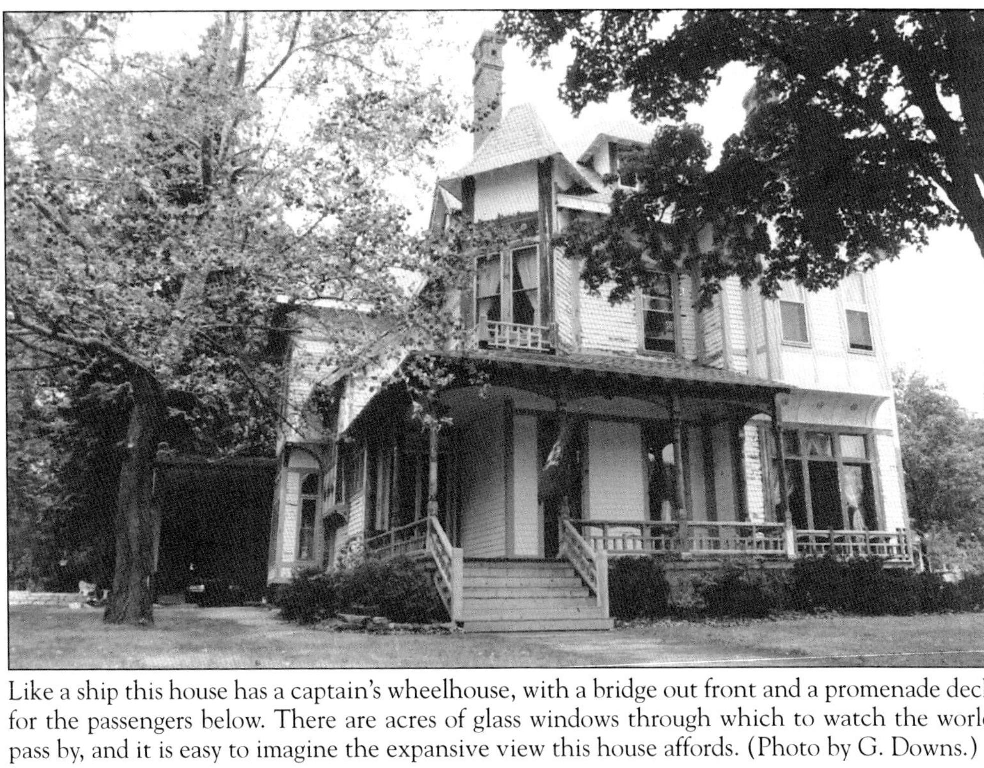

Like a ship this house has a captain's wheelhouse, with a bridge out front and a promenade deck for the passengers below. There are acres of glass windows through which to watch the world pass by, and it is easy to imagine the expansive view this house affords. (Photo by G. Downs.)

The mansard roof, with its protected third-floor window, make this small house on Arch Street look interesting. Although the windows have been updated, the rounded-border garden, the porch pillars, and the generous overhang of the roof maintain this home's links with its past. (Photo by G. Downs.)

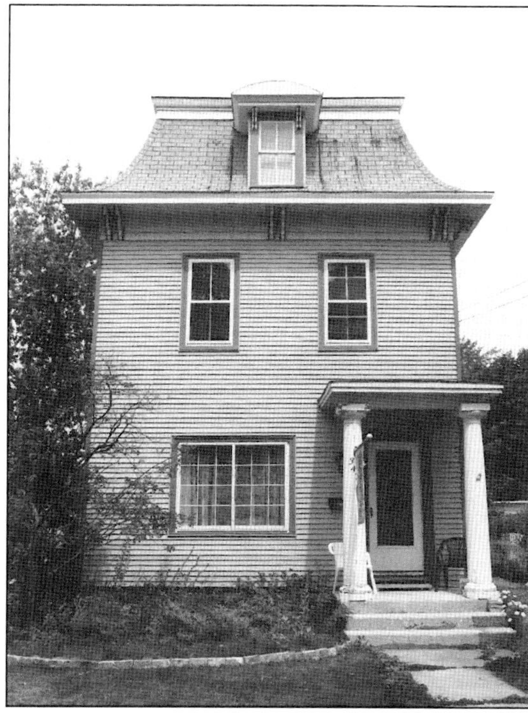

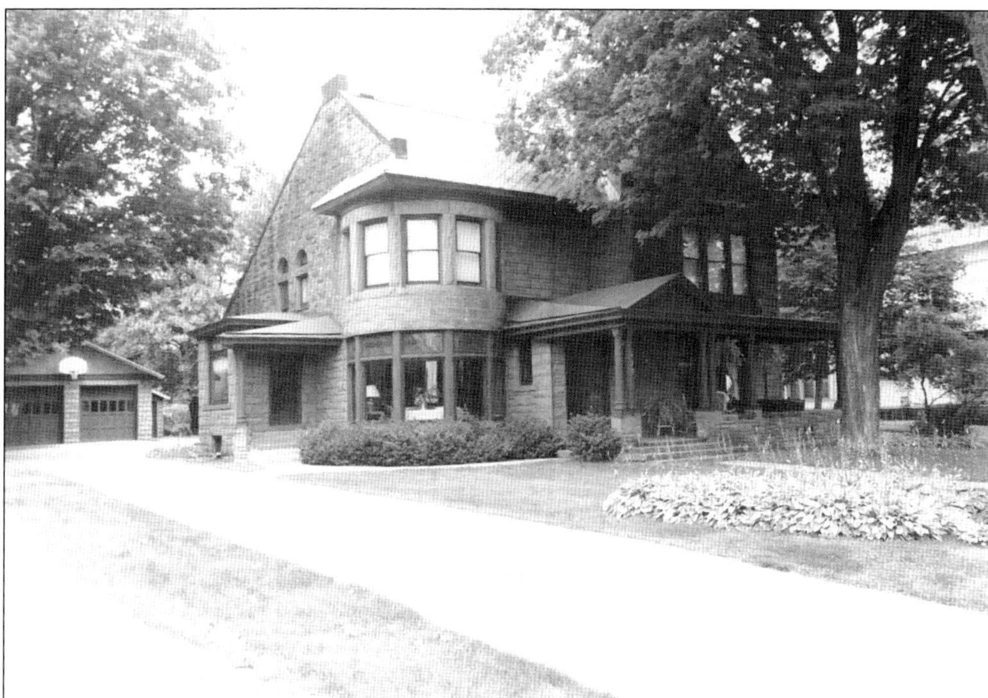

This grand house at 433 East Ridge Street deserves attention. Its interesting design includes a rounded, corner tower, a pillared porch, variegated stone walls, and two arched windows under its steeply pitched, rear roof line. It is imaginatively assembled to create an imposing effect. (Photo by G. Downs.)

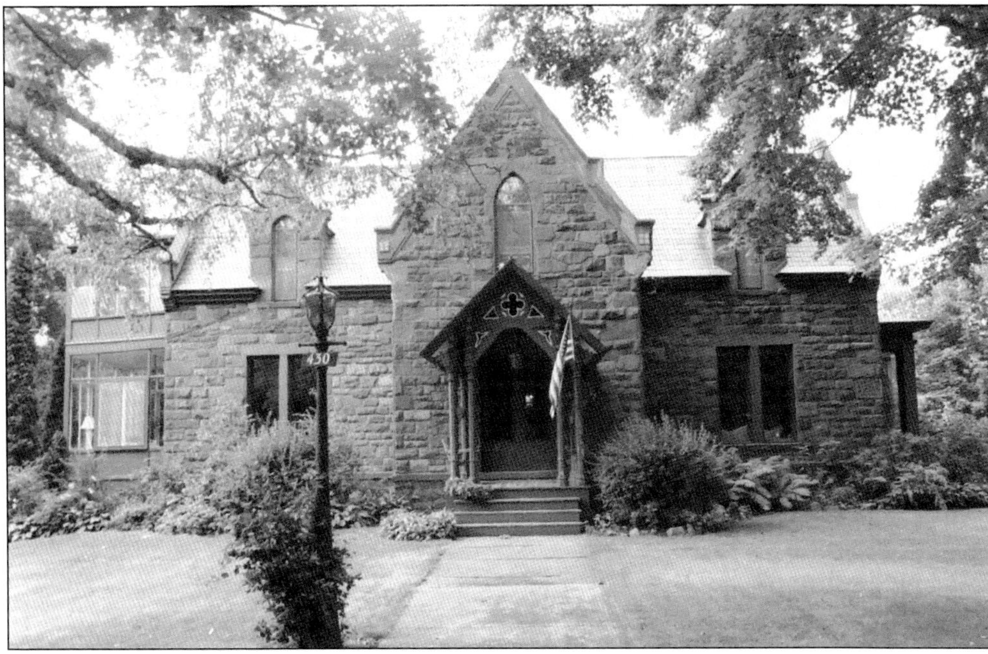

In this contemporary photograph, the Andrew A. Ripka House at 430 East Arch Street carries its age with grace. Designed by Carl F. Struck, who practiced as an architect in Marquette in the 1870s, this Gothic revival house sports parapets, random stone facing, and a particularly attractive entry. The original owner was employed as a railroad and ore dock supervisor. (Photo by G. Downs.)

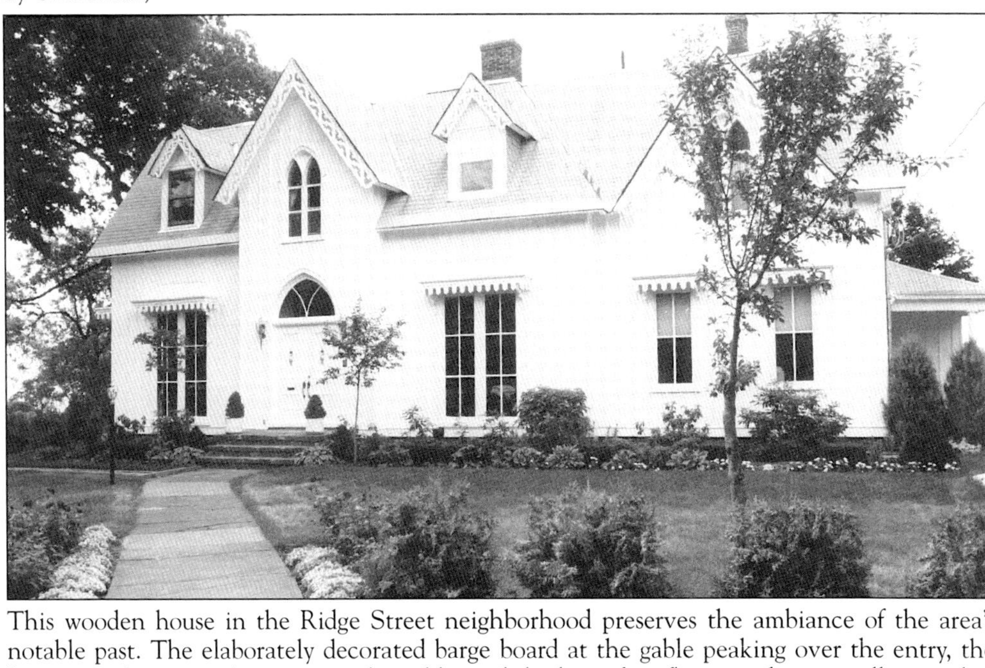

This wooden house in the Ridge Street neighborhood preserves the ambiance of the area's notable past. The elaborately decorated barge board at the gable peaking over the entry, the lancet window extending up into the gable, and the long, first-floor windows are all reminders of the degree to which the Gothic Revival often dominated residential architecture, especially in wealthy neighborhoods before the turn of the century. (Photo by G. Downs.)

Nine

PEOPLE AND PASTIMES

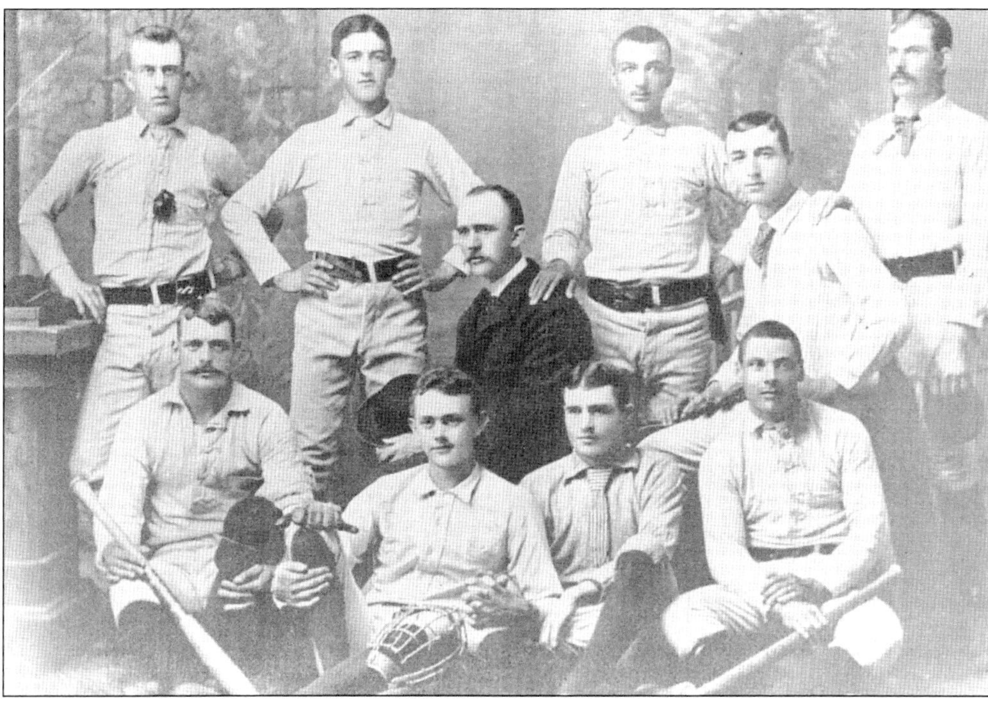

This men's baseball team, the Marquette Nine from 1888, had barely enough players to avoid a forfeit. The catcher and first baseman can be identified by their distinctive equipment, and the manager is wearing his street clothes. The game was still evolving, but its professional structure had been in place since 1876; almost every town throughout the United States was represented by a team. (Courtesy Peter White Library.)

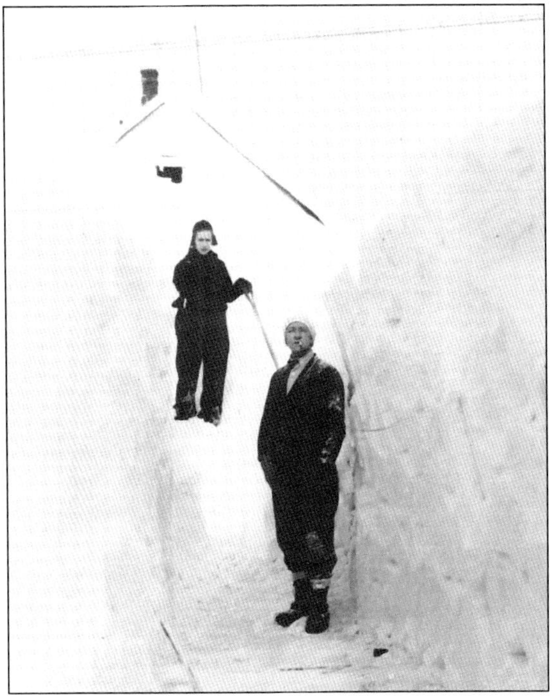

Winters in the Upper Peninsula are character builders. Snow has fallen during every month except August, although not every year. Shoveling out is a frequent occupation. In this picture, the couple has just finished a shoveling, and, warmed by their effort, are appraising their accomplishment. If they look less than exultant, it is understandable. This was an April storm in 1930 that came near the end of a punishing winter. (Courtesy Marquette County Historical Society.)

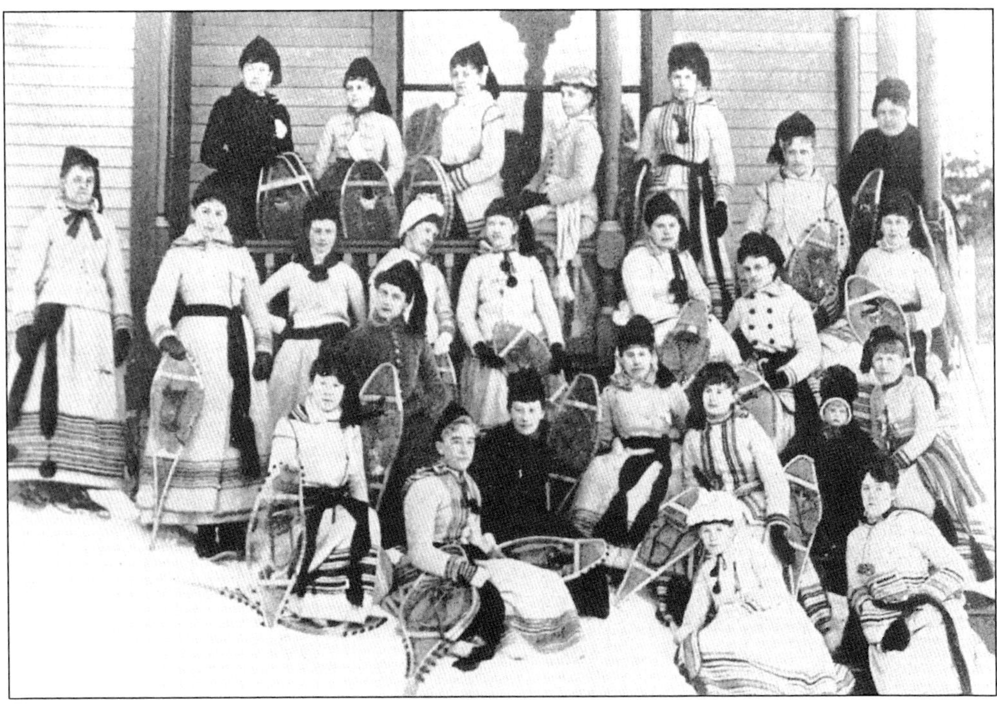

Before hockey and skiing developed into sports, snowshoeing was a popular winter pastime. In 1886, this group of Marquette women gathered with their equipment for this photograph. The style of the shoes is remarkably uniform. A close examination uncovers only one set of bear paws, and more than 14 pairs of the "Michigan-style" shoe, which are still worn in the Upper Peninsula. (Courtesy Peter White Library.)

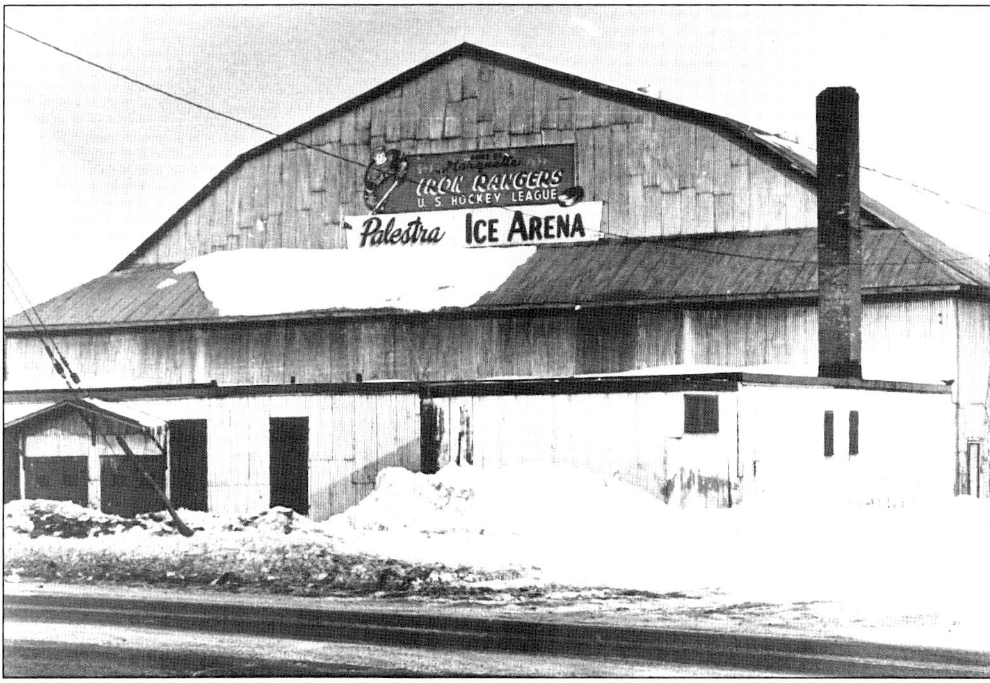

Nobody ever said it was a beautiful building, but there were times when the Palestra was the beating heart of the city; for residents, it was probably one of the most important-places. The Iron Rangers played hockey at this site, years after the Millionaires and the Blackbirds. Couples courted, bands played, people danced, and, during WW II, Marquette's young men began their long journey by waiting for induction at the Palestra. (Courtesy Marquette County Historical Society.)

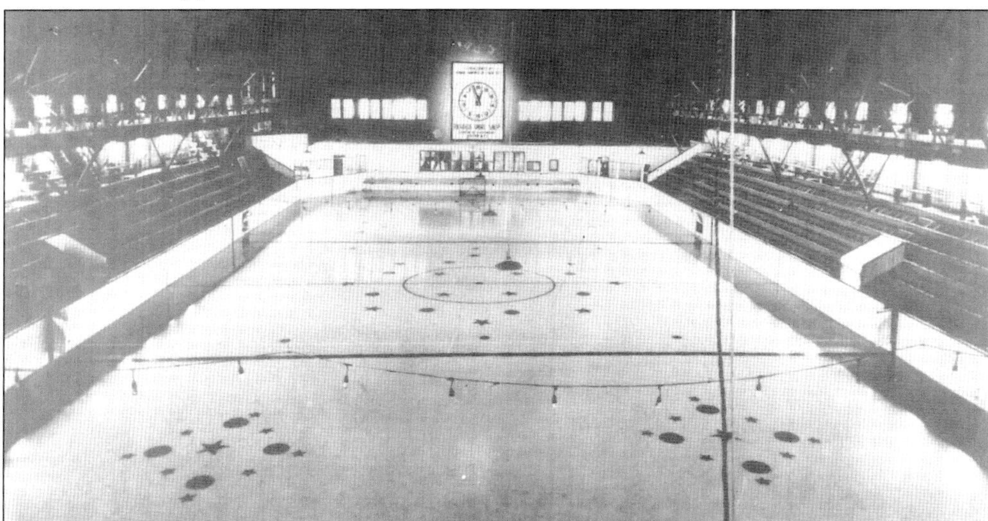

Shown is the interior of the Palestra during the hockey season in the 1970s, near the end of the old building's life. Fans took their chances at games. The front rows at rinkside had no protection from pucks and sticks, and the shared dangers created a kind of emotional intimacy between local teams and their supporters. The view from the gallery was great, however, and fans weren't as edgy. (Courtesy Marquette County Historical Society.)

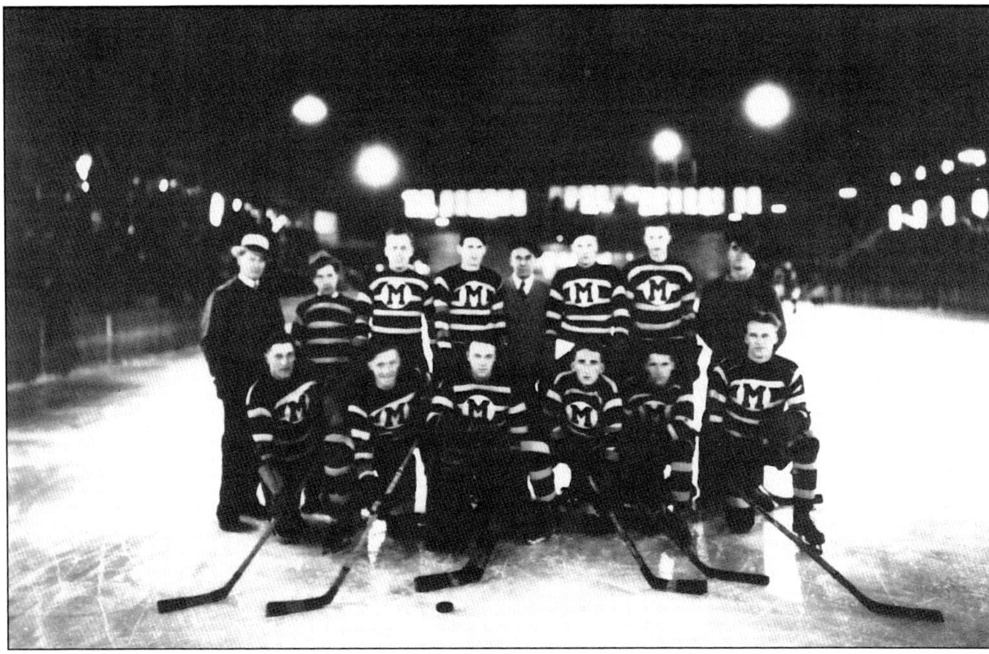

The Marquette Millionaires pose near center ice at the Palestra in 1935. During the Depression, this team helped build the community's reputation as a good hockey town. The Millionaires were mostly local talent, which ensured enthusiastic support, and their name was a match for the hopeful and defiant spirit of the Marquette Range at a time when work was scarce and wages were low. (Courtesy Marquette County Historical Society.)

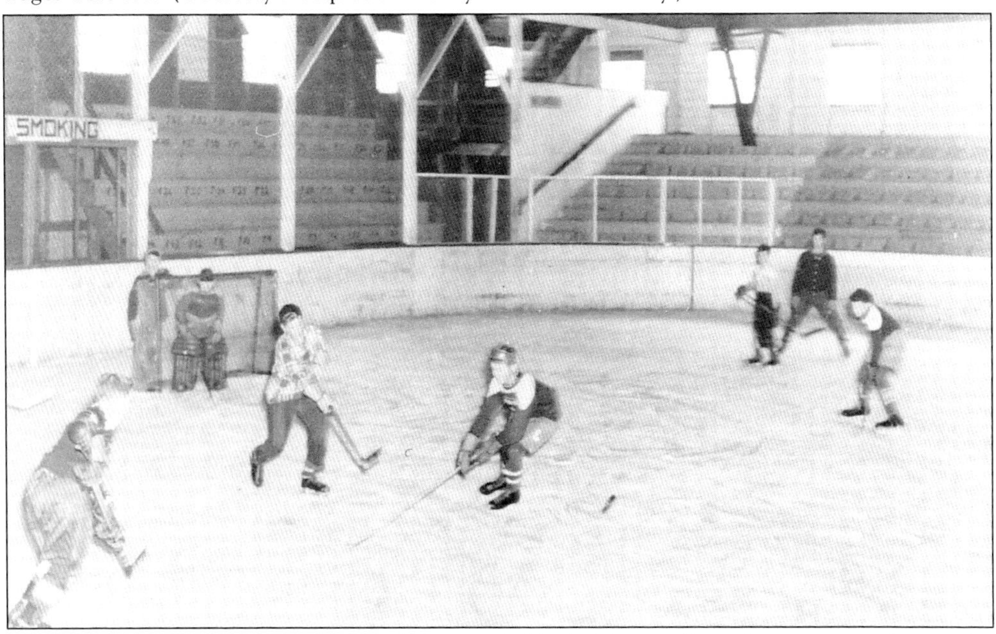

This youth hockey session at the Palestra, probably held on a Saturday morning during the 1960s, is more evidence of the influence the game has had on Marquette and its people. The uniforms don't match, but everyone is focused, and the young players have begun to develop some moves. (Courtesy State Archives of Michigan.)

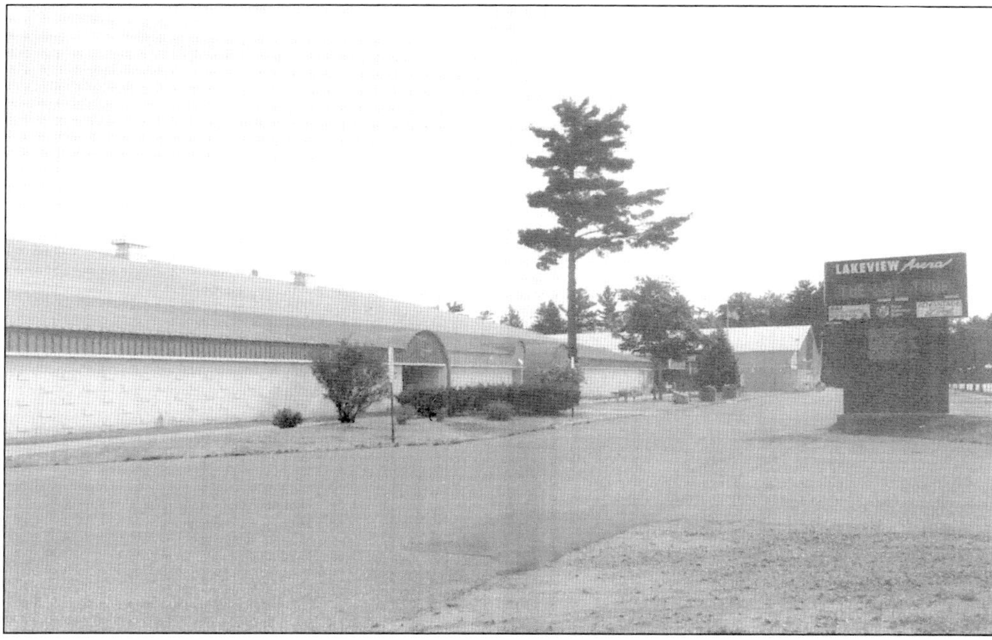

When the Palestra was finally pulled down in 1974, after 53 years of service, the Lakeview Arena replaced it. This modern facility, pictured here in 1998, is many things the Palestra couldn't be. The pattern of life in Marquette has changed, entertainment opportunities are much greater, and the competition for attention is more intense. The arena is popular, but it doesn't generate the same affection. (Photo by G. Downs.)

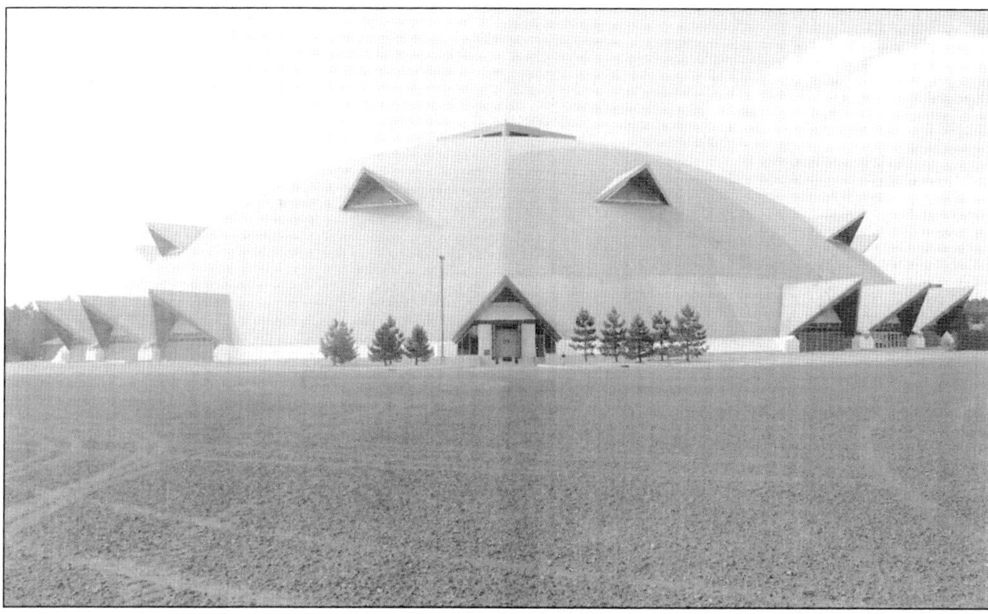

Built to stand up to the Upper Peninsula's strong winds and heavy snowfall, the Superior Dome is the largest wooden sports dome in the world. It was constructed in 1990–1991 by the State of Michigan to serve as a training site for Olympic athletes and others attending the Great Lakes Sports Training Center. Interior space covers more than 5 acres, and the facility seats 8,000. (Photo by G. Downs.)

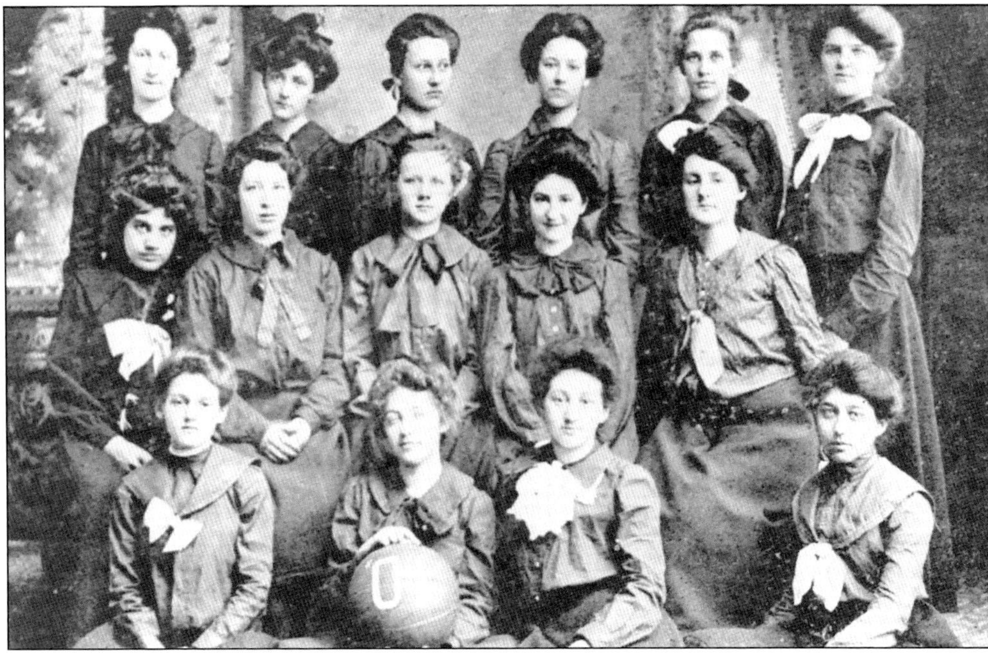

Although they are overdressed by contemporary standards, the 1901–1902 Marquette High School women's basketball team played a form of the game we would still recognize today. Their style was much more static, the rules far more restrictive, and there wasn't much scoring, but it was still basketball, and we would share their pleasure if we saw them play. Team pictures had already settled into the rigid arrangements still used today. (Courtesy Peter White Library.)

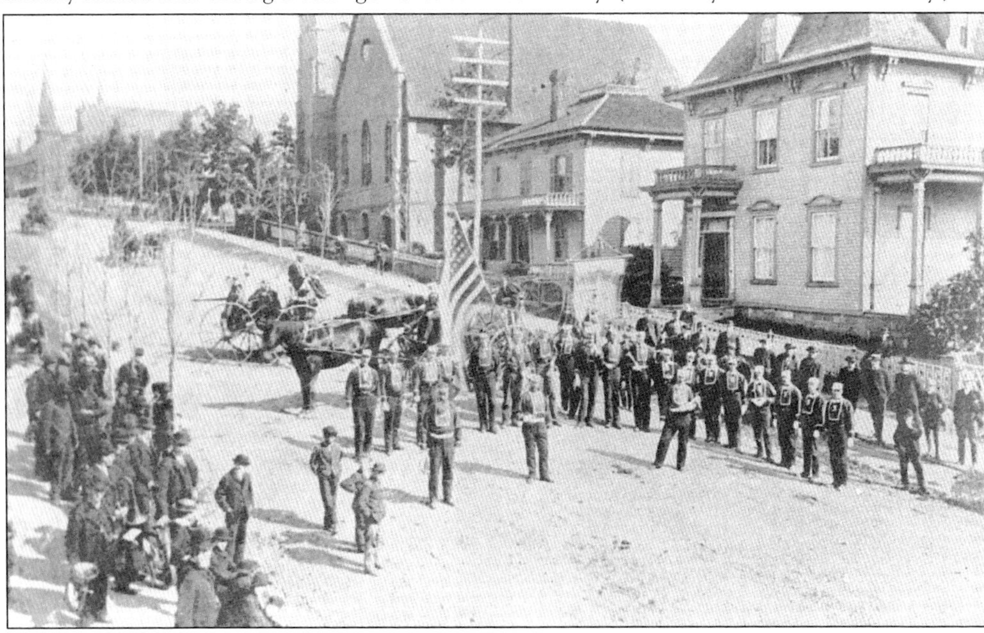

Americans in frontier towns were joiners. Their clubs, teams, and service organizations immediately established networks of friends, companions, and clients, and made the experience of living in a new and strange place manageable. This volunteer fire department has assembled on North Front Street to march in a c. 1880 parade. (Courtesy Peter White Library.)

Harlow's Wooden Man was conceived and assembled by Amos Harlow. The durability and popularity of this curiosity dates back to 1875. It was made of cedar, fungi, untwisted hemp, birch, and cedar bark, with a pine burl for a head. Featured in *Ripley's Believe It or Not* in 1930, the "man" was married to a local woman in a mock marriage ceremony in 1891. (Courtesy State Archives of Michigan.)

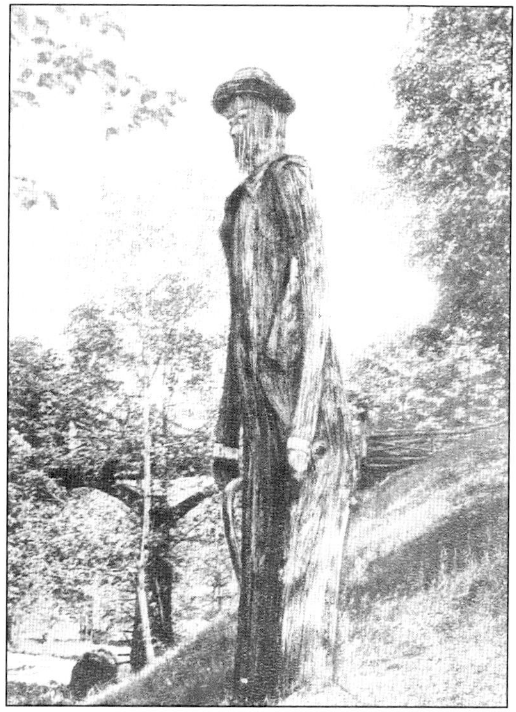

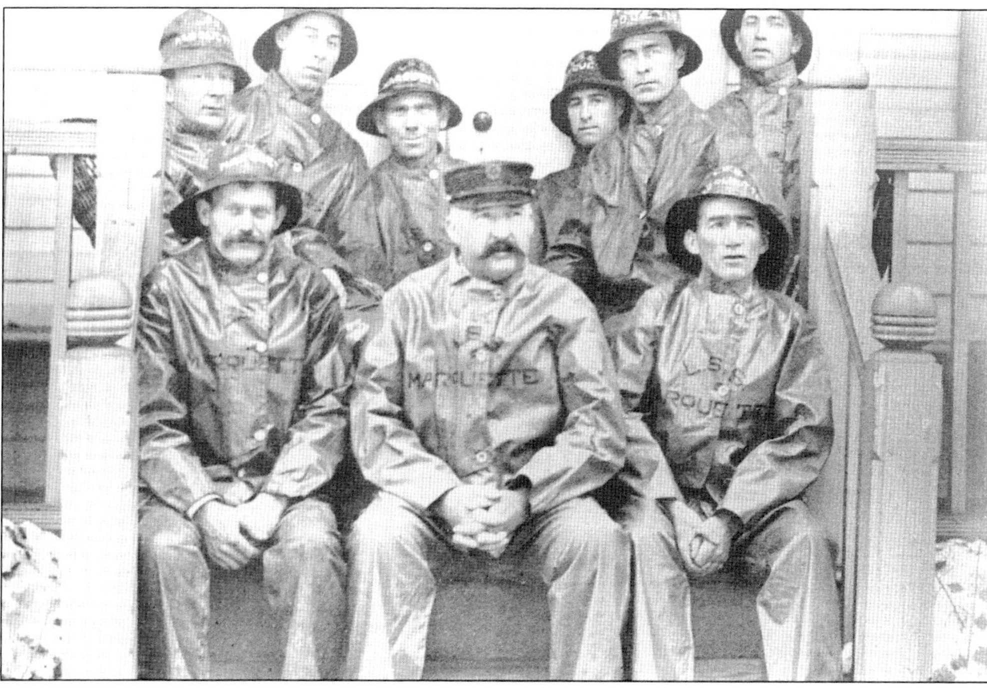

On September 29, 1895, Captain Cleary and his lifesaving crew, pictured here, rescued the men of the S.S. *Kershaw*. It was a challenge for which they were well prepared. Their training and the quality of their leader had been recognized in 1893, when they were chosen to give demonstrations of the latest techniques in lifesaving at sea at the World's Fair in Chicago. (Courtesy Peter White Library.)

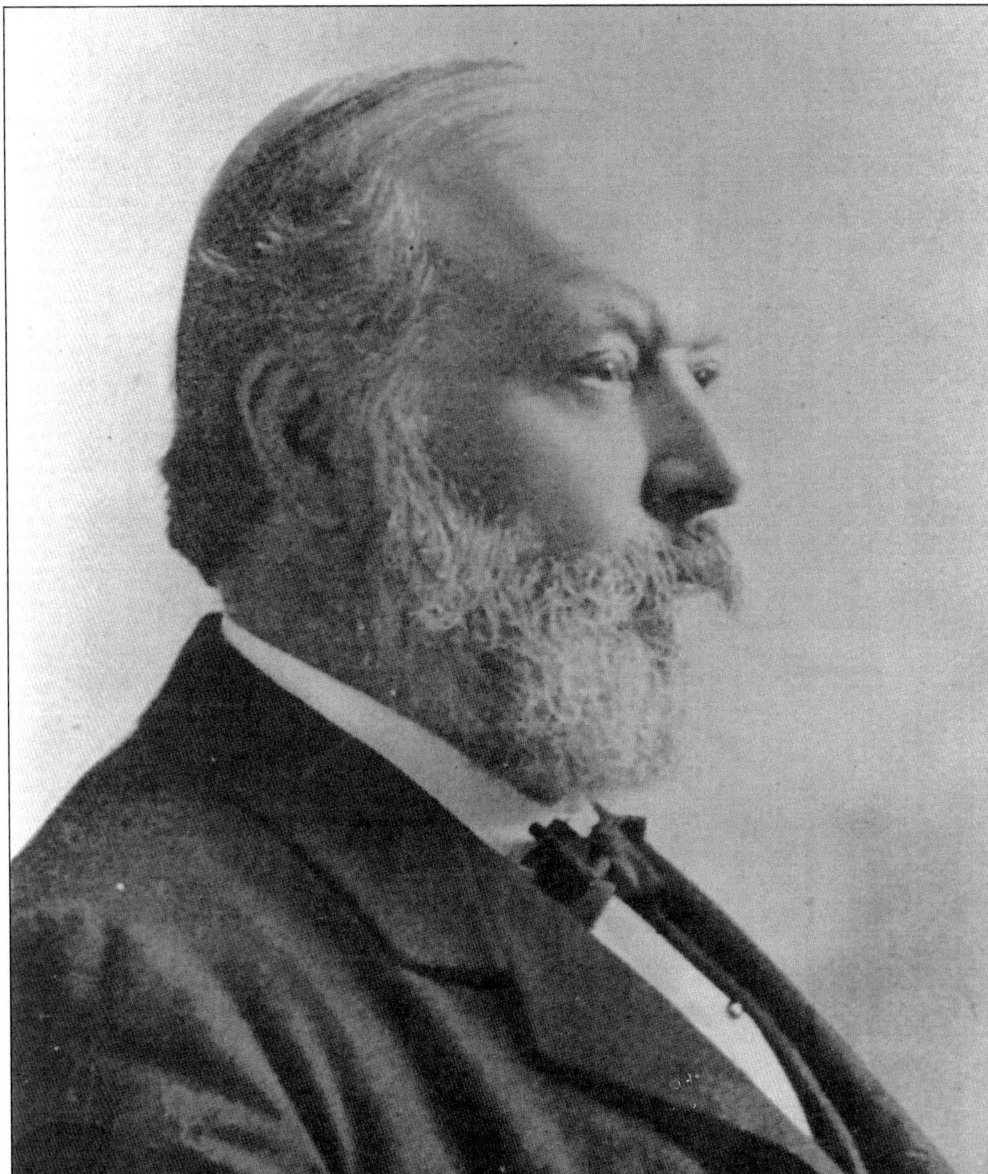

Peter White (1830–1908) came to Marquette before the city even had a name, and he possibly contributed more to the development of the area than any other person. This is not written to minimize the contributions of Amos Harlow, Robert Graveraet, Philo Everett, or other remarkable individuals, nor those of the groups of miners, lumberjacks, land agents, engineers, teachers, and homemakers who played a role in the area's growth and prosperity. Peter White arrived in the area in 1849, and lived here the rest of his life. His efforts to develop Marquette were enormous; he assisted in the building of the library, the university, and the park; he put his hand to large public tasks, serving as mayor, state representative, and state senator; he established an insurance office and a travel agency; he helped construct buildings of beauty and substance—a bank, a library, a chapel; and he became a local celebrity in the eyes of residents. The model for the character, Mr. Black, in *The Dandelion Cottage*, White also appears in Traver's *Laughing Whitefish* as himself. (Courtesy Peter White Library.)

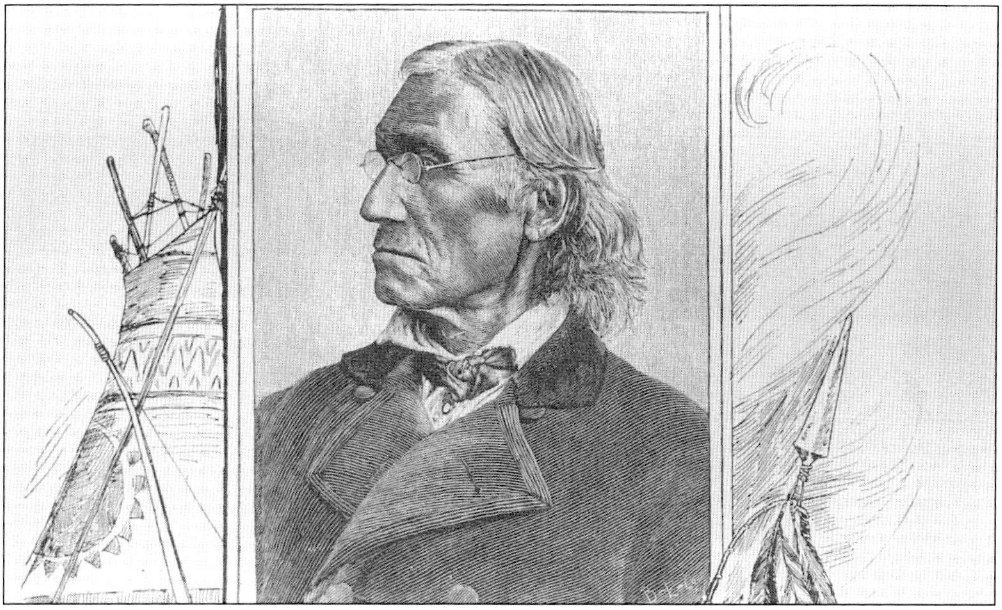

When the Citizens' Association published a promotional book, *Marquette, Michigan Illustrated*, this engraving of Charles Kawbawgum was included. He was an Ojibway Chief and a member of a family who played a significant role in the early history of the area. It was Marji Kawbawgum, his father-in-law, who guided William Burt on the expedition that led to the discovery, and later, the development of the Jackson Mine and the Marquette Iron Range. (Courtesy Peter White Library.)

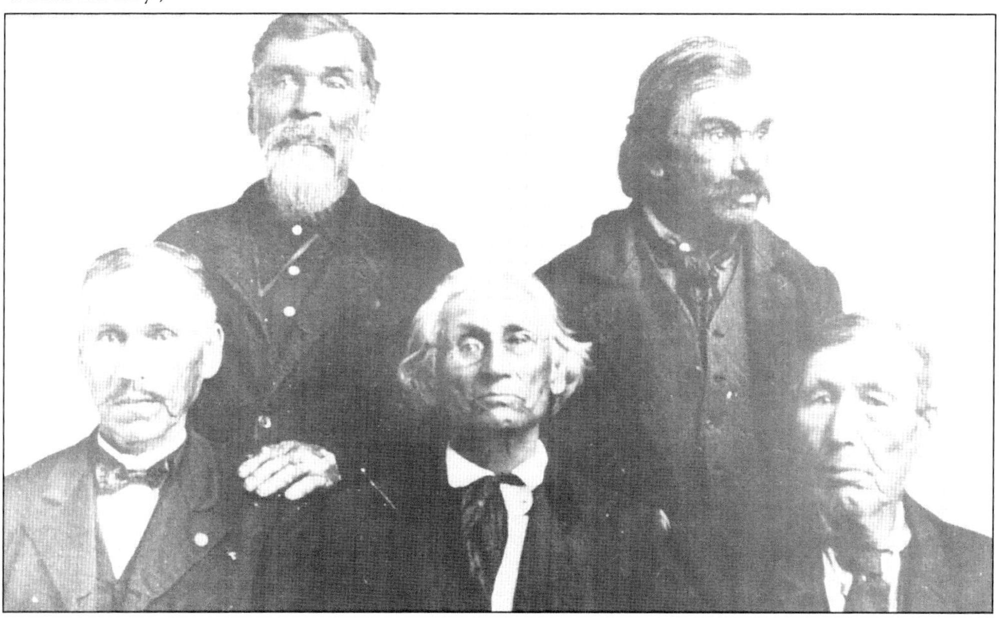

Charles Kawbawgum (center front) and four other Native Americans from the Marquette area are pictured here after testifying in the case that established the claim of Charlotte Kawbawgum, Charles's wife, along with other members of her family, to a part of the profits from the Jackson Mine, which her father, Marji, helped discover. (Courtesy State Archives of Michigan.)

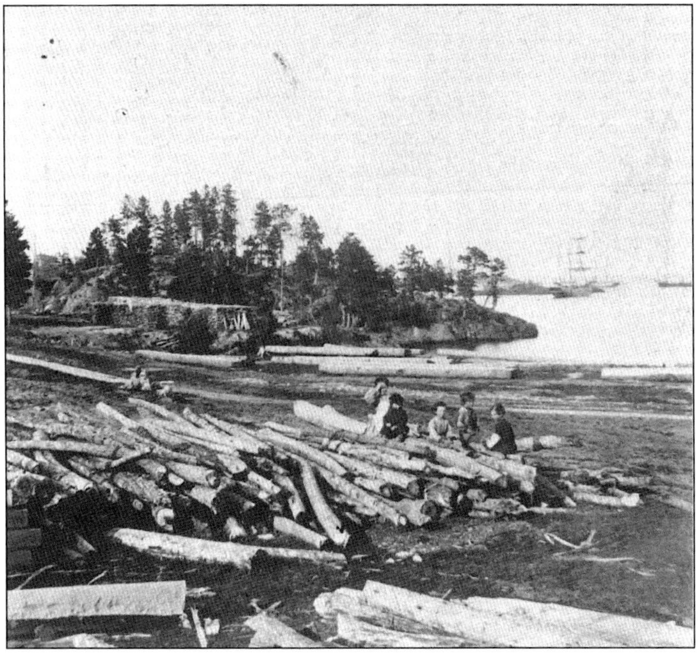

These children are at play on a log pile on the shore near Marquette in this 1860s photograph. By that time treaties had arranged for the cession of Native American lands to the United States Government; the land east of the Chocolay River had been ceded earlier, and the Treaty of La Pointe, in Wisconsin, opened the land around Marquette for settlement in 1842. (Courtesy State Archives of Michigan.)

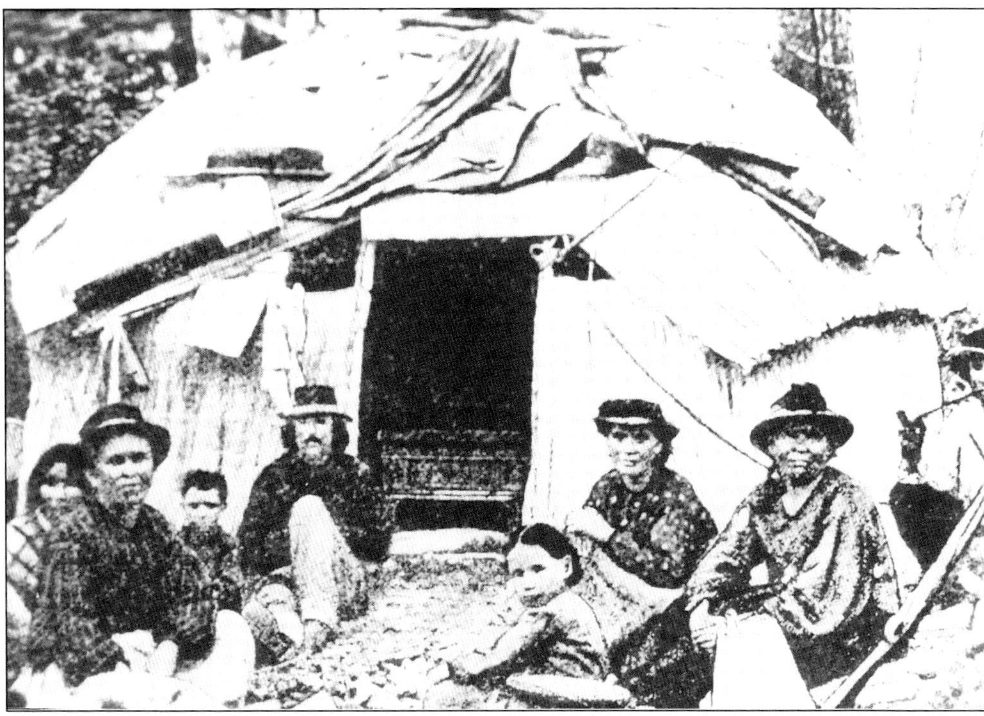

Early white settlers were usually quick to point out that there weren't many Native Americans in the vicinity of Marquette when they arrived, and there were no permanent Native American settlements. Seasonal bands of Ojibways summered at the mouths of the Dead and Carp Rivers, but spent their winters on the southern side of the Upper Peninsula. This photo shows a group at the Carp River encampment in the 1880s. (Courtesy State Archives of Michigan.)

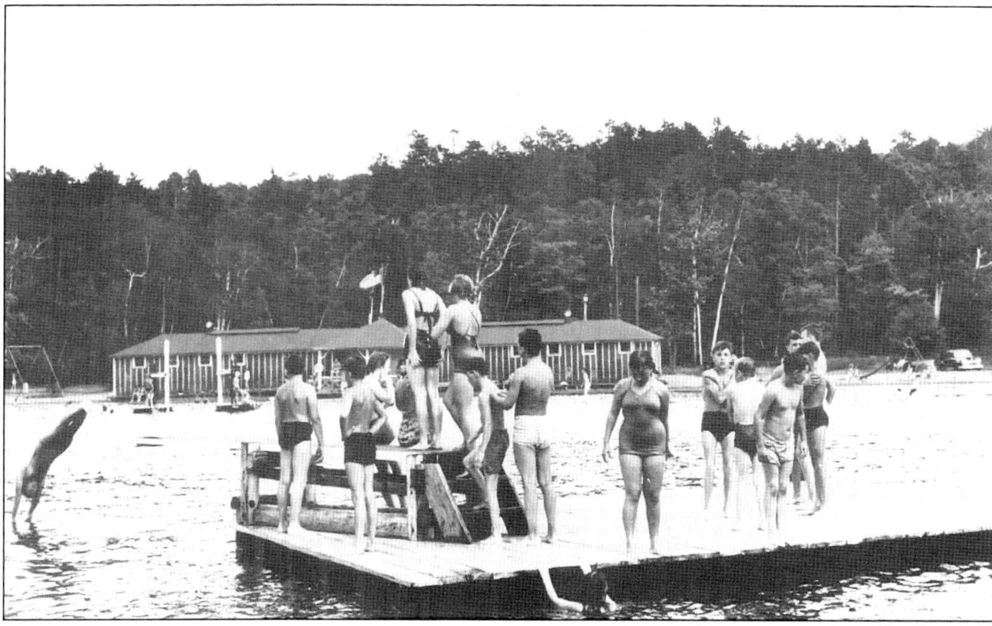

On a warm summer day in the 1950s, the diving platform at Presque Isle was a good place to hang out. Even in the height of summer, the water was so cold that there were more kids on the raft than in the water. The beach wasn't fancy or exclusive, but parents didn't worry about their children when they were there. In the short Marquette summer, everyone tried to soak up as much of the sun as they could. (Courtesy State Archives of Michigan.)

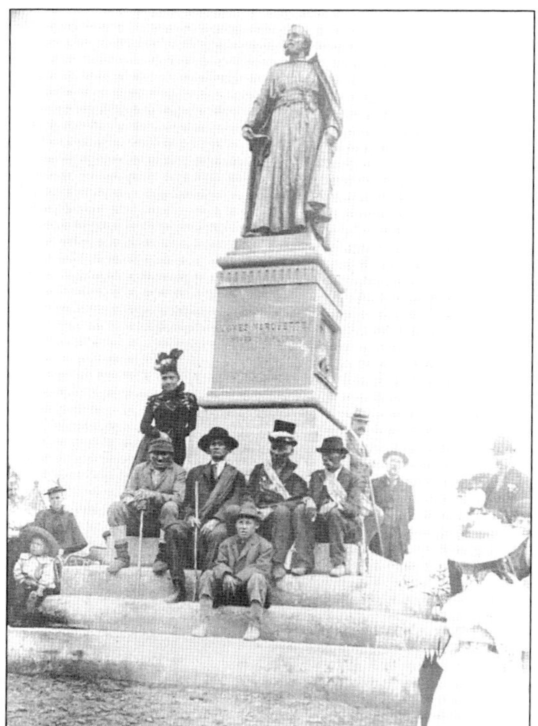

This 1897 photograph was an attempt to establish continuity between the city's roots and the bustling port that it had become after the civilizing and christianizing mission of Father Jacques Marquette. The city's namesake, Marquette was a missionary and an early explorer of the Great Lakes and the Upper Midwest. Seen at the foot of his statue are Native Americans of the Ojibway Tribe, whose ancestors lived in the vicinity of Marquette many years earlier. (Courtesy Peter White Library.)

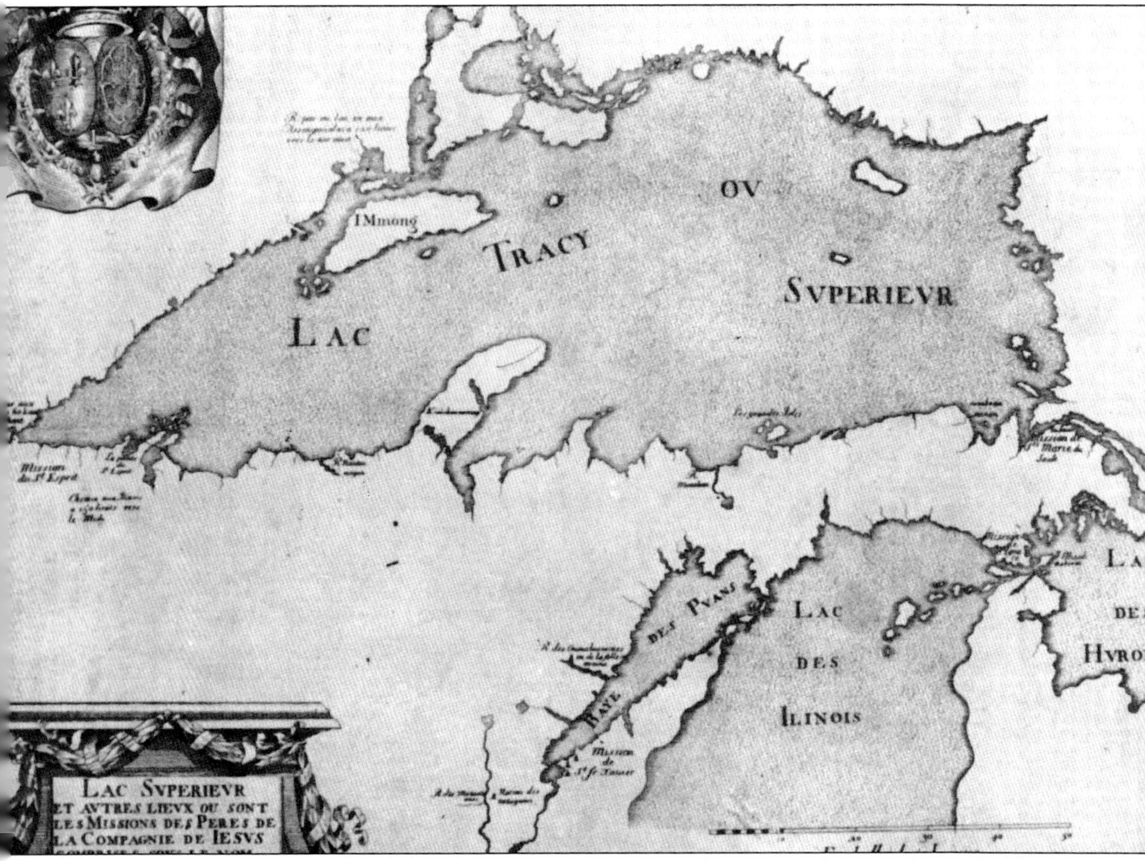

This detail of a map drawn in 1671 was published in *The Jesuit Relations*, the earliest-known tour guide of the Upper Great Lakes. The intent here was to show the location of the Jesuit missions among the Native Americans. The missions were usually established near the more permanent settlements of Native Americans or astride their main trade and migration routes, for example the "mission de Marie de Sault." The map maker also wanted his audience to be able to find important geographic features or landmarks such as "les grande isles," which are located near present-day Munising. Note that while we can place the site of Marquette on this map, the Jesuits didn't bother. Neither they nor the Native Americans were interested in mining iron ore. Marquette wasn't on the map until the advent of mining. (Courtesy State Archives of Michigan.)

Ten

IRON ORE AND LUMBER

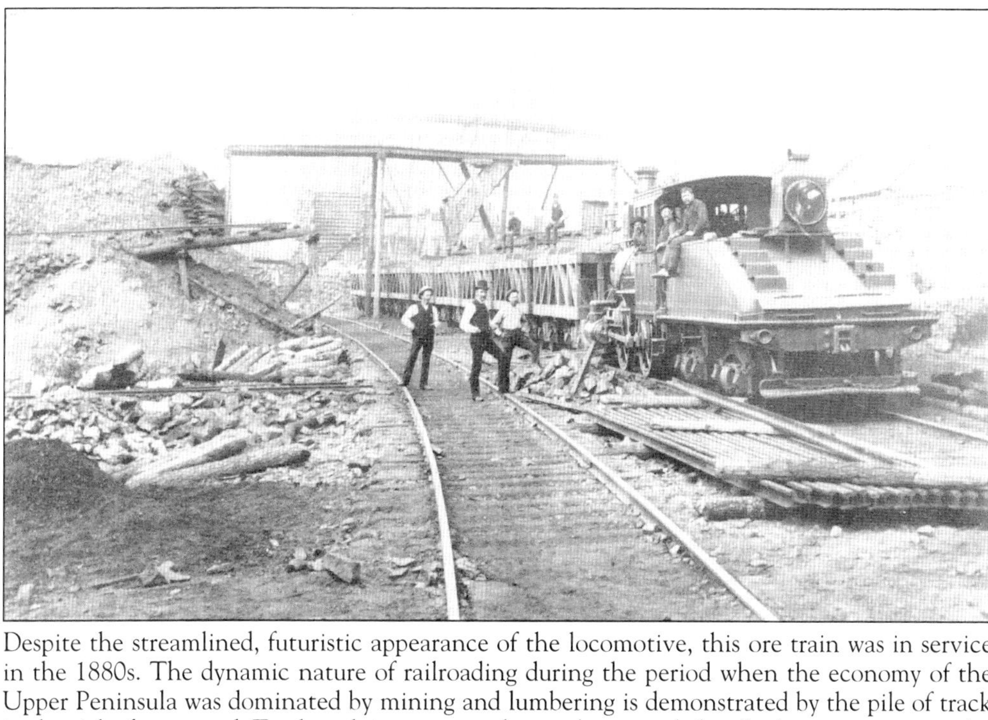

Despite the streamlined, futuristic appearance of the locomotive, this ore train was in service in the 1880s. The dynamic nature of railroading during the period when the economy of the Upper Peninsula was dominated by mining and lumbering is demonstrated by the pile of track in the right foreground. Track and ties were set down where needed and taken up as soon as the need passed. (Courtesy State Archives of Michigan.)

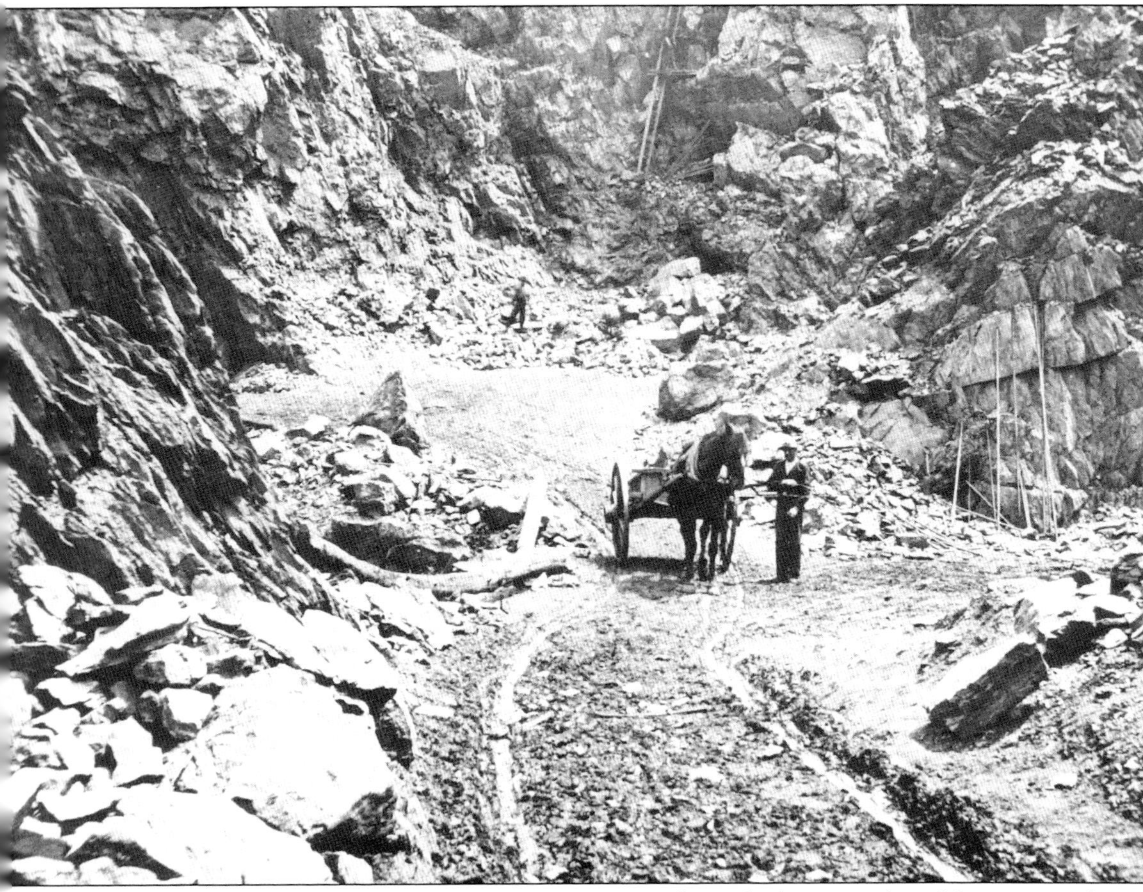

This 1850s view of the Jackson Mine, near Negaunee, shows the location where Marquette took root, very near the moment that it did. The Jackson was the first great mine on the Marquette Range, and its nearly infinite potential for producing huge amounts of iron ore and immense profit drove the early development of the region; the mine existed before Marquette was begun. The first ore was mined here in 1846, and the first iron "bloom" was produced at the Carp River Forge in 1848. It was not until 1 pm, on July 10, 1849, that workers began clearing the trees from the Marquette town site. By 1850, Marquette had its own forge, and in July of that year, the first shipment of ore from the Jackson Mine, five tons, was on its way down the lakes to Newcastle, Pennsylvania. At first, the ore was transported by horse and wagon from mine to harbor, from there to Sault Ste. Marie by ship, around the rapids on land, and by ship again to the lower lakes. The completion of the Sault Locks and the arrival of the steam engine changed everything. (Courtesy State Archives of Michigan.)

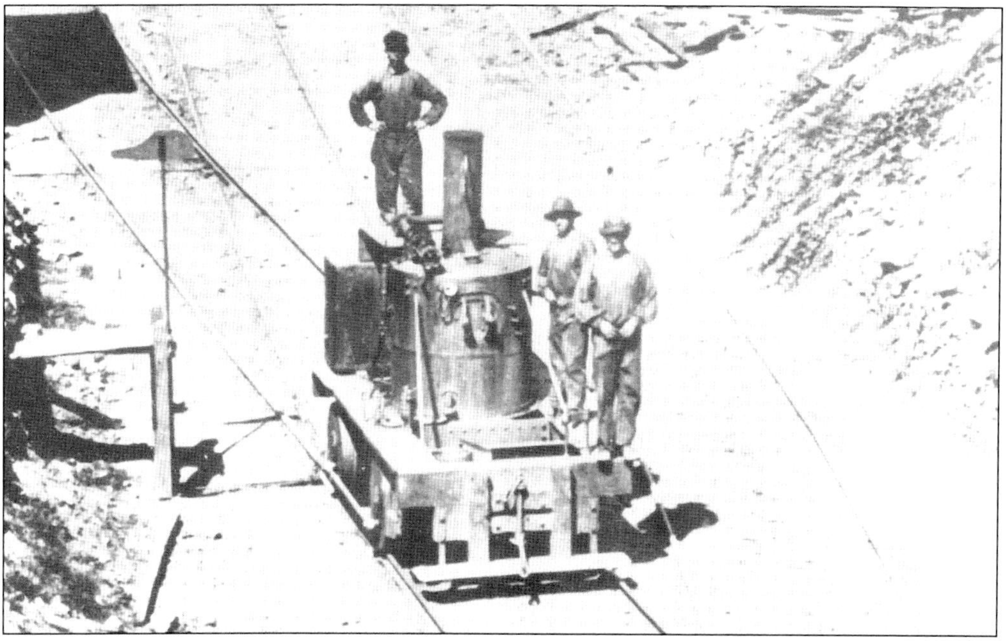

This 1857 image shows the John Bull locomotive on its tracks, near the Jackson Mine. Though by no means powerful compared to what came later, the John Bull was an enormous advancement over the horse-pulled wagons that were used when the mine first opened. Ore was moved from the mines to the Marquette docks, and from there to the steel mills at the foot of the Great Lakes. (Courtesy State Archives of Michigan.)

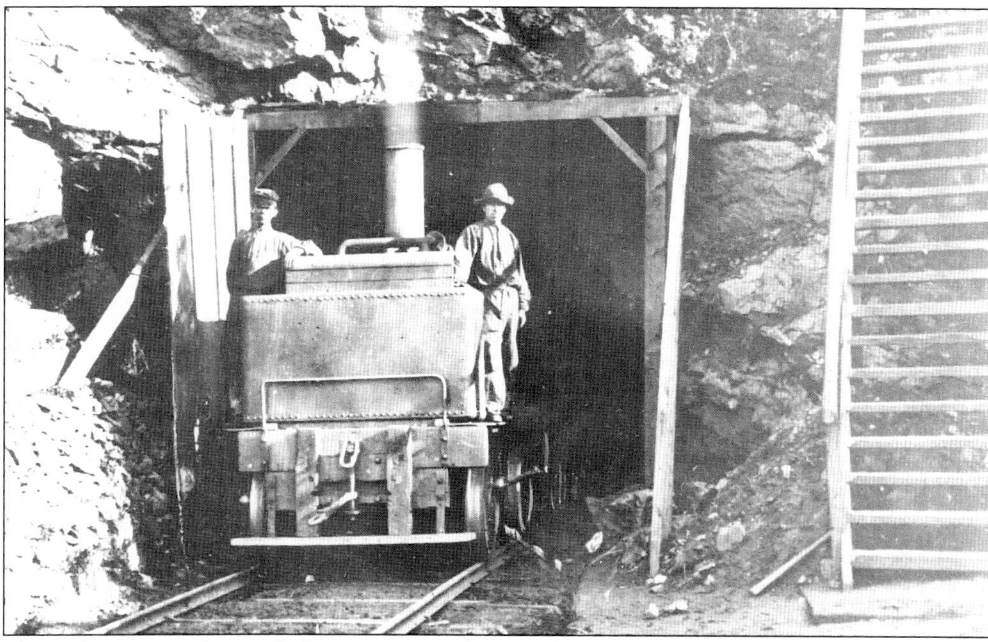

Shown here is another early locomotive at the mouth of the mine. The engine is under way in this 1860s picture, moving slowly from the tunnel with a load. When the Sault Canal opened at Sault Ste. Marie in 1855, coal and machinery became abundant as shipping costs fell. These two inputs made ore production expand quickly. (Courtesy State Archives of Michigan.)

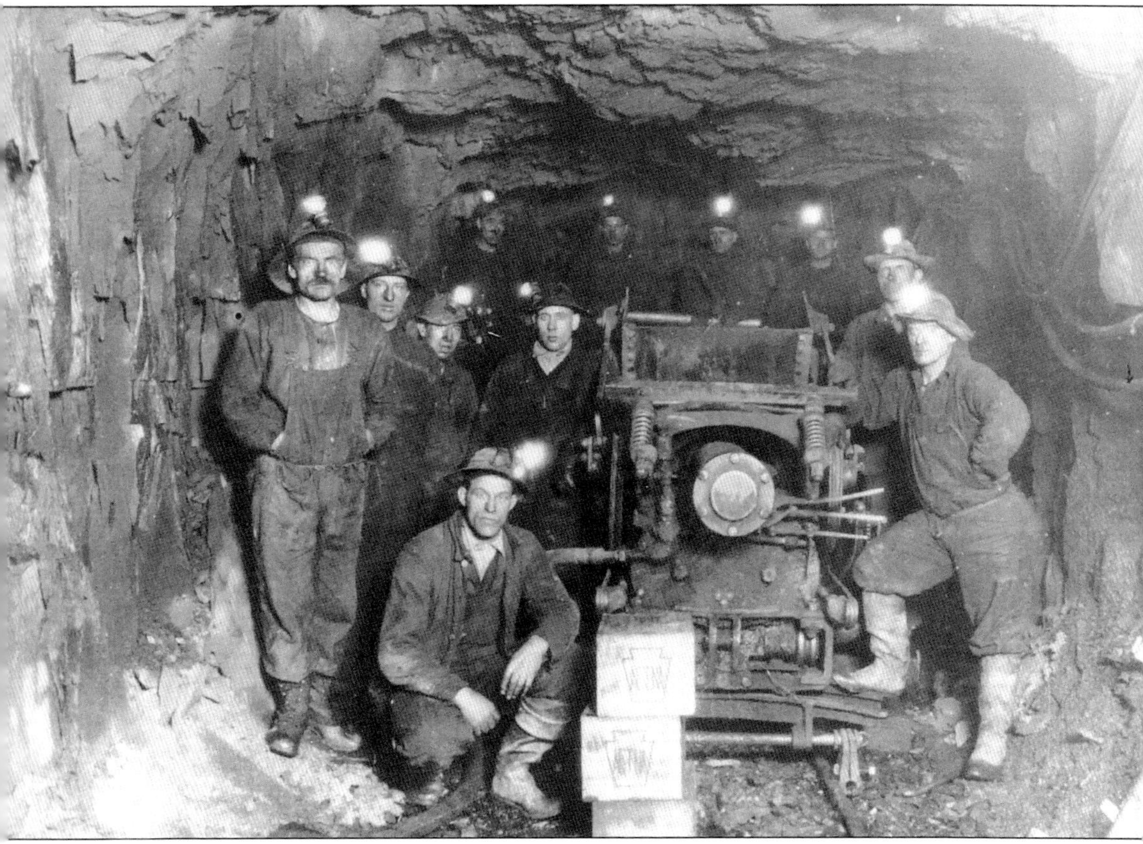

Iron mining was hard, dirty, and dangerous work. Although the mines lay beyond the Marquette city limits, and the majority of the miners lived elsewhere, the mines provided Marquette with its economic sinew, and in its early days, the city's reason for being. This picture was taken underground in the Barnes-Hecker mine near Ishpeming in 1926. The name of the mine is no longer familiar and the miners, with their headlamps lighted, look tired and show only a trace of the swagger of men who do risky work; they give no sign that they know what is in store for them. Less than six months after the picture was taken, 51 miners, several of whom appear here, were killed in this mine in the worst underground disaster in Michigan history. Connections between the iron mines and the city, the miners in their homes, and the houses and people on Ridge Street, are needed for a whole history of the community. (Courtesy State Archives of Michigan.)

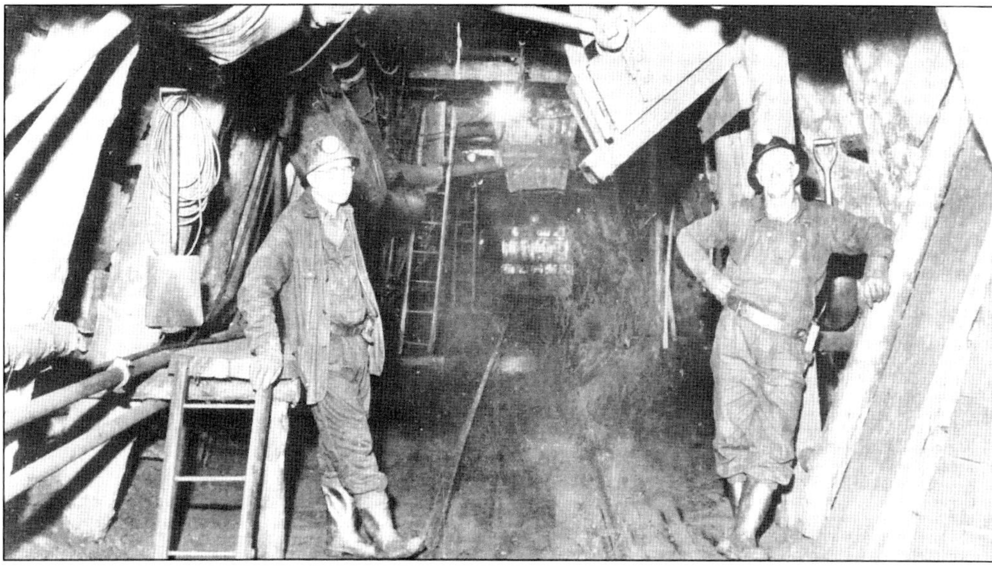

Pictured are two miners standing at ease at the fifth level of the Mather Mine on the Marquette Range. They appear to be well into—or near the end of—their shift. The clutter, the tracks, and the production development around them indicate that this level has been well worked for a long time. The photo was taken in the 1920s or 1930s. (Courtesy State Archives of Michigan.)

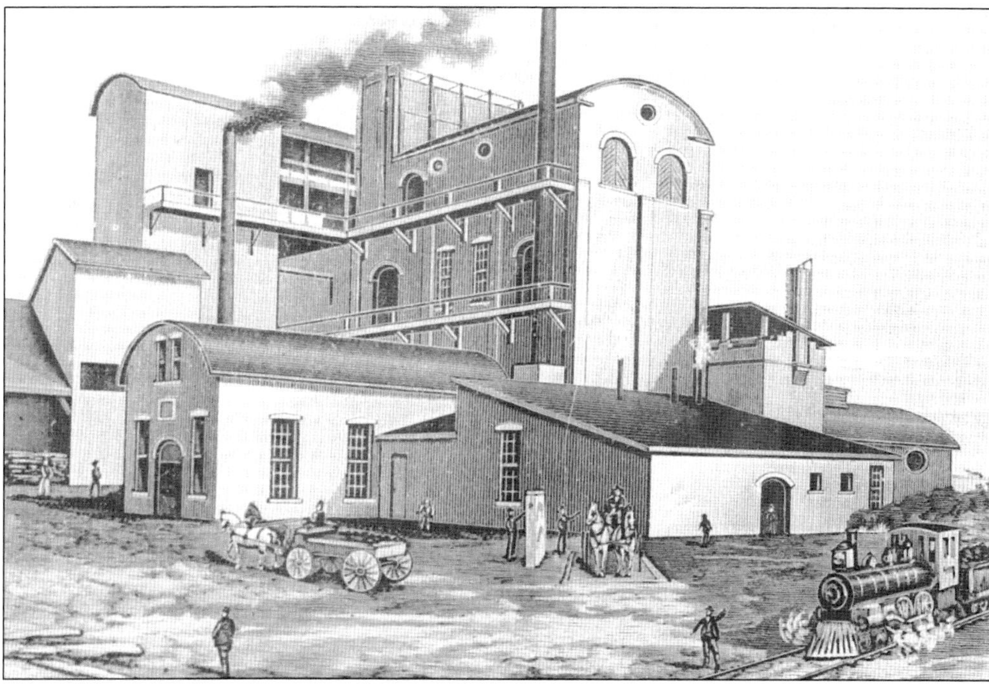

In this lithograph from the 1890s, the Northern Furnace is in full production, advertised at 60 tons per day. Lithographs were based on photographs, but they were artfully (and sometimes not so artfully) enhanced for promotional purposes. The train in the lower right-hand corner is so out of proportion it appears toy-like. In the context of the late 19th century, however, the image is persuasive. (Courtesy Peter White Library.)

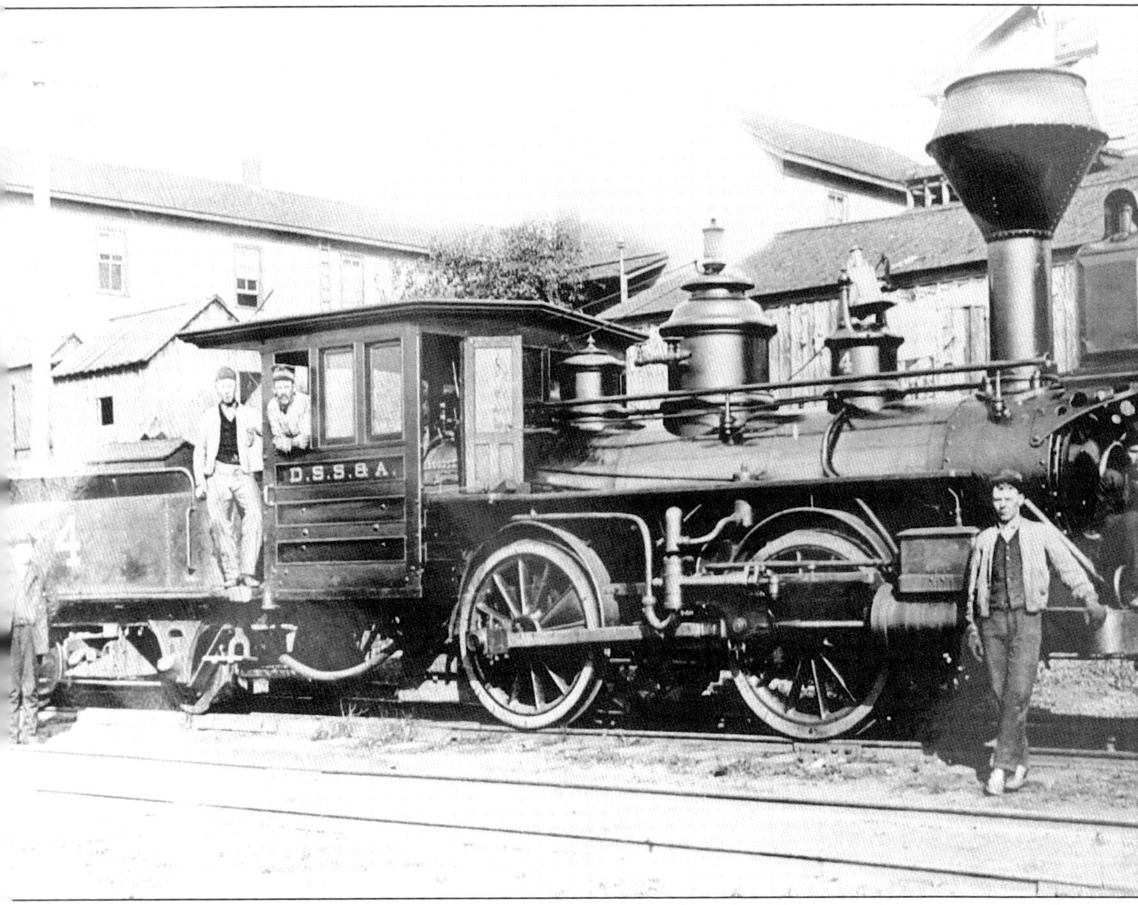

Nearly as complex and dizzying as the mergers and hostile takeovers that occur in today's corporate jungle were the maneuvers of 19th-century railroads. Engine No. 4, of the Duluth South Shore & Atlantic Railroad, was part of one of Marquette's two surviving railroads; the other was the Lake Superior & Ishpeming. The D.S.S.&A. Railway Company was organized in 1886, and in 1890, merged with the Marquette, Houghton, & Ontonagon Railroad Company. The M.H.&O was itself the product of an 1872 merger of the Houghton & Ontonagon with the Marquette & Ontonagon. A year earlier, the Marquette & Ontonagon had been consolidated with the Bay de Noquet & Marquette Railroad Company. Along the way, the M.H.&O also scooped up the Houghton & L'Anse. Meanwhile, another set of consolidations, mergers, and acquisitions was moving toward what became the Lake Superior & Ishpeming in the 1890s. By 1887, about the time when Engine No. 4 posed for this picture, the D.S.S.&A. owned or leased 78 locomotives and 4,700 cars. (Courtesy Peter White Library.)

Winter is the logging season, and in the vicinity of Marquette, the snowy woods produced thousands of board feet every winter until 1900. In that year, logging operations had exhausted the nearby resources, and the wood that came to the city traveled from farther away. This sled, and the logger riding it, was typical of small operations in the 1890s. (Courtesy State Archives of Michigan.)

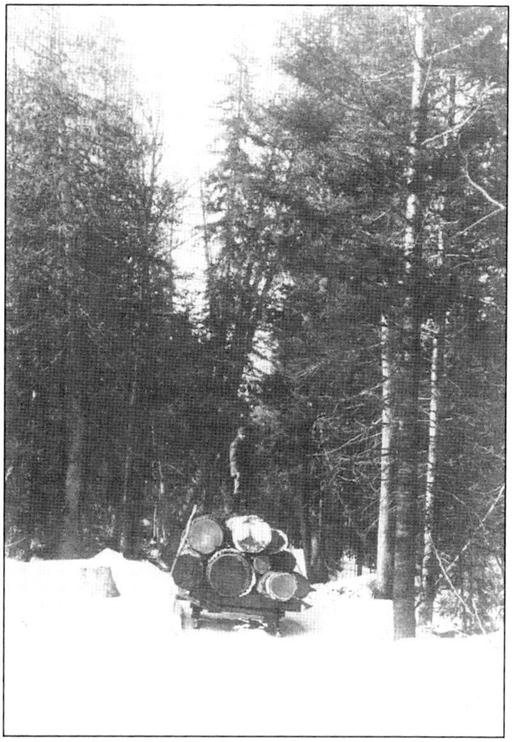

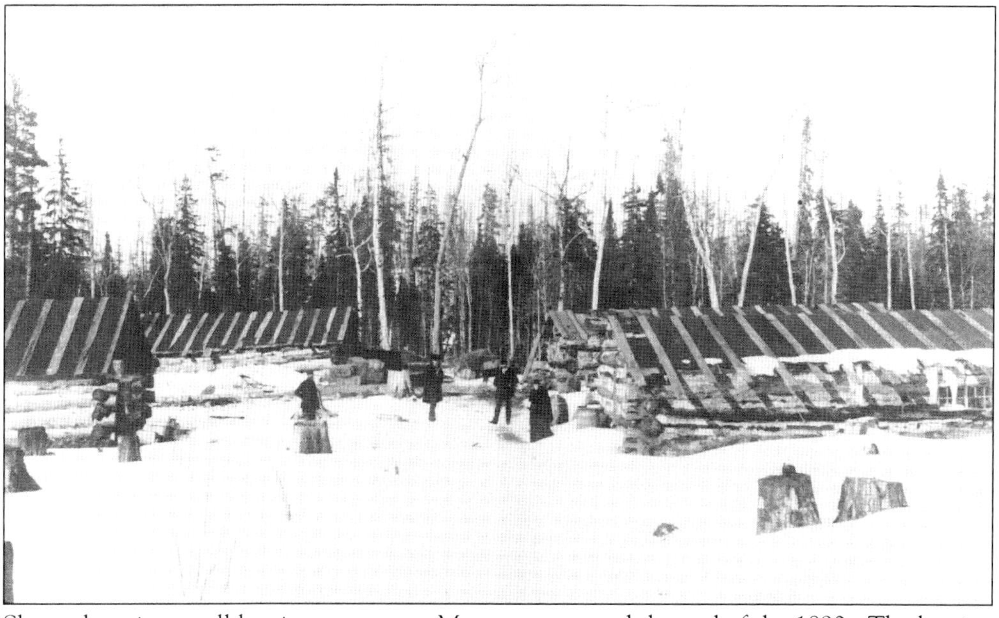

Shown here is a small logging camp near Marquette, toward the end of the 1890s. The logging life was very difficult, the work was unremitting, the pay was low, and the amenities were very few. In this picture, the isolation and primitive living conditions seem to be part of the static, enduring appearance of the crew and cook. (Courtesy State Archives of Michigan.)

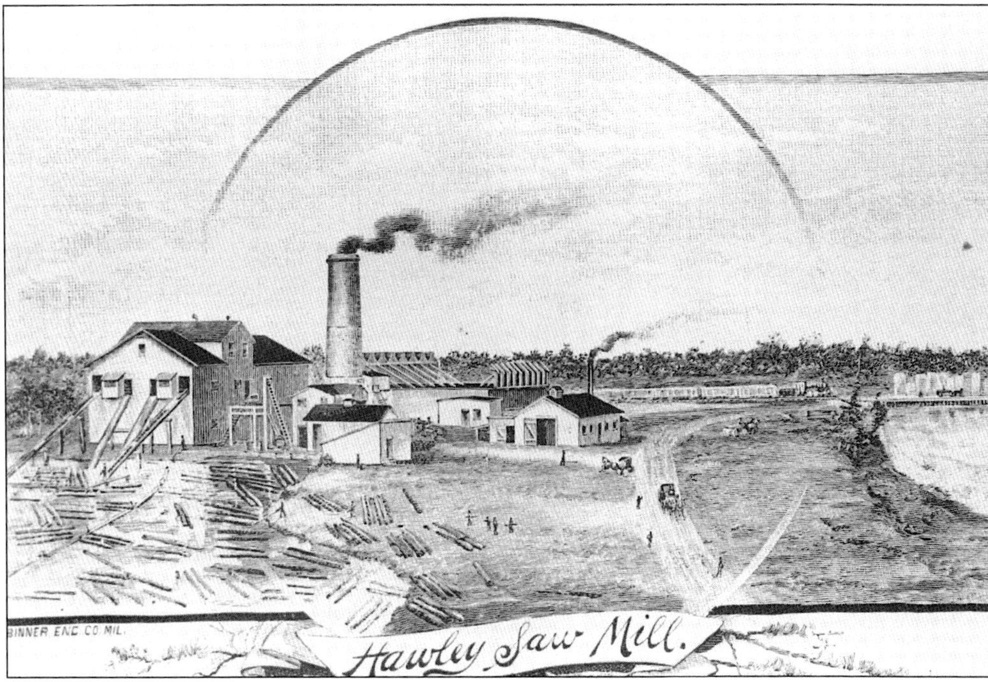

The Hawley Sawmill was built by the Cleveland Sawmill and Lumber Company in 1891, just north of the Dead River. The mill had four band saws and two railroad spurs and, at first, production boomed. It was sold to the South Arm Lumber Company in 1901, and by 1906, the business went bankrupt, a victim of a volatile market and the depletion of local lumber sources. (Courtesy Peter White Library.)

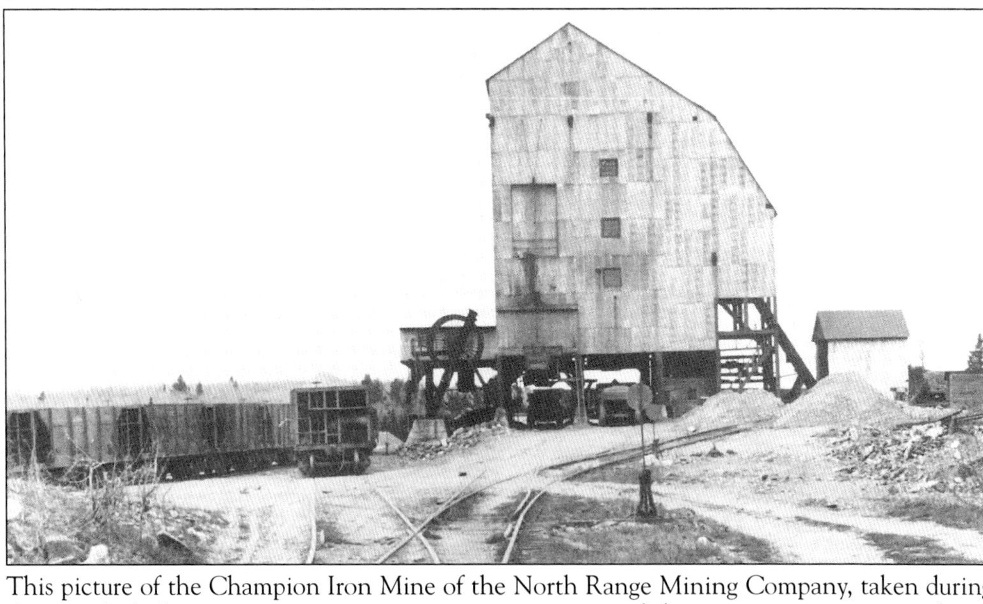

This picture of the Champion Iron Mine of the North Range Mining Company, taken during the mine's declining years, is an accurate representation of the entire iron-mining industry throughout the Upper Peninsula. It was more than a boom—after all, it started in the 1850s and continues today—but it is less than a shadow of its former self, and the ruins are sad. (Courtesy State Archives of Michigan.)

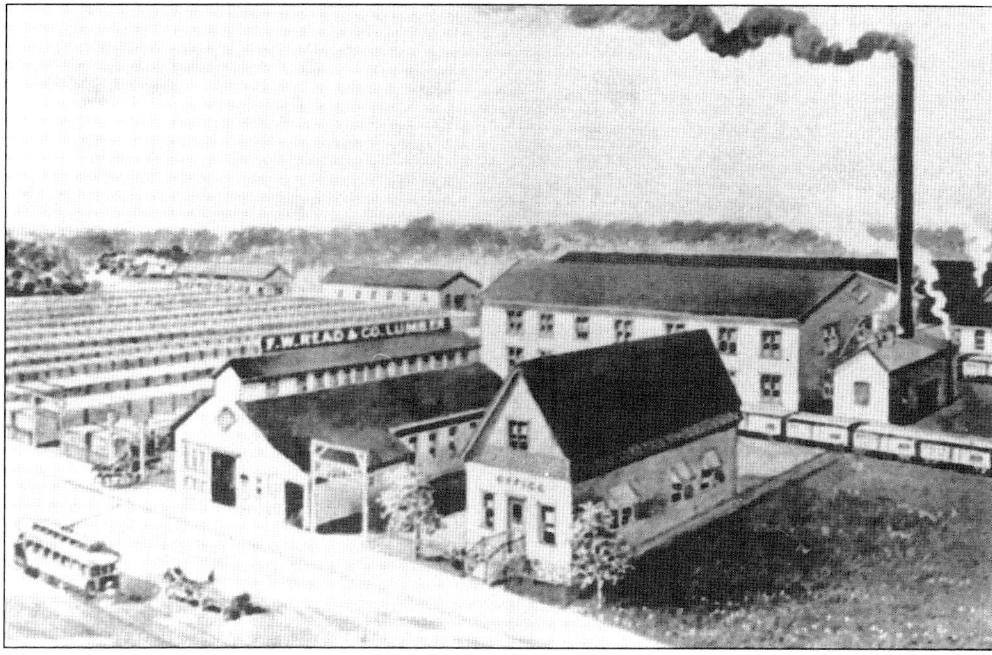

F.W. Read and Company was in the lumber business in a big way. Incorporated in 1887, it had been in business for four years when this lithograph was produced. Its offices and mill were located west of Marquette on Washington Street, and yes, eventually the trolley cars did get that far out. Read and Company milled between 18 and 20 million board feet of lumber per year, with much of it in sash, doors, interior trim, and flooring. (Courtesy Peter White Library.)

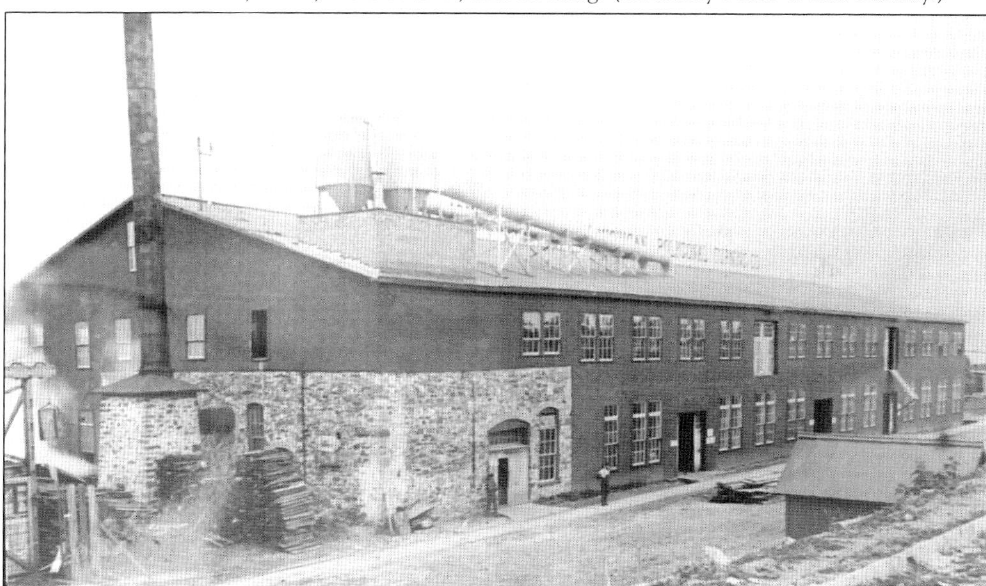

The Polygonal Turning Corporation operated in Marquette on the south side of Washington Street from 1890 to 1895. Affectionately called the "polliwog factory" by its employees, Polygonal milled fancy wooden products such as gingerbread, balustrades, and veranda posts for the finish carpentry in Victorian-era homes. Undercapitalized and vulnerable to a volatile market, the polliwog factory had short legs. (Courtesy Peter White Library.)

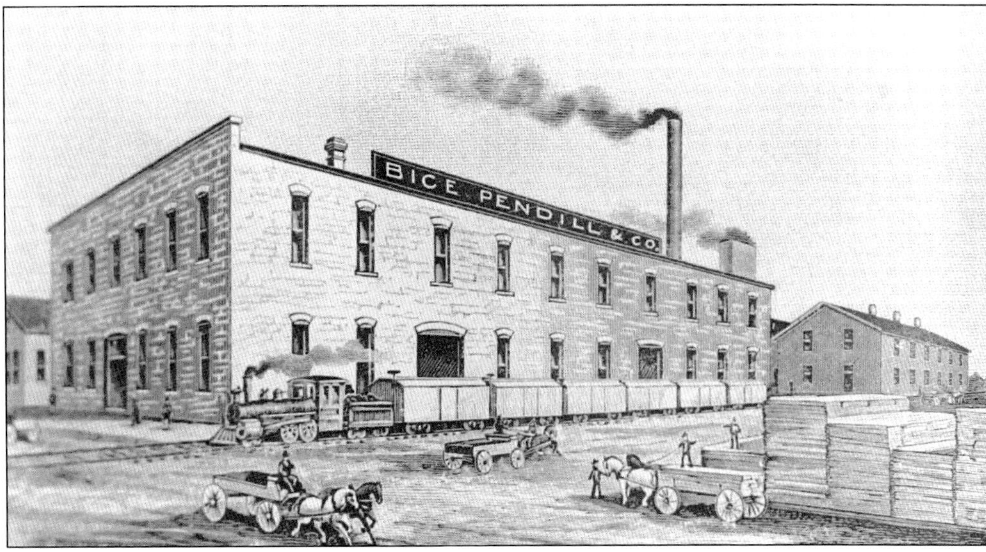

Pictured in this 1851 view is the South Marquette factory and the mill of Bice, Pendill, and Company, manufacturers of sash, doors, and blinds. This lithograph gives the impression that a lot was going on. Bice, Pendill, and Company took over the facilities of the Polygonal Turners in 1896, and by 1900, was no longer listed in the city directory. This building was taken over by E.L. Fraser and Company. (Courtesy Peter White Library.)

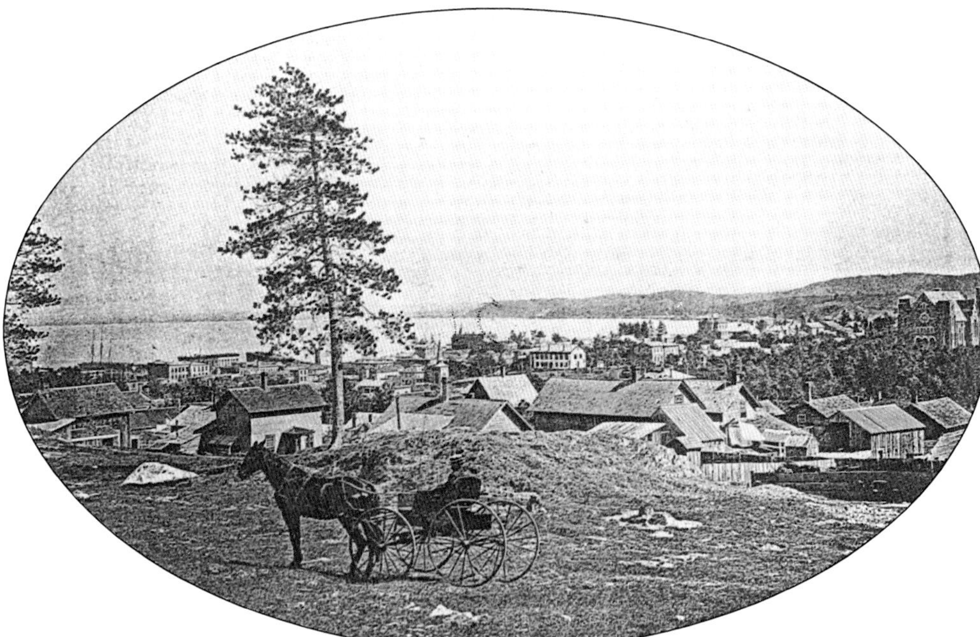

In the distance, to the south, is St. Peter's Cathedral. The rest of Marquette is still mostly a wooden town with homes and commercial buildings intermixed. This view, which was carefully arranged for artistic effect, dates from 1891. It was published in a book promoting Marquette's commercial possibilities. (Courtesy Peter White Library.)

Eleven

The Lake and the Shore

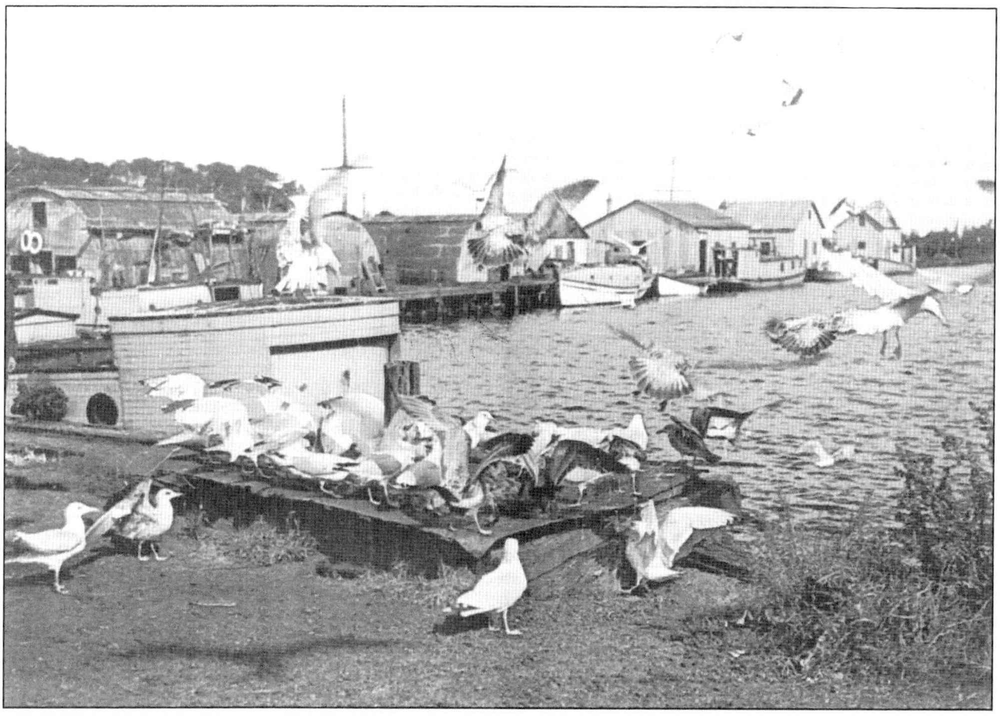

There have always been gulls. In this 1950s postcard photo they are feeding at the fish dock in the lower harbor. Though beautiful in flight and an important part of the image people have of the sea and the Great Lakes, gulls at their dinners are not elegant and graceful; they tend to be raucous and ugly when feeding. They do, however, help keep a waterfront clean. (Courtesy Peter White Library.)

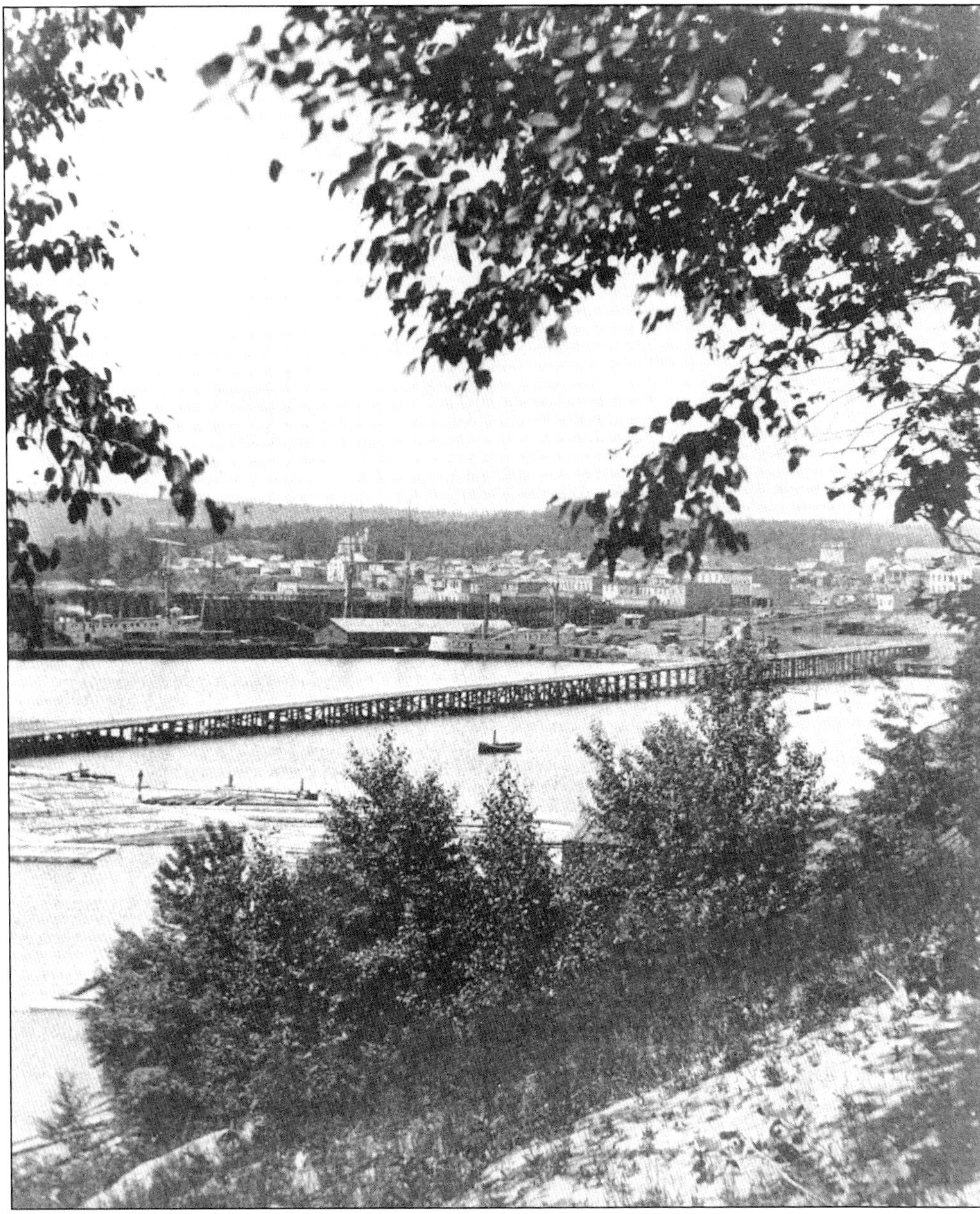

This image is one side of a stereopticon view of the Marquette harbor in the 1880s. It is a handsome shot; the photographer was standing near the end of Ridge Street looking southwest and took care to provide an attractive leafy frame for the picture. In the immediate foreground are the trestle and tracks of the Ransom, Burtis, and Marsh Sawmill, and beyond that, to the left across the harbor, is the ore dock of the Marquette, Houghton, & Ontonagan Railroad. Just left of center is the old Marquette County Courthouse with its distinctive cupola; the present St. Peter's Cathedral had not been built yet, and Marquette's new courthouse, now a historic building, would not appear on its hill for another 20 years. The harbor is not particularly active; there is a passenger steamer at the Monahan Dock and several other craft about, but the scene has the air of a quiet summer day, trees in full leaf and, because the leaves appear still, no breeze. (Courtesy State Archives of Michigan.)

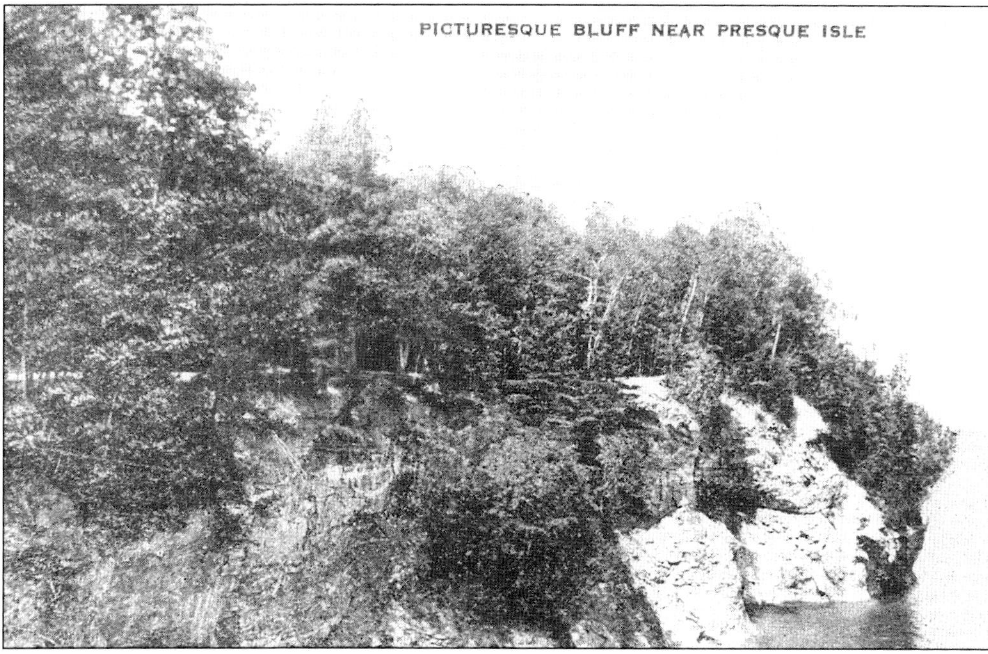

This "picturesque bluff near Presque Isle" is a 1930s postcard view of the shoreline of the park of that name. The one-way drive through the park can be seen on the crest of the bluff through the trees. Although Presque Isle is one of Marquette's prime tourist attractions, it was originally intended for use as a lighthouse site, and the land at first belonged to the federal government. (Courtesy State Archives of Michigan.)

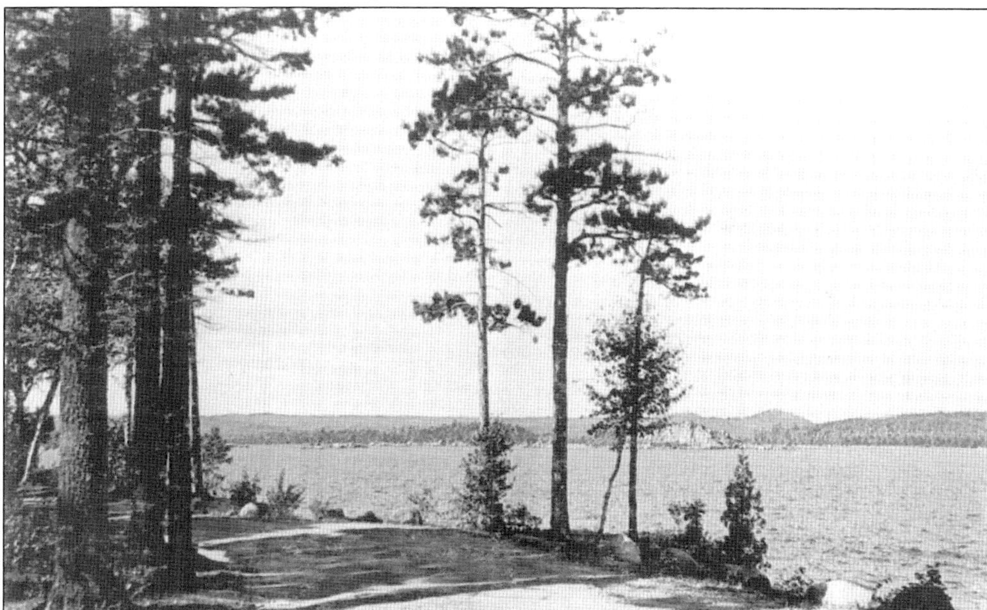

The traffic sign on this section of Sunset Drive bears the direction "slow." This is good advice. The view is beautiful enough to be distracting, and the road does make an abrupt turn. In summer, watching the sun go down at this point is an inexpensive excursion for anyone who enjoys watching a sunset. (Courtesy Peter White Library.)

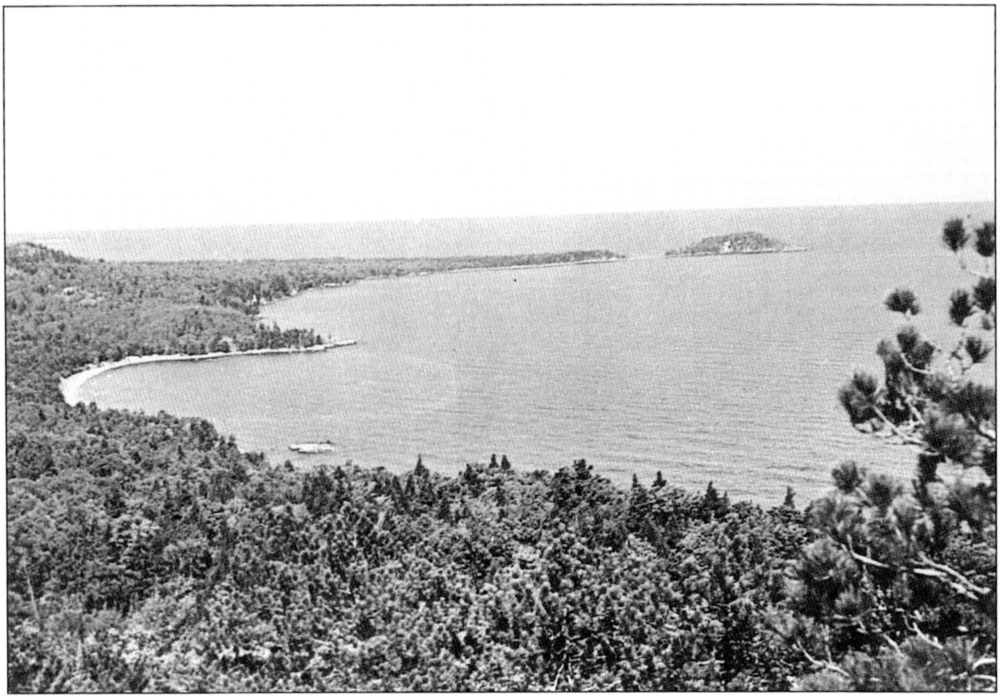

Presque Isle is a large, 328-acre park located near another popular tourist attraction, Sugar Loaf Mountain. After driving around Presque Isle, walking up Sugar Loaf salves the consciences of those who think they should get more exercise. The view from the peak, like the hike up, is breathtaking. This postcard photo was taken looking east. (Courtesy Peter White Library.)

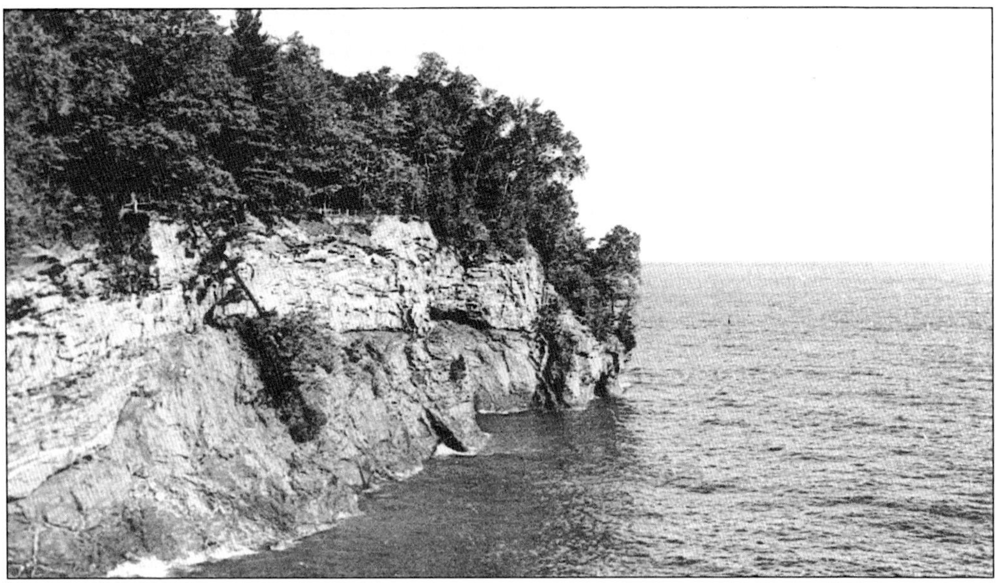

In the 1950s, Ernie's Photo Shop in Marquette published a collection of postcards showing scenic sights in the city's vicinity. Presque Isle was a favorite subject in this series. These pictures are skillfully composed in the commercial style of the time, and the photographer had an excellent sense of what tourists wanted to send to their family and friends. (Courtesy Peter White Library.)

This image brings several Marquette themes together: Lake Superior, powerful storms, and ships. Winter is thrown in as a bonus. The *Plymouth* ran aground at Presque Isle on October 23, 1887, while hauling coal to Ashland, Wisconsin. She was one of three ships wrecked near Marquette in that storm. (Courtesy Peter White Library.)

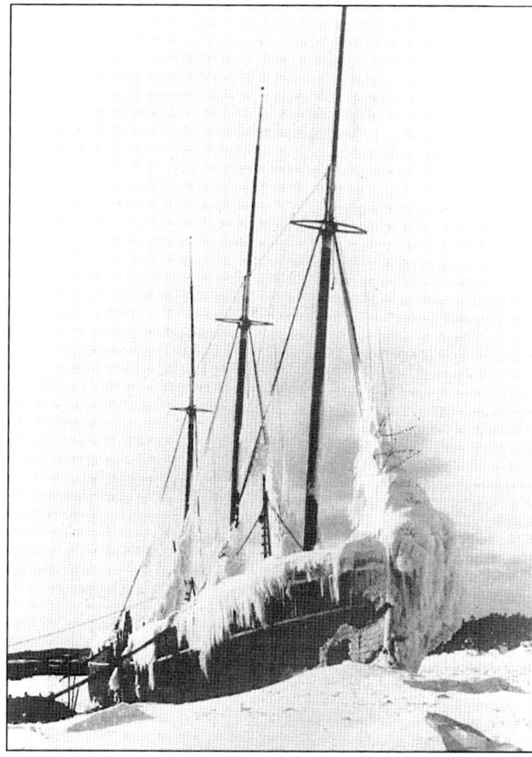

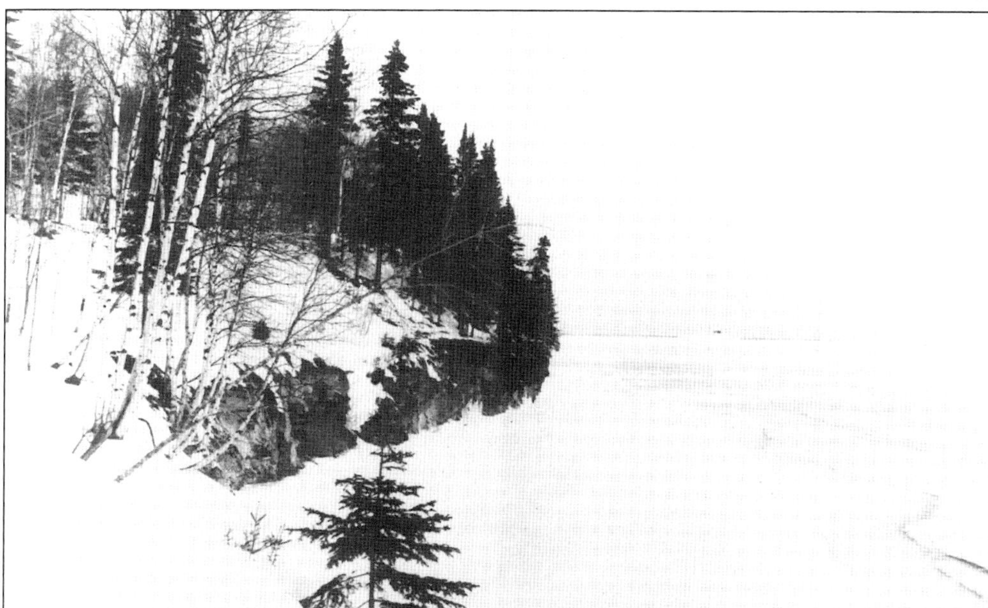

Wintertime at Presque Isle provides visitors with a different sense of the park. The shoreline is slippery and dangerous, but there are fewer people, and the quiet is strangely liberating. Because the leaves are gone, more of the park's natural beauty is visible. Though the color tones are nearly monochromatic, the contrasts are dramatic and the images are sharper. (Courtesy State Archives of Michigan.)

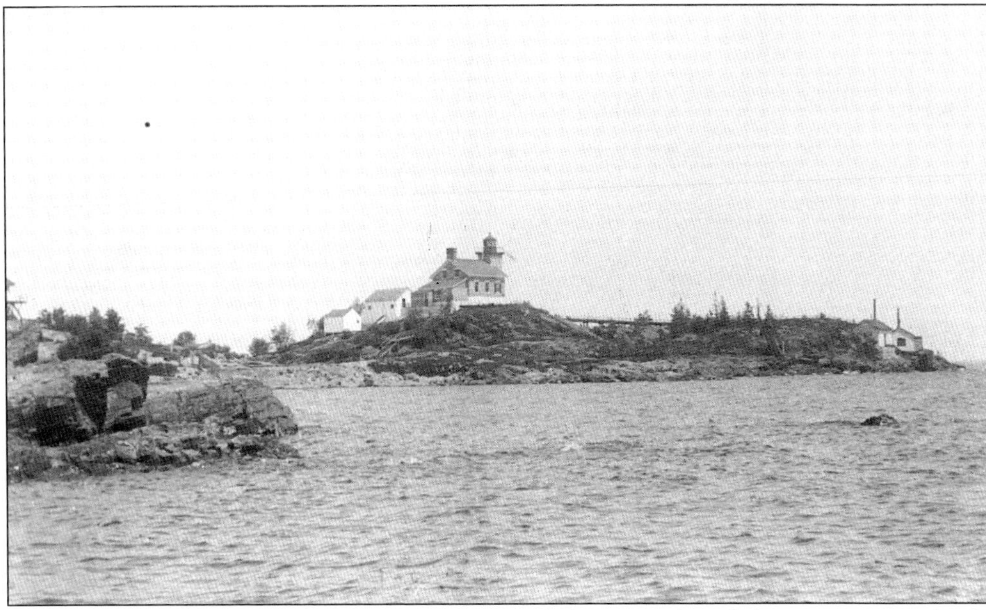

Compare this photograph of the Marquette Lighthouse and Lighthouse Point with the contemporary picture below. One hundred years ago, the point was relatively barren and the site was less developed. There was, however, a tramway from the lighthouse to the shore as well as more elaborate docking facilities. Additional supplies required to maintain the light were delivered by boat. (Courtesy State Archives of Michigan.)

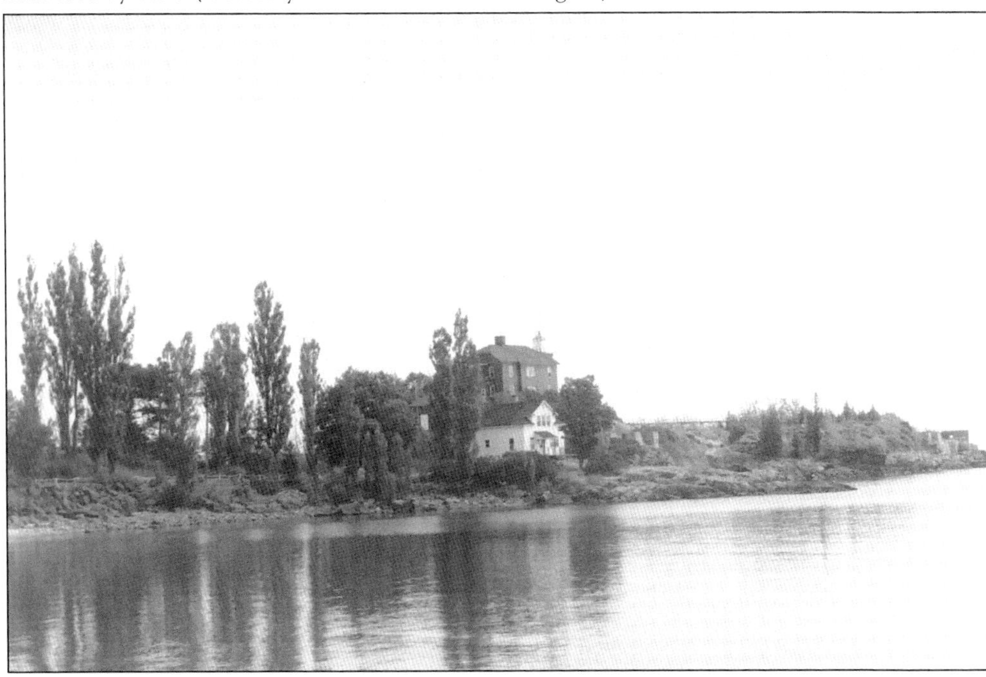

The Marquette Lighthouse on Lighthouse Point has been a staple for postcard publishers and tourists since its beginning. Part of this is due to the romance of lighthouses in general, but the rest, and probably the greatest part, consists of its scenic locale and its solid, indomitable, and persistent aura. (Photo by G. Downs.)

The lighthouse intended for Presque Isle was eventually built on Stannard Rock, which is far offshore in Lake Superior. A group of Marquette's leading citizens, led by Peter White, were persuaded by the unspoiled tract's proximity to the city, its recreational potential, bold cliffs, and rugged hills (seen in this early 1900s postcard) to petition the federal government to deed the land to the City. (Courtesy State Archives of Michigan.)

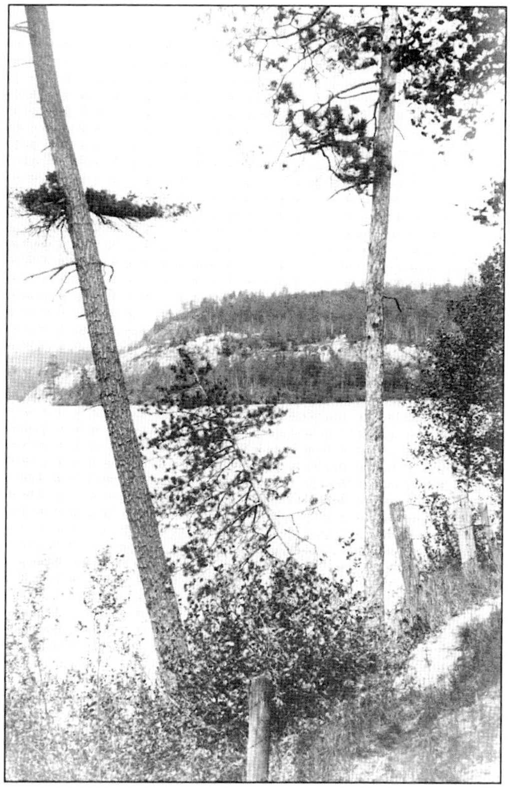

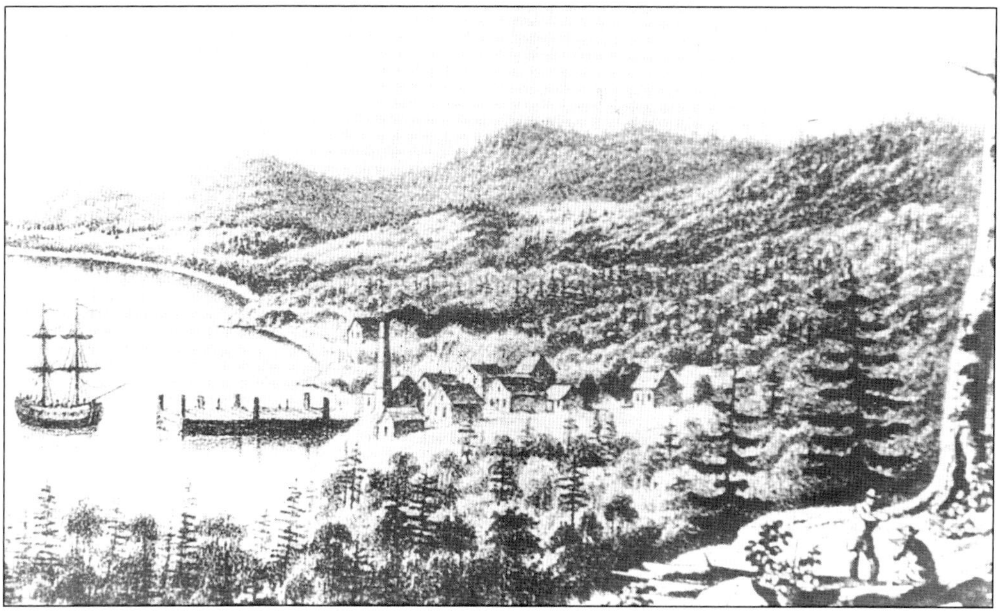

This romantic rendering of Marquette is an artist's view of the earliest ore dock and iron forge as they appeared in 1850, the year following the city's founding. The two figures are posed near the point where Ridge Street was later laid out, and the ship, with its sails furled, stands off the dock. Marquette's harbor was a shoal anchorage at the time. (Courtesy State Archives of Michigan.)

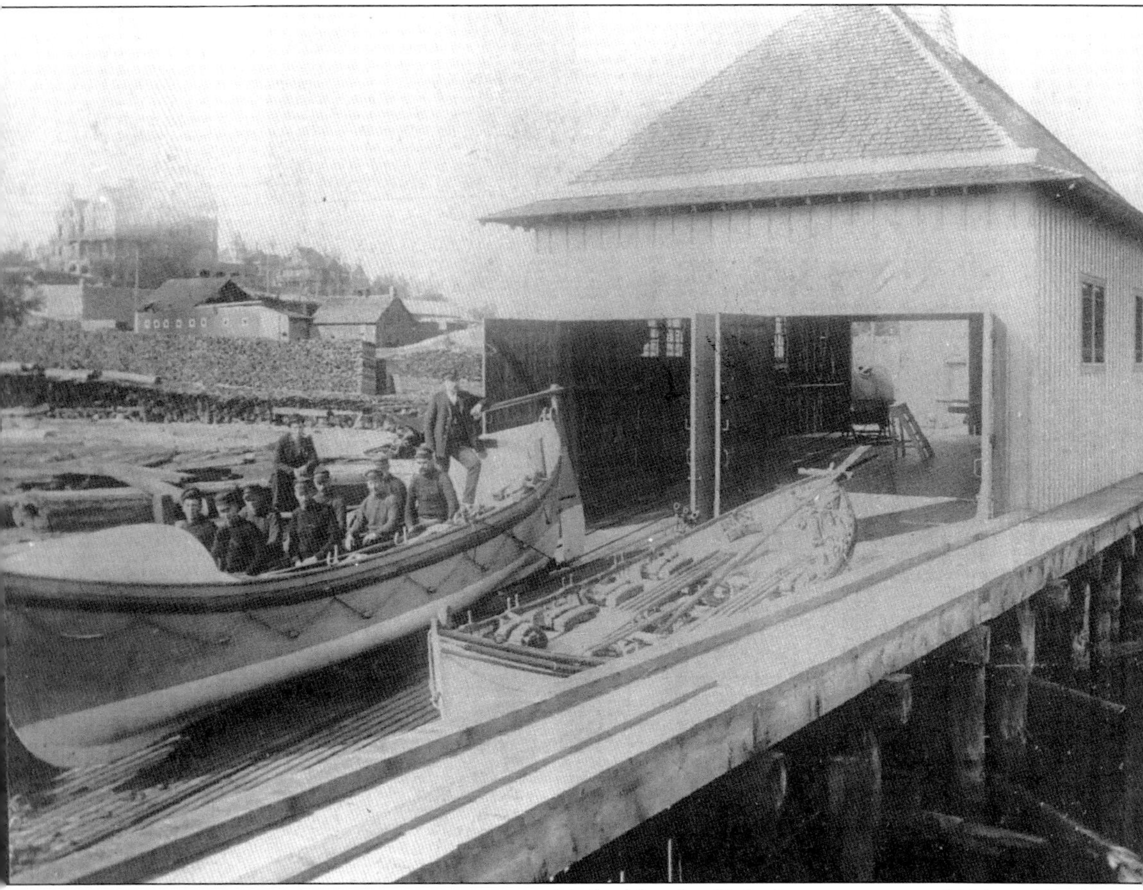

The Marquette Lifesaving Station was established by the U.S. Government in 1891 and built at Lighthouse Point. This picture was taken during the station's first decade of operation and shows the crew in its large, double-ended life boat. These boats were double ended to protect them in a following sea and to make them more maneuverable. The ropes on the sides provided convenient hand-holds for those sailors or passengers in the water. For speed and efficiency, the boats were launched on tracks down an inclined ramp, which can be seen in this picture. At a time when Great Lakes shipping still depended in large part on sailboats and an unperfected steam technology, the personnel at the station had enough to do, and practice drill for their hazardous work occupied a lot of their time. The small vessels of the commercial fishing fleet were particularly vulnerable to storms since the weather science of the time could not make accurate predictions. (Courtesy State Archives of Michigan.)

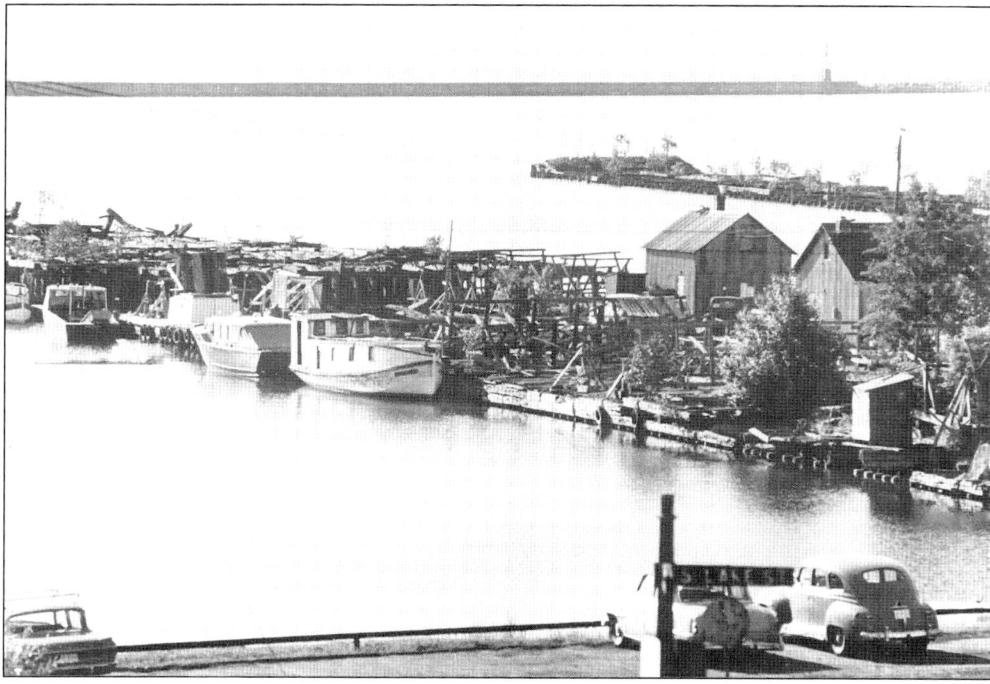

Commercial fishing was still a lively, even dominant, presence on the Marquette waterfront when this picture was taken in the 1950s. Fish houses and racks for drying nets co-exist easily with pleasure boats, indicating that both kinds of connection with the big lake had fair claim on space at the dock. (Courtesy State Archives of Michigan.)

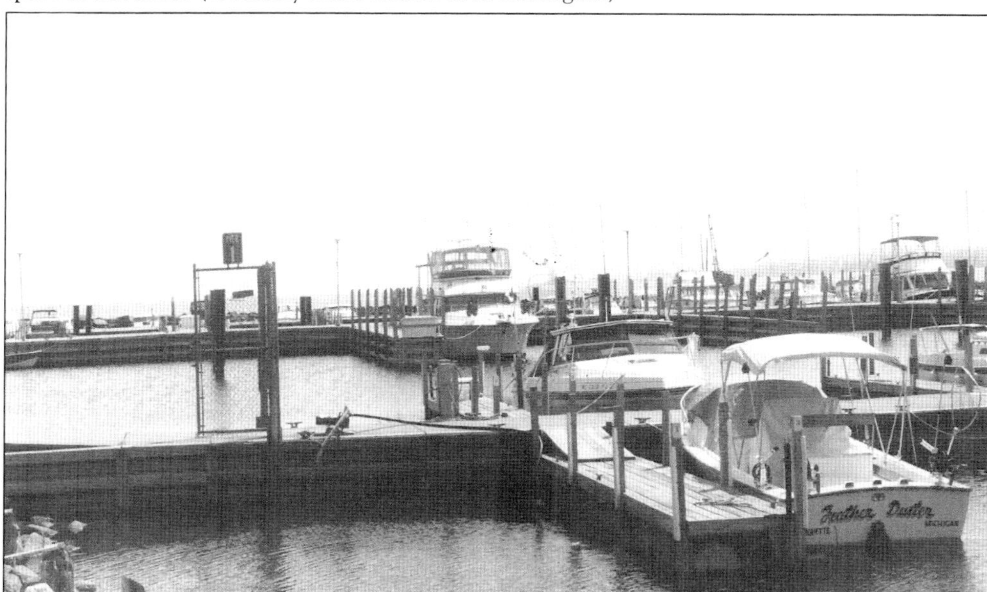

The modern facilities (1998) at the marina are clearly intended for recreational boats. They mark the transition from a waterfront setup to service commerce of shipping, fishing, and iron ore to one given over to tourists and the summer trade. Chances are that the crew of the *Feather Duster* never hauled net. (Photo by G. Downs.)

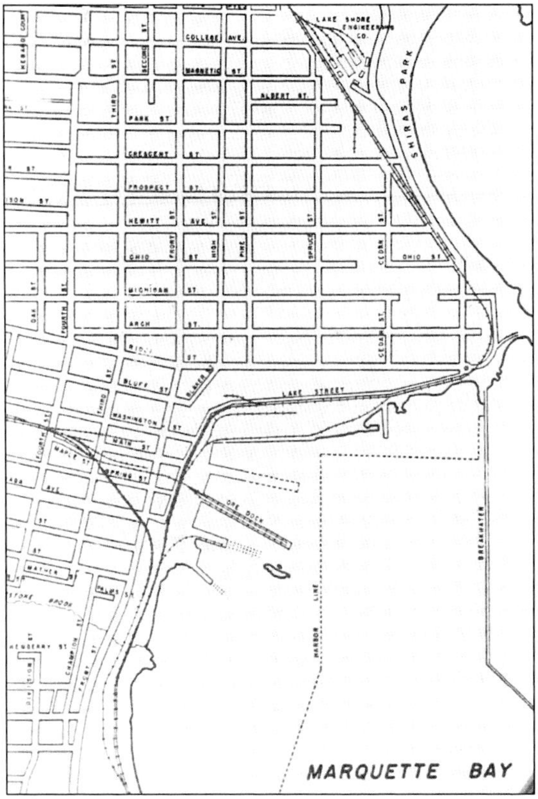

This 1950s map of Marquette shows how the central business district filled in during the city's first 100 years. Highway traffic was still being funneled through the downtown area on Front and Washington Streets. New businesses were pushing west on Washington and south on Front, and new centers of commercial activity were developing around Northern Michigan State College on North Third Street. (Courtesy Peter White Library.)

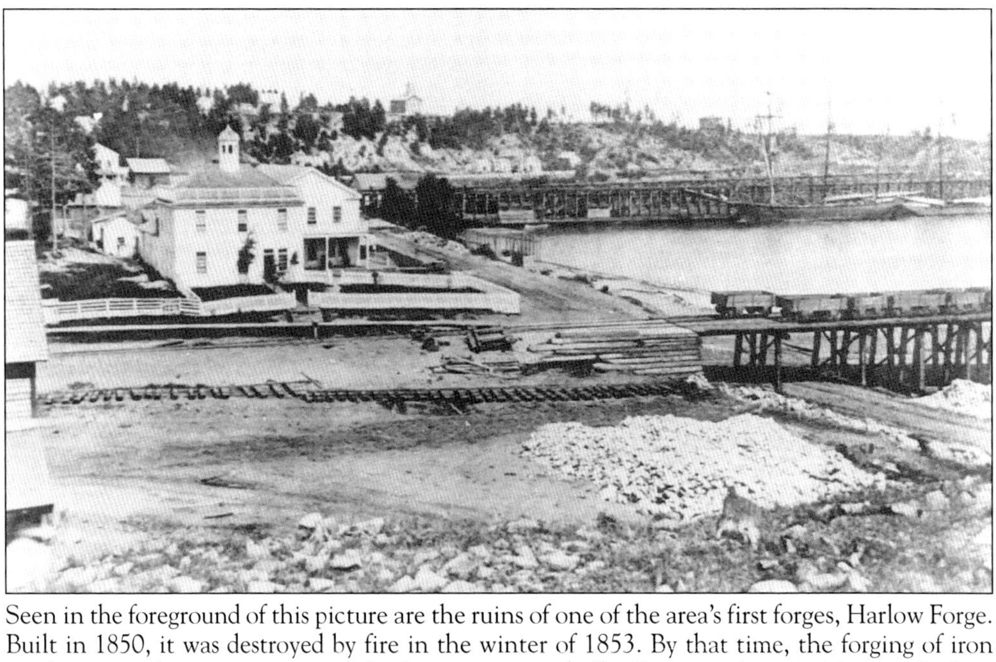

Seen in the foreground of this picture are the ruins of one of the area's first forges, Harlow Forge. Built in 1850, it was destroyed by fire in the winter of 1853. By that time, the forging of iron was becoming less important, and the forge was not rebuilt. Compare the primitive ore dock in the middle distance with the larger, much improved model across the harbor. (Courtesy State Archives of Michigan.)

Twelve

THE DOCKS

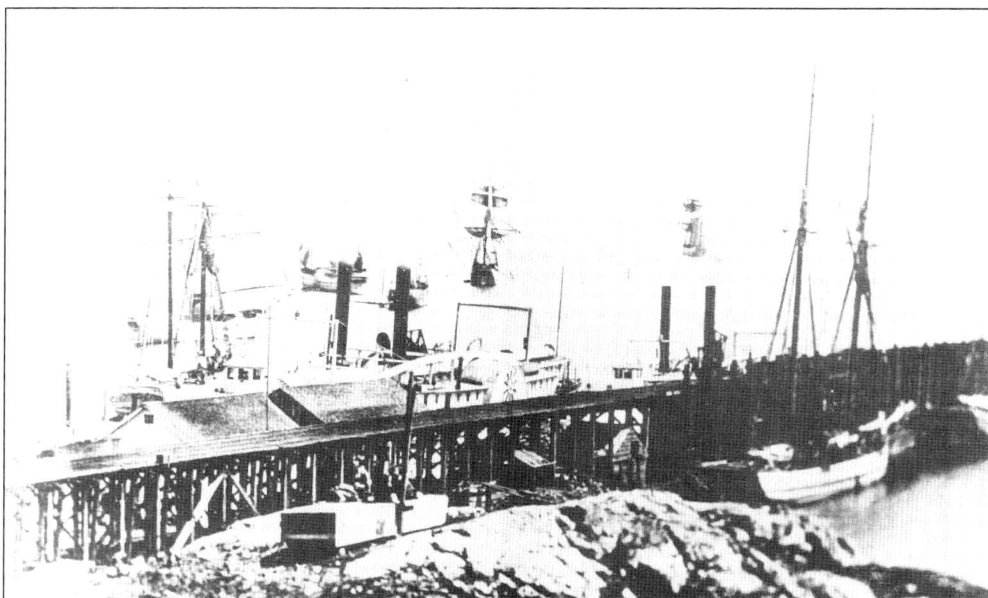

Several schooners are drawn up at the Cleveland Iron Mine Dock in this 1862 photo. This was the first ore dock constructed with pockets and chutes, and it revolutionized the loading process, improving its speed and efficiency. Built in 1857, it was destroyed by fire late in 1868. Fire was a progressive force; the new dock was bigger and better. (Courtesy State Archives of Michigan.)

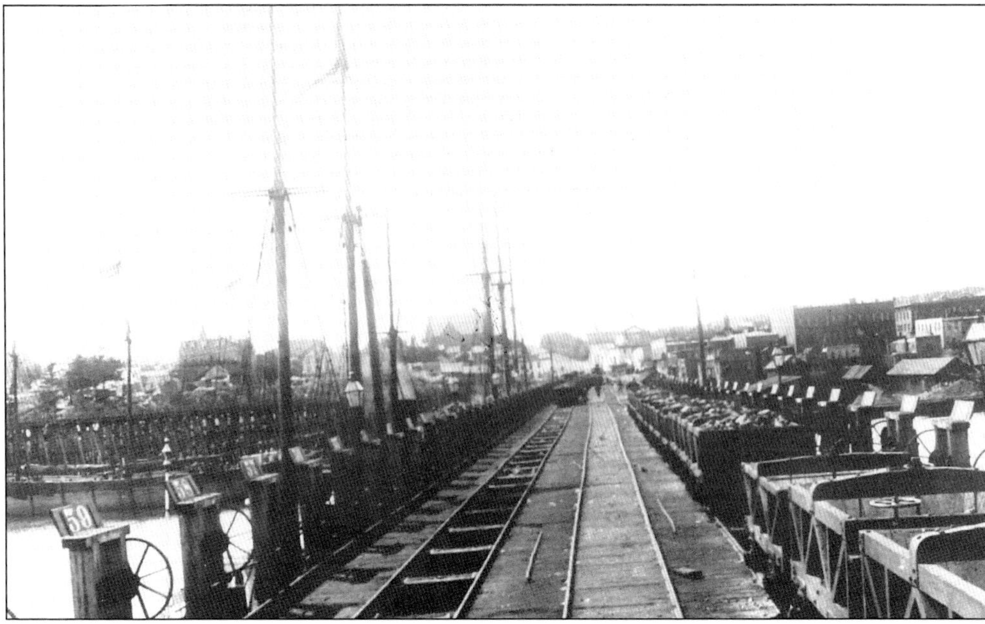

The ships seen at dockside, ready for loading, in this 1870s view were wind driven. Although the ore was brought to this dock in cars pulled by steam locomotives, much of the loading machinery required manual labor. Marquette's growing business district can be seen in the background on the right. (Courtesy State Archives of Michigan.)

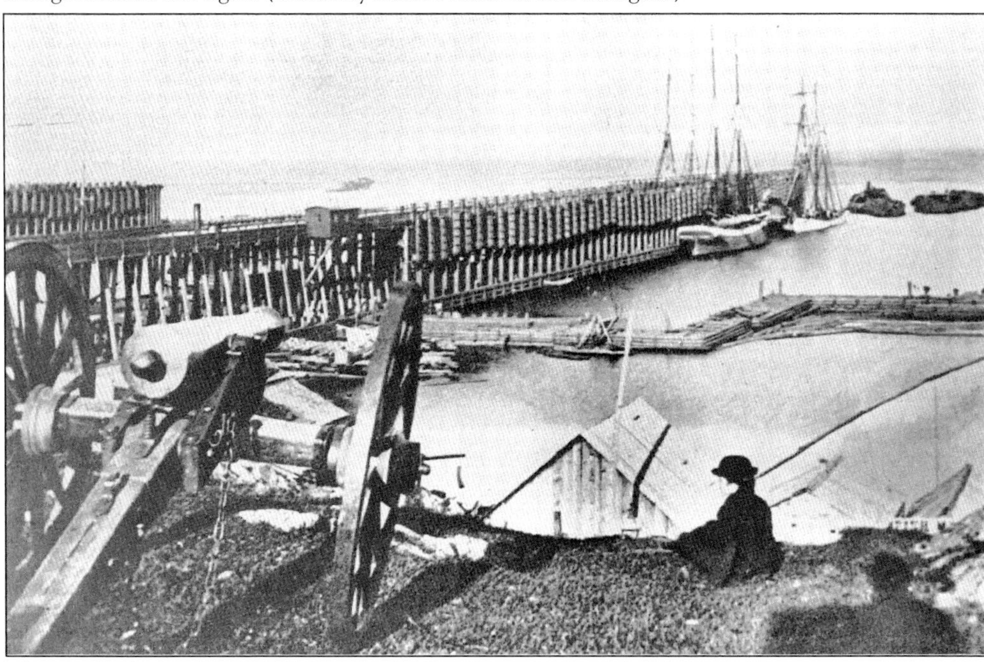

This carefully composed image is packed with interesting distractions. The Civil War cannon and the seated figure indicate the photographer's taste for artistic composition. Judging by the length of the shadows, the time of day was probably late afternoon. It appears that this made it possible for the artist himself (lower right-hand corner) to be part of the picture . By 1873, there were two modern-style ore docks in the harbor. (Courtesy Peter White Library.)

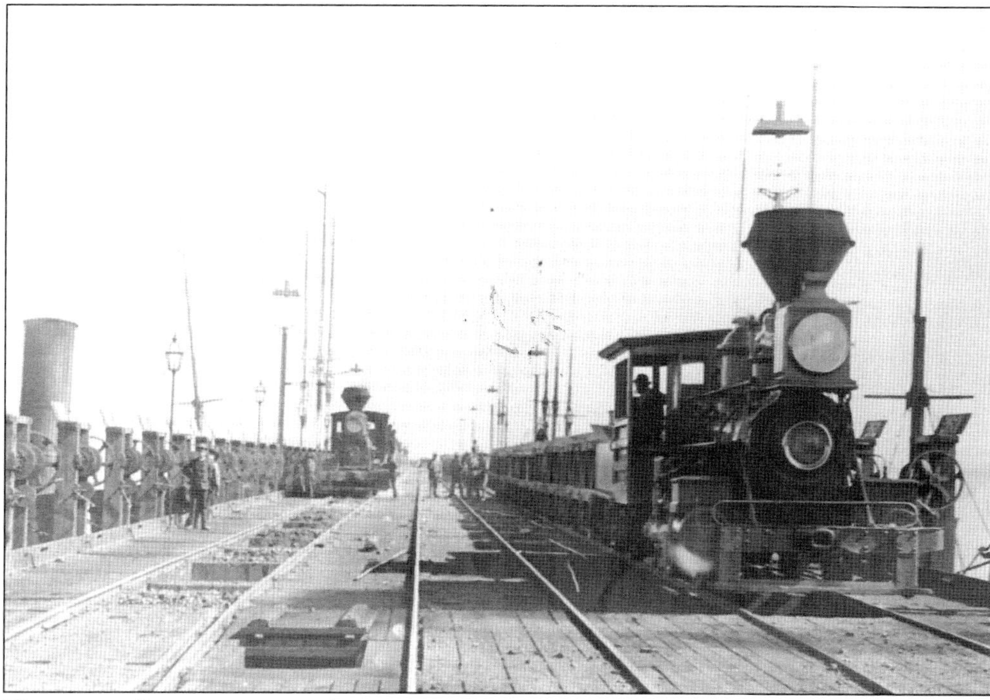

This view of a vintage steam locomotive atop an ore dock is an impressive example of the muscular technology of the 19th century. Although the ship masts in the background are from a more traditional mode of transportation, the funnel (left) represents the future. The layout of the dock, its loading capacity, and its massive scale all show how iron mining was growing. (Courtesy Peter White Library.)

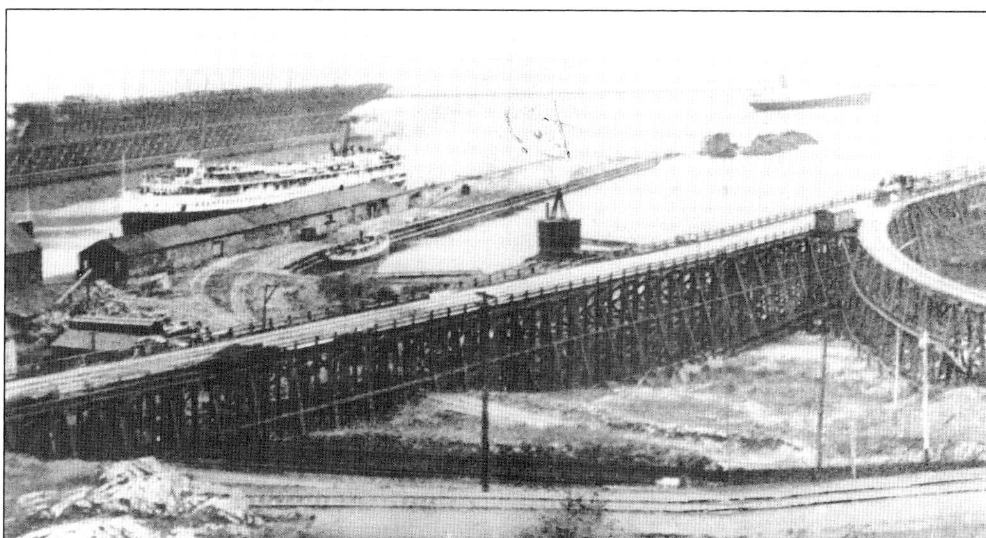

During the shipping season, there was regular and frequent lake steamer passenger service between Marquette and the lower Great Lakes ports of Detroit, Chicago, and Cleveland. Then the automobile and state truck road system transformed travel. The steamer docked between the ore docks was a common sight in 1905; another can be seen departing in the upper right-hand corner of the picture. (Courtesy State Archives of Michigan.)

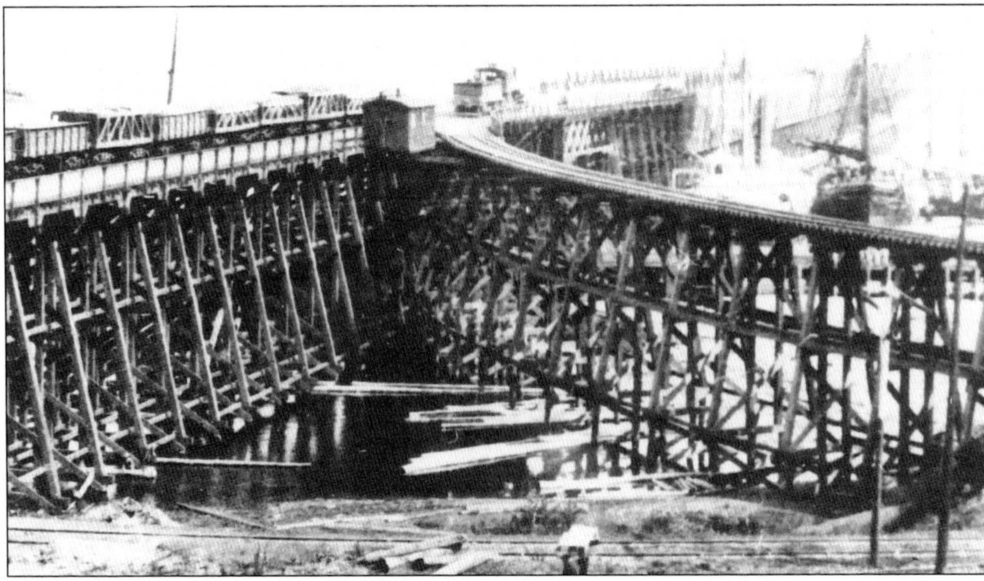

The elaborate trestle works of the Duluth, South Shore, and Atlantic ore dock lend visual drama to this 1880s picture. As the iron mining industry grew, the dock facilities became more and more elaborate. Until the beginning of the 20th century, wooden timbers were the construction material of choice. Plenty of lumber was available in the forests near Marquette and, obviously, wonderful things could be built with it. (Courtesy State Archives of Michigan.)

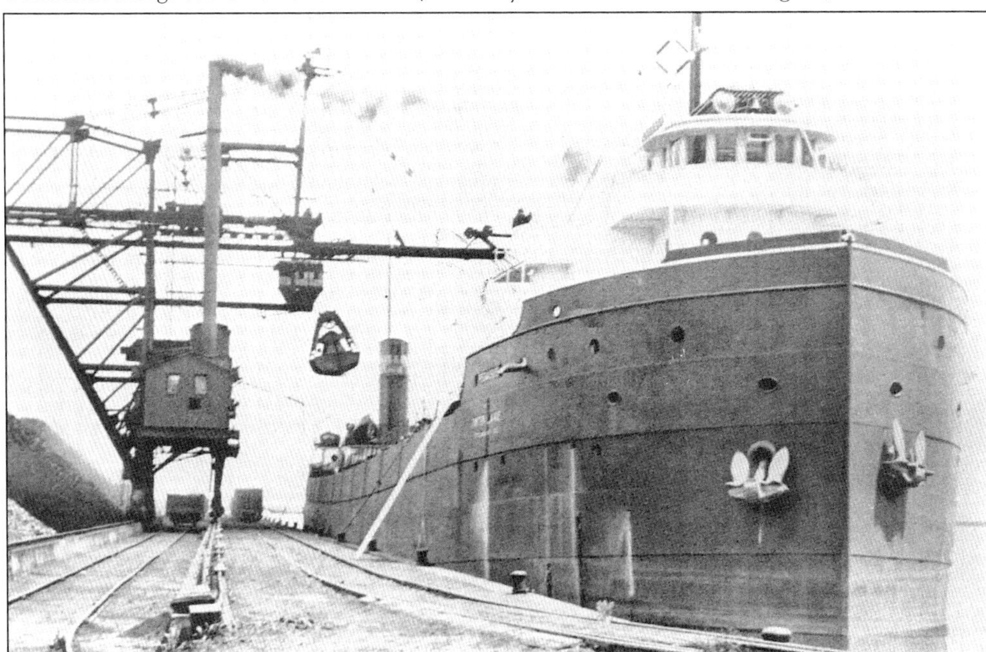

In this picture from 1949, a steam-driven derrick is being used to unload coal from a lake freighter. In this earlier technology, the coal industry had a greater variety of uses—and more consumers—than it does now. First wood, then coal supplied Marquette's heat during the long winters. Local industries used coal for most of their heavy tasks. (Courtesy Peter White Library.)

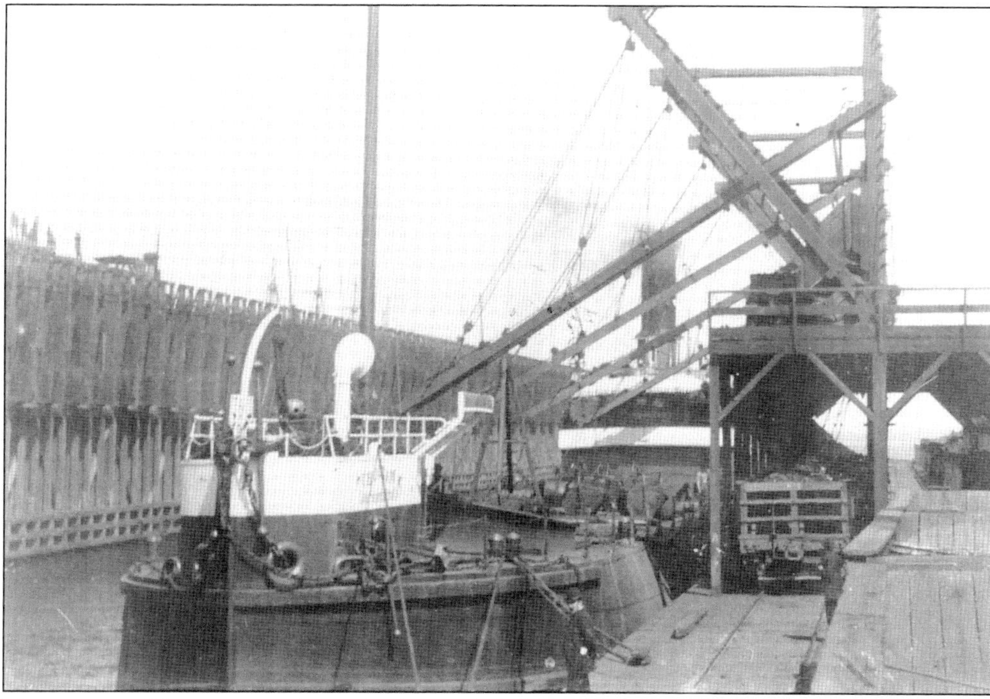

The steamer *Choctaw* was alongside the coal dock in the lower harbor when this picture was taken. Conveyor belts on adjustable arms moved coal from the hold of the ship up to a scuttle and chute above railroad cars. The coal fell into the scuttle, down the chute, and into the cars. (Courtesy State Archives of Michigan.)

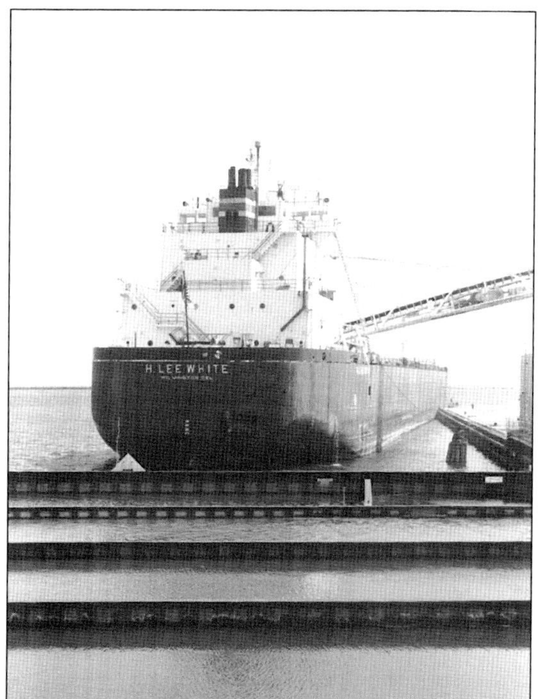

From its earliest days, Marquette has depended on coal for energy, and most of that coal has come by ship up the lakes. These days the fuel is used to generate electricity, and the largest coal piles are found near local generating plants. In the summer of 1998, the *H. Lee White* was photographed unloading near the site of the city's plant on Lake Shore Drive. (Photo by G. Downs.)

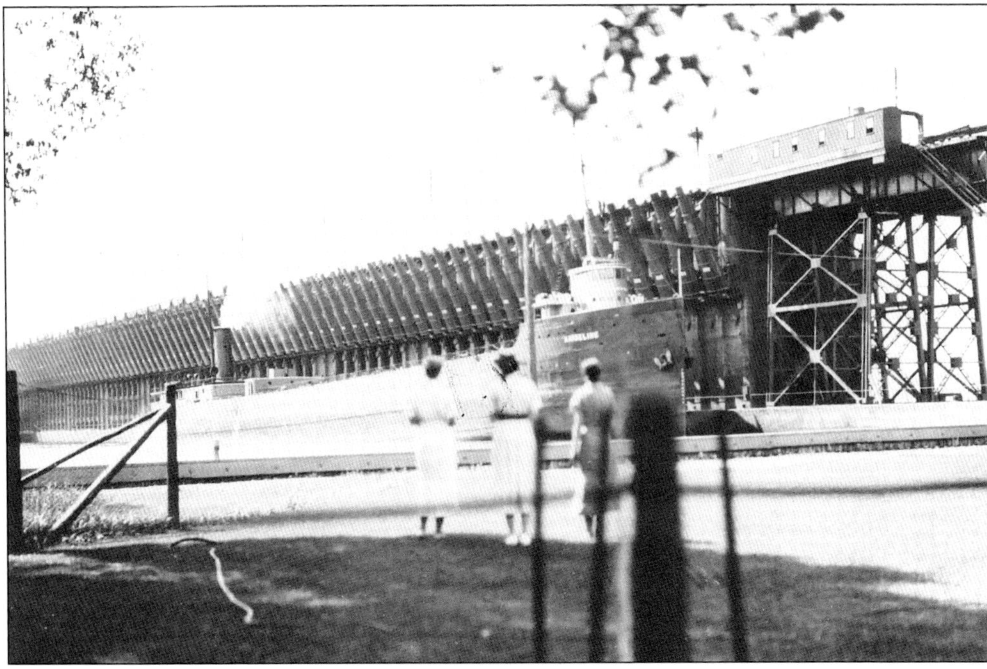

This photograph captures the impressive symmetry of the L.S.&I. ore dock during a loading in 1929. It is an interesting process. Spectators gathered to watch and listen as the iron ore rustled and rumbled down the chutes and the crew carefully distributed the weight of the load in the hold. (Courtesy State Archives of Michigan.)

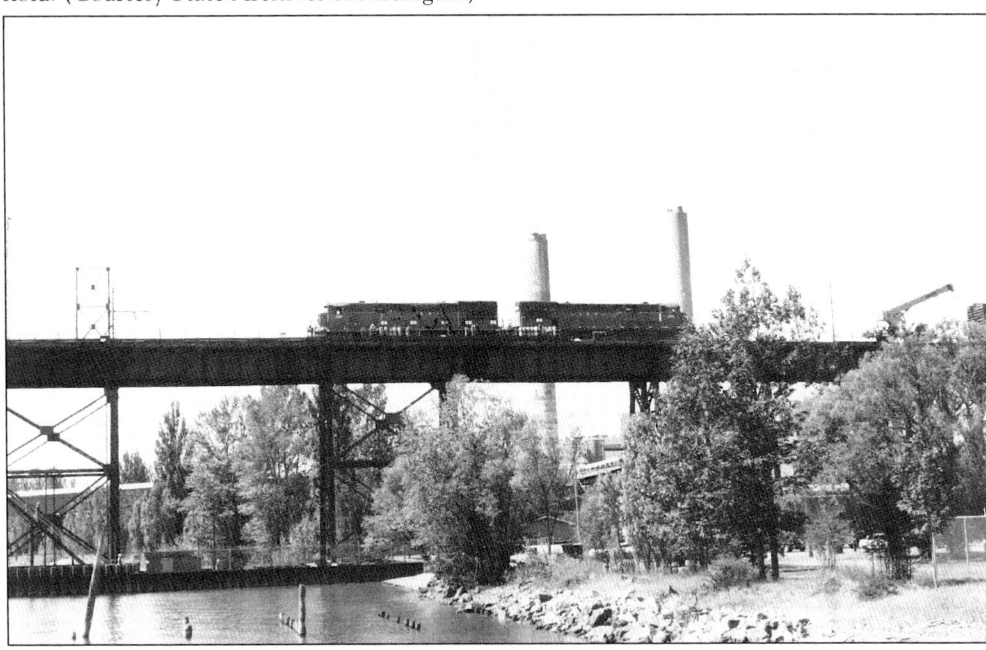

Although iron-ore mining, like lumbering and fishing, is no longer a commanding industry in Marquette, there are still days at the Lake Superior and Ishpeming ore dock when the mighty past is present. This 1998 photograph shows a diesel locomotive on the approach trestle of the dock during the loading process. (Photo by G. Downs.)

On an August morning in 1998, the *Kay E. Barker* slips carefully along the side of the L.S.&I. ore dock to take on a shipment of palletized iron ore. With 200 pockets and chutes, this facility is capable of loading the *Barker* and getting her under way in less than two hours. A modern ore boat can be back for another load in less than five days. The problem posed by a short shipping season is not great. (Photo by G. Downs.)

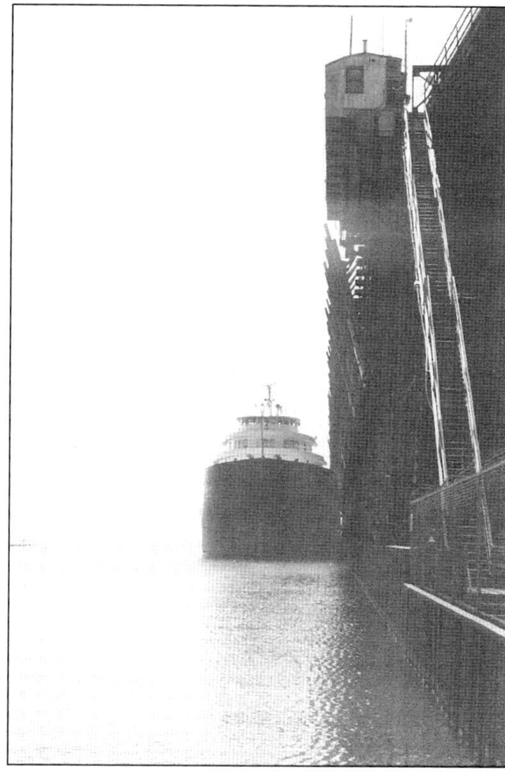

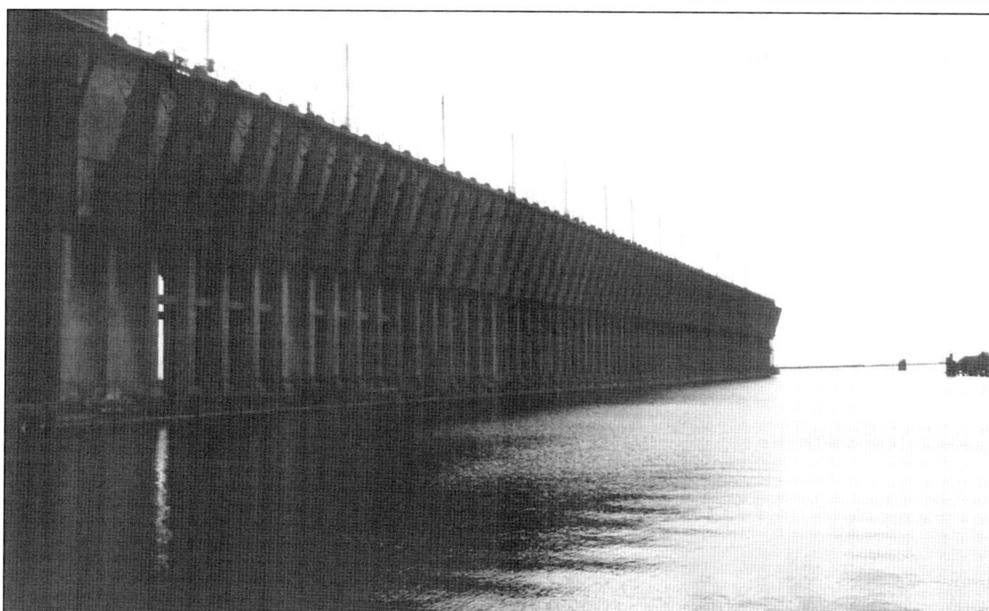

No longer in use today, the D.S.S.&A ore dock is too massive to be dismantled and trucked away. In 1930–1931, the prospects for the iron-ore industry were so bright that an investment in this cement and steel state-of-the-art dock seemed reasonable. It was built on a scale that is monumental and constructed with materials that defy time. It has outlived the reason it was created. (Photo by G. Downs.)

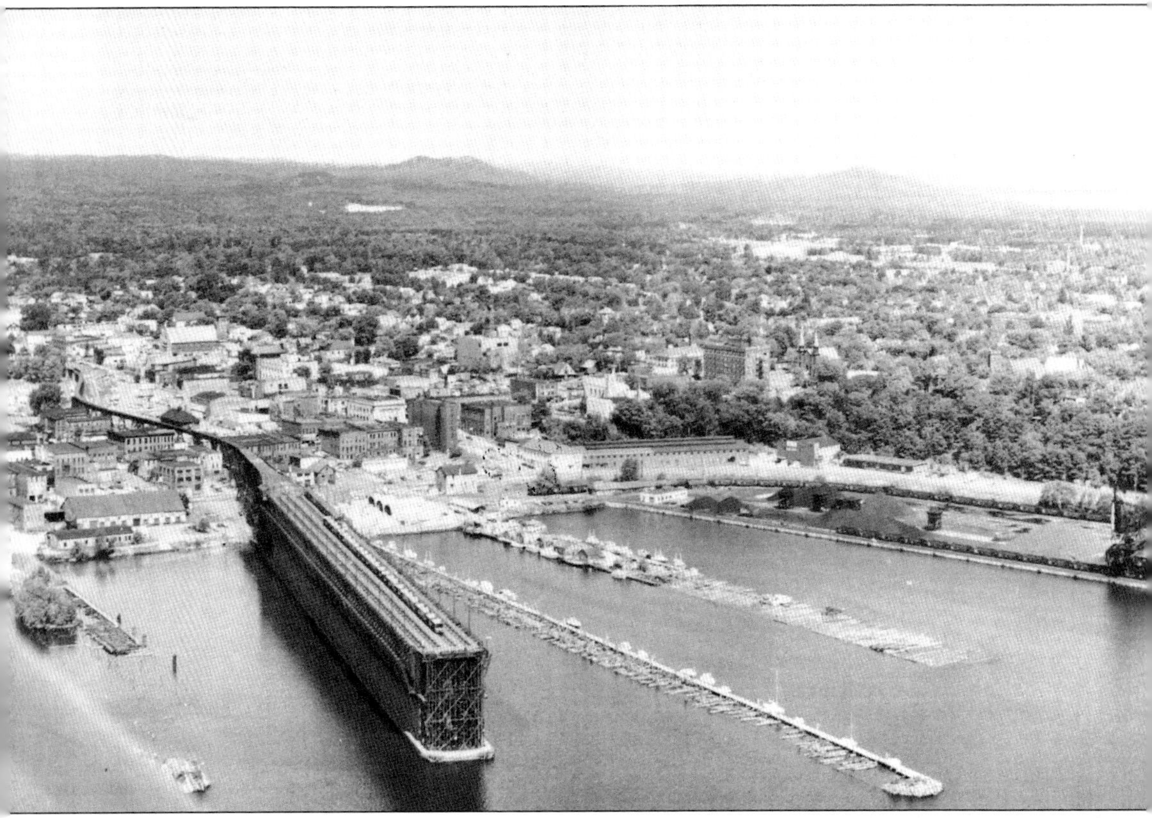

This aerial view of Marquette City and its harbor was taken in 1948. The dramatic thrust of the D.S.S.&A. ore dock provides the photo with some interest. Some of the landmarks seen in this view include the railroad trestle to the dock, the Marquette County Savings Bank building, the Hotel Northland, the Union Bank, the L.S.&I. shops, and the boat dock. Marquette was emerging from the Depression and WW II and entering an era of expansion and change. The earlier reliance on iron mining and lumbering would give way to a new and more diversified economy in which tourism, public sector services including the Branch Prison, Northern Michigan University, Marquette General Hospital, and K.I. Sawyer Air Force Base, and a variety of small, light industries played more prominent roles. (Courtesy State Archives of Michigan.)